The Dog in Your Life

The Dog in Your Life

A
COMPLETE GUIDE TO
CHOOSING, RAISING, FEEDING,
TRAINING AND CARING FOR YOUR
DOG *PLUS* SECTIONS ON SHOW DOGS,
HUNTING DOGS, COURSING DOGS,
HERD DOGS, SLED DOGS, GUARD
DOGS, GUIDE DOGS, AND
A DISCUSSION OF
COMMON CANINE
ILLNESSES

Matthew Margolis
&
Catherine Swan

CONSULTANT: SUSAN MCLELLAN, D.V.M.

VINTAGE BOOKS
A DIVISION OF RANDOM HOUSE
NEW YORK

Frontispiece photo by Victoria Wilson

Some of the material in Chapter 9, "Educating Your Dog:
Obedience Training and Correcting His Faults," has previously
appeared in different form in Good Dog, Bad Dog, published by
Holt, Rinehart and Winston, and in Underdog, published by Stein
and Day, both co-authored with Mordecai Siegal, also The
Liberated Dog, published by Holt, Rinehart and Winston and is
used by permission of Mordecai Siegal and the publishers. The
temperament test in Chapter 2, "Choosing the Right Dog," has
previously appeared in different form in Underdog and is used by
permission of Mordecai Siegal and the publisher.

Library of Congress Cataloging in Publication Data
Margolis, Matthew.
The dog in your life.
Bibliography: p.
Includes index.
1. Dogs.   I. Swan, Catherine.   II. Title.
SF426.M36 1982   636.7   82-4941
ISBN 0-394-71174-2   AACR2

Manufactured in the United States of America
987
Cover photograph by Harry Langdon

To Ira, a good friend,
and to Mike

PREFACE

As a dog trainer, my main concern has always been the relationship between the dog and his owner. My idea about obedience training is that a well-mannered dog who does what he is told when he is told to, and does it cheerfully, is more fun to live with and more apt to get on well with his owner than an untrained dog. I believe the best place to teach a dog is at home where he can learn not to do the things that make dog ownership difficult, like climbing on the sofa, chewing the upholstery, soiling the rug, barking and disturbing the neighbors. And I believe that the dog should be taught with love and affection, never punished, and that the owner should learn along with him.

In the course of my training career I have co-written four obedience books, *Good Dog, Bad Dog, Underdog* (about mutts), *The Liberated Dog* (about off-leash training) and with Maurice Sendak, *Some Swell Pup*, a book about dogs and dog training for children. One day, however, it occurred to me that among all the dog books on the market, there did not seem to be a single one that covered all the different things a dog owner needs to know about to make his relationship with his dog a happy one. Around that time I met Catherine Swan, a writer whose recalcitrant five-year-old Weimaraner was in desperate need of training. In the course of working with her dog, we began to plan this book.

The Dog in Your Life is as complete a manual as we could make it. It covers everything from choosing and raising to training and traveling, plus a good solid section on the different kinds of dogs there are and what they were bred for. Many people buy specialized kinds of dogs without understanding the purpose for which these dogs were developed, and therein lies the crux of a problem relationship. They blame a hunting dog for being nervous in a small apartment, when hunting dogs are bred for nervous energy, which helps them endure long hours in the field. They blame a herd dog for toppling over the children, when he was bred to circle, direct and drive. Or they buy a show dog without realizing that he requires many hours of grooming and ring training and thousands of dollars' worth of travel. Many people, if they knew these things, wouldn't buy the kind of dog they buy; others might still do it, but at least would be forewarned.

In addition to this kind of information, we also include a section on canine illnesses. Many books on the market describe the same subject matter, but few do it so that the average person can understand it. We had the advantage of working closely for several months with Susan McLellan, D.V.M., who has a remarkable ability to describe complicated medical subjects in everyday language. She was the third person needed to make this book possible.

—Matthew Margolis

CONTENTS

1 WHAT IT MEANS TO OWN A DOG IN THE CITY, THE
  SUBURBS, THE COUNTRY   3
2 CHOOSING THE RIGHT DOG   13
3 BRINGING YOUR DOG HOME   57
4 THE INNER DOG: PROPER FEEDING   71
5 HOUSEBREAKING AND PAPER TRAINING   86
6 A DAILY HEALTH EXAMINATION   96
7 YOU, YOUR DOG AND THE VETERINARIAN   110
8 A CATALOG OF COMMON CANINE ILLNESSES   121
9 ÉDUCATING YOUR DOG: OBEDIENCE TRAINING AND
  CORRECTING HIS FAULTS   146
10 GROOMING AND EXERCISE   197
11 HOW TO DEAL WITH EMERGENCIES   213
12 SEX, REPRODUCTION AND BIRTH CONTROL   235
13 THE TRAVELING DOG AND THE DOG AS BOARDER   265
14 THE AGING DOG   290
15 DOGS FOR SPECIAL PURPOSES   295
   Show Dogs   295
   Coursing Dogs   303
   Sled Dogs   307
   Earth Dogs   311
   Water-Rescue Dogs   312
   Hunting Dogs   315

Police/War Dogs
Guard Dogs
Herd Dogs
Guide Dogs
INDEX

The Dog in Your Life

KATHERINE HOWARD

1

WHAT IT MEANS TO OWN A DOG IN THE CITY, THE SUBURBS, THE COUNTRY

A dog can be a rewarding friend and companion who adds greatly to the quality of your life, or he can be a persistent care and nuisance. Which he is will depend largely on the way in which you approach the subject. If you take the trouble to learn in advance what owning a dog entails, and if you decide that the dog is well worth it, he will repay you tenfold. If you don't, you may constantly be unpleasantly surprised. Here are the major points to bear in mind:

A dog's owner is responsible for keeping the dog healthy, happy and under control. This means a proper feeding program, daily grooming and exercise, housebreaking and basic obedience training, regular medical examinations, an immunization program (including yearly boosters against rabies and the big three)* and the securing of immediate veterinary attention if the dog is hurt or ill.

The owner is also responsible for the dog's sex life: preventing conception if breeding is not desired, introducing correct breeding programs if breeding is desired, and understanding the basic genetic principles as well as the mechanics of the mating process. If you breed your bitch, you should know how to care for her while she is pregnant and while she is nursing, how to assist if delivery proves difficult, and how to hand-raise her pups if the bitch cannot or will not raise them herself. If you want your dog to be a stud, you should know how to make sure that he impregnates the bitch.

The dog owner has further obligations to the community in which

* Distemper, hepatitis, leptospirosis (DHL).

he and his dog live. Before getting a dog, you should learn what laws governing dogs are in effect. Contrary to popular belief, these laws have been made not to punish the dog lover but rather to protect both the community and the relationship between the owner and his dog. Among the more important laws enacted to keep this relationship harmonious are:

• **Abandonment**   Sometimes when a dog seems to be more trouble than he is worth, his owner releases him in the surrounding community, hoping that someone else will fall in love with him. "It is bette " he thinks to himself, "than taking him to a shelter, where he will be gassed."

In most states it is against the law to abandon your dog: first, because it's bad for the community, and second, because most abandoned dogs die—and die cruelly. The majority are struck by cars or become diseased.

• **Licensing**   Licensing protects a dog from the gas van if he is lost or injured and provides him with identification. License fees also supply the dog pound with much-needed funds. Guide dogs must be licensed, but they are usually exempt from the license fee.

• **No Dogs Allowed**   In most places in this country (including rural areas), the local board of health prohibits dogs from grocery stores, restaurants and other public places that have anything to do with food. Public playgrounds are also usually off-limits. On public transportation, dogs must be leashed, or in many cases contained in carriers or kennels.

Guide dogs are exempt from such laws. In fact, the guide dog and his owner are protected by state law against discrimination in hotels, restaurants, public conveyances and other places where dogs are not usually allowed.

• **Curb Laws**   These laws were established to protect the health of the surrounding community. Curbing means that the dog's urine and feces are deposited in the gutter, where they are less likely to offend pedestrians or transmit disease and more likely to be swept away by the street cleaner.

The scoop law has become increasingly popular in overpopulated areas of the country. This law requires owners to clean up after their dogs.

• **Leash Laws**   Such laws require that dogs be kept on a leash at all times on the street and in the public places where they are allowed.

Margolis' Law: The owner's responsibilities tend to increase as the area of confinement decreases. Among other things, a city dog has to be walked on a leash.

You may have additional responsibilities depending on where you live with your dog.

The City

• Regular, scheduled exercise is a must, both because the dog needs the opportunity to relieve himself and because exercise is necessary for his physical and mental health.

• A regular grooming program is essential wherever you live, but if you live in an apartment, regular bathing is also necessary, for the welfare of the apartment dwellers as well as of the dog. Left uncontrolled, fleas and lice breed profusely in the apartment milieu.

● Obesity is a major problem of the canine city dweller. His daily exercise is limited, which makes it more difficult for him to work off extra calories. And because he is a housemate, he is more likely to share his owner's snacks. Diet and food intake must therefore be constantly supervised—especially with dogs who seem to have no natural appetite control.

Dog-food companies have compounded this problem in two ways: the recommended amounts on the backs of packages are frequently in excess of the city dog's daily caloric requirements, and some dog foods concentrate on taste appeal, which interferes with the dog's natural sense of surfeit.*

● Boredom is another major problem for the city dog confined in a small area. One common outlet is chewing—which, apart from the destruction, could result in anything from a simple bellyache to a serious electric shock for the dog himself.

Additional hazards present themselves outside the apartment. We recommend the use of a leash for all city dogs whether or not they are off-leash trained—not only because leashing is usually the law, but for the safety of the dog. Even dogs that behave perfectly will sometimes forget themselves at the sight of a neighborhood cat, and one mad dash through traffic could be the last.

● Barking is a serious problem where neighbors live in cramped quarters, often behind paper-thin walls. Some dogs wail sorrowfully when their owners are absent. This problem is complicated by the fact that one of the city dog's *raisons d'être* is the protection of his owner, who must discover a way of teaching his dog when it is appropriate to bark and when it is not. Wailers with nervous, sensitive temperaments require long and tedious training, along with additional exercise to run off steam.

The Suburbs

The suburban dog lives a halfway existence. His owner shares some problems with the city owner and some with the country owner. Many suburban communities enforce curb and leash laws, but suburban dwellers generally have yards, which mean that exercise,

---

* "The obsession by dog-food makers for having every dog devour his food as if it were the dog's last meal defeats completely the built-in mechanism each dog has for preventing obesity: That

"Suburban dogs lead halfway lives," but may enjoy such luxuries as back-yard pools in the summer.

housebreaking and diet control are usually not major problems. Barking, however, can be anathema to suburban neighbors, especially those who moved out of the city to get away from the noise. Other problems are:

● If dogs are not allowed to range freely, the owner may have to invest in a fence if he wants to give his pet access to the outdoors.

● The suburban dog is more subject to accidental poisoning than the city dog, not only from the mysterious sacks and cans stored in the garage but also from leaking antifreeze in the family driveway—antifreeze is sweet-tasting and deadly.

● The suburban dog needs less frequent bathing than the city dog, but fleas, ticks and mosquito bites, the last of which can transmit heartworm, are easier to acquire.

● The bitch in heat is more of a problem in the suburbs than in the city. If she spends any time at all in the yard, her scent is likely to attract every libidinous male in the neighborhood.

mechanism is the instinct for eating only enough food to meet its caloric needs. Housepets offered these highly palatable canned foods quickly learn to eat to satisfy their palates" Donald R. Collins, D.V.M., "The Housepet," *The Collins Guide to Dog Nutrition* (New York, 1976), p. 234. Collins also notes that taste tests are the first tests that dog-food manufacturers make. This means, of course, that the nutritional value is of secondary importance.

● The damage the city dog does with his teeth in an apartment is paralleled by that the suburban dog inflicts on the yard with his paws and urine. Dog urine is not beneficial to flowers, shrubs or grass, and digging is an age-old canine instinct, especially if there is a bone to bury and then disinter.

● Many plants are poisonous to dogs. Indoors, you can solve the problem by hanging them out of reach. Outdoors it is harder. Chapter 11 lists common plants that cause trouble. And before you use a weedkiller or a fertilizer, read the label carefully and consult your local poison-control center.

The Country

Most people erroneously believe that the country is the ideal place for dogs. But city dogs, unlike city owners, tend to live longer, perhaps because city owners, aware of the additional strain confinement places on their animals, tend to be more conscientious. They also have more control over their dogs' daily activities.

● Country dogs are apt to encounter pesticides, poisons, bones and fetid garbage, all of which can bring about an early death.

● Country dogs may be wounded or killed by shotguns or wild animals. Many are killed by cars.

● External and internal parasites are easy to come by and much easier to neglect in the country, where the dog is out most of the day. The country dog who does not kill an occasional rabbit is not worth his salt, but rabbits are notorious tapeworm hosts.

● Barking is seldom a problem, but interference with livestock frequently is. Hunting dogs have the taste for birds bred into them, and a sudden lapse of training may result in death in the chicken pen. Other dogs like to chase cattle. Laws against such behavior are strict, and those who shoot dogs engaged in these pursuits are not held liable.

● The bitch in heat can be a major source of agony for the country owner unless she is sent away to a kennel for the entire period, although in general we are opposed to kenneling the bitch in heat because she will drive the rest of the kennel crazy.

Once you know your responsibilities, you need to make practical decisions about just what you will do when you bring a dog into your home.

The country isn't always an ideal place for a pet, but it can provide a perfect setting for an American Eskimo Dog.

Assign a Caretaker   If you're single, who the caretaker will be is obvious. If the family contains two or more members, the problem becomes increasingly complex.

In a family situation, it's often the kids who first ask for a dog, pestering their parents until finally one or the other gives in. "But," the kids are told, "we can't get a dog unless *you* [meaning the kids] promise to take care of it." Immediately this calls to mind a TV tear-jerker in which a small boy spends his first hard-earned fifty dollars to buy a Redbone Coonhound, lavishes attention on it and trains it to become the best coonhound in the county.

The principle of the story is a valid one. The boy did pay for the dog, did take complete responsibility for it, and was repaid for his efforts to the extent that he was able to contribute to the family income. But certain underlying facts make this situation unalterably romantic. The boy lived in farm country, and because his family enjoyed a certain amount of isolation, he had no human companionship to distract him from his single-minded purpose. Although children can learn a great deal by caring for pets, most of them are really not capable of taking full responsibility for one.

In most cases, the woman of the household, simply because she's home most of the day, becomes the dog's caretaker. She housebreaks, feeds and waters him, and is probably the first to know when he's sick. If she doesn't want these responsibilities, she ought to say so from the start so that other arrangements can be made. On the other hand, if the responsibility is spread over three or four family members, nothing gets done. This doesn't mean that the entire family shouldn't be involved, but simply that one person should be designated chief.

Consider the Season   If you really hate cold weather, we recommend that you put off buying a puppy until the spring. After the puppy receives his final shots at about twelve weeks, housebreaking can begin. The problem is, if you get the puppy in winter and it's really cold out, it will be unpleasant to walk him. The puppy can probably take it, but how will you like to stand outside in 15° weather and wait for him to defecate in the snow? Of course you'll always have to walk him in bad weather, but it's usually only the early stages of housebreaking that require long walks, patience and fortitude.

Housebreaking should not be a torture for either you or your animal. It should be a relatively pleasant task, and if it is done properly and under the right conditions, it should provide excellent results. Not only will your carpets and floors be clean, you will feel fully satisfied that you are well on the road to being a happy and successful dog owner. (See Chapter 5 on housebreaking.)

WHEN SHOULD YOU NOT BUY A DOG?

1.   Never buy a dog on impulse.

2.   Never buy a dog to keep a problem dog company. Many people think that if they have a badly trained dog or a dog with a bad temperament, they can ease the situation by introducing another dog into the household. More likely than not, this simply multiplies the problems.

3.   Never buy a dog as a gift. First, you can't know whether another person really wants a dog and is prepared to care for it responsibly. Second, even if you know what kind of dog he wants, you can't know how he'll feel about the particular puppy you bring him. It's like trying to pick out a wife for someone else. Choosing a dog is very personal. There's an attachment that occurs almost immediately. One person may feel this attachment when a puppy wiggles his way over and nibbles on his shoelaces, another when the puppy cocks his head in a certain way or licks his face. You can't possibly know what it is that someone else is looking for because usually he doesn't know himself until it happens.

4. Never buy a dog if you're not willing to spend the time and do the research to make a proper choice. It's not something anyone else can do for you, although it may be a family affair, where you all go together and say, "Hey, this is the breed, and this is the one we like."

Ultimately, owning a dog means being willing to face the problems it may entail and being able to consider practical solutions. Too many people at the first sign of difficulty rush their dogs to the pound. If we did this with our children, we would live in a society of orphanages. Like a baby, a dog is a living creature, and a particularly valuable one when we consider the many services he performs for us and the many hours of affection and pleasure he is capable of giving. Yet thousands of these potentially pleasant creatures are legally destroyed every year. The best way to prevent this kind of unfortunate occurrence is for every owner to find the kind of dog he can live with most comfortably. And that's what the next chapter is all about.

"The mutt is an unknown quantity," and often turns out to be, as above, handsome, alert and intelligent.

2

CHOOSING
THE
RIGHT DOG

Puppies are one of the biggest impulse-buy items in this country.
Many people put less thought into getting a dog than into buying
a car, which they will own probably less than half as long. They
would not dream of getting a car without first studying catalogues
and consumer reports, considering the specifications and estimated
maintenance costs of different makes and models. Yet they will walk
into a pet shop with an attractive litter of puppies in the window
without any thought that dogs, too, come in different models which
satisfy different needs and wishes. The important thing is to find the
right one for you.

Purebred or Mixed Breed?

You buy a purebred for one of two reasons: because you want to
show him or because you want an animal whose appearance and
temperament are more or less predictable. The mutt is an unknown
quantity. Even if you know his parents, you can't be sure of the
result. If you cross, say, a German Shepherd with a Collie in the
hope of getting a longhaired watchdog with a calm, easygoing
temperament, it is just as likely that you'll get a shorthaired, high-
strung, nervous animal who barks at the mailman. There are too
many genes involved to make predictions. You might get one or two
puppies with some of the characteristics you are looking for, but it
would take many generations before you could sort out all the

undesirable traits. That's why we say that breeds *evolve*. They are not simply the result of mixing and matching.

The authors of this book happen to love mutts, unpredictable as they are, and to feel that they offer certain advantages. The popular belief that mixed breeds are healthier than purebreds is not true, but a first-generation cross does have what geneticists call hybrid vigor and tends to be stronger, sturdier, healthier, perhaps even bigger than both parents. By the next generation, however, all such advantages are lost. A more certain advantage is that mutts are cheaper to come by than purebreds. They are also trainable, lovable, affectionate and willing to please. It's fun to adopt a mutt. It makes you feel good to know that you are saving an animal from the gas chamber or providing a space in the shelter for another stray. And with the help of the temperament test that appears at the end of this chapter, you can determine a mutt's disposition as precisely as you can that of his aristocratic counterpart.

Unlike the mutt, the pedigreed dog has a long line of known ancestors. He has been bred for both physical and temperamental characteristics and for special abilities. If you want to show a dog for quality or for the obedience ring, then you must buy a pedigreed animal complete with American Kennel Club (AKC) registration papers. If you want a hunting companion or a working dog, you have a number of excellent breeds to choose from, although you should remember that there are few tasks that a mixed breed cannot be trained to do.

A Puppy or an Older Dog?

Ideally, you should get a puppy seven to eight weeks old. Puppies adapt quickly and easily to a new environment. They obviously have more years ahead of them than older dogs—an important consideration, since a dog's life span is so much shorter than a human's.

But a puppy also means work. You'll have to housebreak him, and if he lives indoors this will entail walking him every three or four hours. You'll also have to train him. You'll have all the puppy problems to contend with—chewing, jumping, mouthing, going into the garbage, taking food, begging at the table. Before you get a puppy you must think about whether you have the necessary time and energy to devote to him. An older dog is already past the chewing, nipping puppy stages. He may already be obedience-trained. If he is not, he'll learn more quickly than a puppy because his attention span is longer. He may already be housebroken. If not, you can

"The authors of this book happen to love mutts": Catherine Swan and Tammy, a German Shepherd mix.

probably housebreak him within a week or two. And if you're a working person, you have a much better chance of housebreaking a nine-month-old dog than a twelve-week-old puppy who can't possibly hold his urine for the eight or nine hours you are gone.

If you adopt an older dog, on the other hand, you may also inherit problems. If he has bad habits you will have to take the time and trouble to train him out of them, while if you start with a young puppy you can train him correctly in the first place. Puppies begin to relate to human beings between seven and twelve weeks of age. If you get a puppy at this age, you'll have considerable influence over the final product.

The older dog has an already established size and weight, which is particularly important if you're getting a mixed breed. A mongrel puppy so small he can fit into the palm of his master's hand, may, by the time he is a year old, be the size of a Great Dane.

If you have your heart set on a show dog, you should wait until he is at least six months old before you buy him. By that time both you and the breeder will know whether or not he adequately represents his breed standard. Even pedigreed dogs come in varied shapes and sizes. The Weimaraner, for example, weighs on the average about 75 pounds. If you buy a Weimaraner puppy, and she grows up to weigh 47 pounds and measures two inches short of the standard, she is automatically disqualified from the AKC dog shows.

You must, however, resign yourself to the fact that a clear show-quality six-month-old puppy automatically commands a higher price than an eight-week-old one, not to mention the fact that the breeder will have invested a lot of money in the puppy's upkeep which he plans to get back. Furthermore, if the puppy has been kenneled for a substantial part of his six months, he may have a difficult time adjusting to family life. For these reasons, and because the socialization period is between the seventh and twelfth week of a dog's life, we prefer the show-potential pup to an out-and-out show dog. Even if he doesn't develop physically as you may have hoped, he can still be an excellent companion.

A Dog or a Bitch?

Everyone has his preference, but there is actually little difference between a male dog and a female one as long as he or she is properly trained and well cared for. Still, there are a few slight differences you should consider.

The male tends to be a better hunter and protector, primarily because in any given breed he is somewhat larger than the female. For example, the desired shoulder height for the German Shepherd is 24 to 26 inches for the male, 22 to 24 inches for the bitch. The difference between the smallest female at 22 inches and the largest male at 26 inches may mean a difference of 15 to 20 pounds in weight. The larger dog will naturally appear more threatening. The female, on the other hand, tends to be more affectionate and better with children, even maternal. She is also slightly more responsive to training. Trainers in guide-dog and police-dog programs have found this to be so.

The male tends to be more aloof and independent than the female.

As a result of scent-post behavior—the need to read all the posts in the neighborhood before going to sleep at night—he is inclined to wander. If he is properly controlled and confined, this is not a problem. The female has more of an inclination to stay home and develops more direct and instinctive ties to her territory and her people.

We prefer the female and are willing to put up with the additional problems of her being in heat or the expense of spaying. The pros and cons of spaying, and the alternatives to it, will be discussed later in this book (see Chapter 12).

The Breeds

If you are in the market for a dog, the first place to go is a dog show where you can see what is available. The dog show is the marketplace for dogs, and the Westminster Show is the biggest marketplace of all. If you don't happen to be in New York City in February, a reasonable alternative is to visit the biggest local AKC show you can find, particularly if it includes an obedience ring where you can get some idea of performance.

A dog's appearance—his carriage, conformation, color and style—is the factor most likely to influence your first choice, but such aesthetic considerations should be weighed carefully against other characteristics. That's why we say a dog show is the first place to go. It is a place where you can acquaint yourself with a variety breeds and discuss them with qualified and competent breeders. But it is not a place to make your final decision for the following reasons:

1. The breeders are partial to the dogs they show. They aren't likely to be truly objective about the breed they have devoted much of their time and energy in developing. Furthermore, they enter their dogs in shows in the hope that they will place and eventually become valuable breeding stock; you, as a prospective client for the pups, are a prime target for a breeder's sales pitch.

2. The judges sometimes make mistakes. Because most shows are primarily beauty contests, little attention is paid to the original purpose of the breed and the temperaments of the contestants. Winners are frequently selected without regard to obvious flaws in temperament. We saw it happen at the 1977 Westminister exhibit when a ribbon was awarded to a beautiful little red Vizsla in spite of the fact that she shivered under the judge's hands and balked when her mouth was pried open for examination. We wouldn't want to take our chances on her pups.

3. You, the spectator, are also subject to failures in judgment. The show is largely a visual experience. You are looking at some of the best examples of a breed, ring-trained, groomed and handled by experts. What you see is not always what you will get. In fact, what you see may lead you to erroneous conclusions. Suppose you fall in love with the enormous Great Dane. You live in an apartment and believe that the only dog you can reasonably keep is a pocket-size Chihuahua. How can you know that a Great Dane is an equally good apartment pet? That in spite of his bulk he is easy to train? That he travels well if you can afford the crate for him? And that he housebreaks more readily?

Many of the accepted "facts" about dogs are based on misconceptions. As a prospective owner, it's up to you to find out what is *really* true. Breeders will give you some information, books will give you some more. But it's ultimately your responsibility to sift through the facts and theories and apply both knowledge and instinct to your final choice. If after all that you are still at a loss, consult a reputable dog trainer. Many trainers provide consultation services to help you choose the breed that's most appropriate to your tastes and life style.

How to Choose

RULE 1:   KNOW THE GROUP.

For purposes of classification, the AKC has divided dogs into six general groupings, based on the original purposes for which the breeds were developed. Because task and temperament bear some relationship to each other, brief summaries of the temperamental characteristics of each group are useful, although there are wide variations among the breeds within each group.

GROUP I: SPORTING DOGS

Pointer	Golden Retriever
German Shorthaired Pointer	Labrador Retriever
German Wirehaired Pointer	English Setter
Chesapeake Bay Retriever	Gordon Setter
Curly-Coated Retriever	Irish Setter
Flat-Coated Retriever	American Water Spaniel

Golden Retriever

Brittany Spaniel
Clumber Spaniel
Cocker Spaniel
English Cocker Spaniel
English Springer Spaniel
Field Spaniel

Irish Water Spaniel
Sussex Spaniel
Welsh Springer Spaniel
Vizsla
Weimaraner
Wirehaired Pointing Griffon

This group includes the hunting breeds. Generally speaking, they are active, high-spirited, affectionate and occasionally high-strung. Breeds like the German Shorthaired Pointer and the Weimaraner adapt best to the country, where they can run freely. But if they are given plenty of exercise and obedience training, they can also adapt to an apartment. Retrievers, both the Golden and the Labrador, are easy to train and adapt to any environment, although in the suburbs and country they often get into trouble because of digging, fence-leaping or barking. Longhaired breeds like the Irish Setter are also plagued by burs and ticks.

Irish Setter being judged at an outdoor show

OPPOSITE: Weimaraner

Confined to a city apartment, a sporting dog may chew you out of house and home. As a puppy he must be supplied with plenty of rawhide toys to keep him from gnawing on the furniture. The more high-strung breeds—the Pointer, German Shorthaired, Irish Setter and the Weimaraner—sometimes howl when confined or left alone and must be trained not to do so. They must also be trained not to jump on the furniture, or they will dig a nest in the cushions and turn your upholstery to rags. All sporting dogs have a tendency to drool, though not excessively. Although sporting dogs in general shed copiously, this is only a minor problem with the shorthaired breeds, who require little grooming. The longhaired breeds need a longer daily brushing.

Sporting dogs are highly responsive to training, especially the Golden and Labrador Retrievers. Breeds such as the Chesapeake, the German Shorthaired, the Irish Setter and the Weimaraner tend to be stubborn and require a firm hand. Because sporting dogs are all active and strong, their training should start at an early age. They are not difficult to housebreak and travel well, but tend to lose weight if confined in a kennel.

Generally good with children and seldom one-person animals, sporting dogs are usually too active and strong for the elderly. Because of their large appetites, they are not economical to keep, but they seldom become obese. Breeds prone to fighting include the Irish Setter (occasionally), the Weimaraner and the Pointer.

Less popular breeds, such as the Springer Spaniel and the Gordon Setter, have escaped the genetic problems that come from overbreeding. The Golden Retriever, sadly, is a prime victim of hip dysplasia,* and both the Irish Setter and the Weimaraner are apt to have overnervous temperaments from overbreeding.

On the whole, sporting dogs are a healthy group. Some, such as the Weimaraner, rarely need to visit the veterinarian for more than the usual once-a-year inspection. Life spans are ten to fifteen years.

GROUP II: HOUNDS

Afghan Hound	Greyhound
Basenji	Harrier
Basset Hound	Irish Wolfhound
Beagle	Norwegian Elkhound
Black and Tan Coonhound	Otter Hound
Bloodhound	Rhodesian Ridgeback
Borzoi	Saluki
Dachshund	Scottish Deerhound
American Foxhound	Whippet
English Foxhound	

Hounds are affectionate and in some cases hypersensitive. They are not the greatest apartment dogs, with the exception of the smaller breeds like the Whippet and the Dachshund. Most, however, will adapt to apartment life if given plenty of exercise and obedience training. They all have a tendency to chew, jump on the furniture and bark, and must be trained out of these habits. Bloodhounds drool badly. The larger hounds need a lot of running exercise, and all of them are apt to dig if given the chance.

Hounds respond to training, but as a group they are stubborn and need a firm hand and considerable time and effort, including long exercise sessions throughout their lives. The Afghan and the Basenji have a reputation as one-person dogs.

* Hip dysplasia is a disease of the hip joint in which the ball and socket are improperly formed, thus causing irritation and a secondary arthritis. The disease is believed to be genetic in origin. It occurs in varying degrees of severity and is often undetectable in the show ring. Responsible breeders try to eliminate hip dysplasia from their breeding stock, but irresponsible breeders take no such precautions.

Bloodhound showing its paces in the show ring

Basenji

Afghans, Basenjis, Borzois, Foxhounds, Greyhounds and Whippets are not recommended for children (Whippets because of their shyness and physical fragility). Bassets, Coonhounds, Bloodhounds and Dachshunds, on the other hand, adapt well to children. The Beagle is famous for his love of children, but we think this is now questionable because of overbreeding. Housebreaking can be a problem with some hounds, especially with Beagles.

Beagles and Afghans fight with other dogs, but most hounds do not. Hounds vary as travelers, depending on their level of activity, and most of them pine when boarded or left alone with strangers. They are economical to feed, especially Whippets and Dachshunds. The smooth-coated hounds require little grooming. Others, such as the Afghan, the Saluki, the Irish Wolfhound, the Borzoi, the Scottish Deerhound and the Norwegian Elkhound require regular brushing. The Afghan also needs occasional styling. Shedding creates problems depending on the color and length of the hair-coat.

Hounds have an average life span of ten to thirteen years.

Black and Tan Coonhound, an American breed

CALLEA PHOTO

GROUP III: WORKING DOGS

Akita	Great Pyrenees
Alaskan Malamute	Komondor
Belgian Malinois	Kuvasz
Belgian Sheepdog	Mastiff
Belgian Tervuren	Newfoundland
Bernese Mountain Dog	Old English Sheepdog
Bouvier des Flandres	Puli
Boxer	Rottweiler
Briard	St. Bernard
Bullmastiff	Samoyed
Collie	Shetland Sheepdog
Doberman Pinscher	Siberian Husky
German Shepherd Dog	Standard Schnauzer
Giant Schnauzer	Cardigan Welsh Corgi
Great Dane	Pembroke Welsh Corgi

Working dogs are the best group as far as training, versatility, adaptability and all-around usefulness are concerned. They are responsive, affectionate, mostly easygoing, good-natured and eager to please. Some, like the Boxer, have a stubborn streak.

In general, working breeds adapt to both city and country if they get a moderate amount of running. Collies and Boxers may have difficulty if they are kept in too much, but the breeds on which city life is the hardest are Malamutes, Komondorok, Rottweilers, Samoyeds and Huskies. The first three need more than the average amount of exercise. The last two breeds like to howl. Country problems are howling and digging.

Working dogs are responsive to training, although the giant breeds require extra patience because they mature late; their serious training should not begin until they are four months old. Until then they should be given plenty of affection and gradually accustomed to the leash. Their attention span lengthens at about twelve weeks, and short obedience sessions may begin then.

Firm handling is essential with working breeds, but it must be adjusted to specific temperaments. Huskies, Boxers, Collies and Old English Sheepdogs tend to be stubborn, and early compliance is a must. Danes, St. Bernards and other giants are sweet-tempered but lazy and require coaxing. German Shepherds and Dobermans are superbly responsive, easily motivated and extremely sensitive. Show them what to do, and they perform willingly. Physical abuse is unbecoming to their dignity—and dangerous, because it can make

Collie

OPPOSITE: Sweetbay's Kestrel,
a Newfoundland trained for
water rescue

Boxer

them touchy. Equally sensitive, slightly shy and extremely responsive to human signals, touch and handling is the delicate Sheltie (Shetland Sheepdog). The Belgian dogs should be investigated by those who seek less popular breeds. For these lovely creatures, breeding is still careful and restrained, and genetic problems are relatively rare.

Most of the working dogs are good for just about everyone. They are wonderful with children, manageable by the elderly, easily handled by both men and women. All the working breeds are protective; in some cases they may attach themselves staunchly to a family, but rarely to just one handler.

Most of the working breeds have good appetites but do not eat ravenously like the hunting breeds. They are not strongly motivated by food and, in spite of their size, *can* be economical to feed. The sheepdogs in particular have been selected for their ability to work long, hard hours with little need or desire for food. The giant breeds, of course, have a reputation for eating their owners out of house and home. Let's face it. Feeding any dog that weighs over one hundred pounds is no small matter. But it must be remembered that after these dogs reach their adult size, they eat less and may be gradually switched to economical all-dry diets.

Grooming can be a complex affair for the working breeds. The one that is particularly difficult in this respect is the Schnauzer. For the massive longhaired breeds like the St. Bernard and the Great Pyrenees, brushing can become tedious. Bathing takes some skill with the giant breeds, especially if they don't like it. These dogs must be gently accustomed to grooming techniques when they are young and small enough to manage. A shower is a good alternative to a tub bath; some dogs, oddly enough, enjoy it more. Shedding is a serious problem with the longhaired breeds and with the thick-coated ones like the Husky, especially if they are kept in apartments where they will shed all year round.

The working breeds don't tend to be dog fighters. Most (but not the Husky) can be left in apartments for long periods of time; all are easily housebroken, are excellent travelers and adapt well to strange environments. St. Bernards, Newfoundlands and Boxers drool.

Indiscriminate breeding has seriously damaged the German Shepherd, the Doberman, the Collie and the Boxer. All these breeds tend to suffer from physical and temperamental problems (although the Boxer has recently improved due to a loss in popularity) The Husky and St. Bernard must also be chosen carefully. Hip dysplasia is a major problem with the working breeds, especially with those that weigh more than forty pounds. This genetic disease is particularly severe in German Shepherds and has been related to breeding for excessively sloping hindquarters.

The working breeds have short to average life spans. The larger breeds tend to live for only nine to ten years.

GROUP IV: TERRIERS

Airedale Terrier	Lakeland Terrier
American Staffordshire Terrier	Manchester Terrier
Australian Terrier	Miniature Schnauzer
Bedlington Terrier	Norwich Terrier
Border Terrier	Scottish Terrier
Bull Terrier	Sealyham Terrier
Cairn Terrier	Skye Terrier
Dandie Dinmont Terrier	Soft-Coated Wheaten Terrier
Fox Terrier	Staffordshire Bull Terrier
Irish Terrier	Welsh Terrier
Kerry Blue Terrier	West Highland White Terrier

The terriers were originally bred to hunt rats and other small varmints. For this reason, they are very active and outgoing, sometimes even stubborn and feisty. They adapt to both city and country life, but an exercise program is essential for the city dweller, especially in the case of the larger breeds like the Airedale. Excessive confinement produces chewing and jumping on people and furniture. In the country terriers dig and bark at other dogs. Terriers are inclined to fight—some, such as the Bull Terrier, were originally bred for this purpose and have a considerable aggressive streak. Early association with other dogs will help control this, but extreme caution and close supervision are required. Terriers take the struggle for dominance seriously. Under laboratory conditions, it has been found necessary to separate terrier pups in order to prevent them from injuring one another in the process of establishing a social hierarchy.

As a rule, terriers are easy to housebreak. Training must begin at an early age, leash-breaking as soon as the dog walks in the door, and serious obedience work by the time he is three months old. A terrier who has been left to his own devices until he is as much as a year old may have already developed serious problems and will be difficult to handle. It is a good idea to plan training sessions after exercise, for the terrier is active, energetic and playful. He loves to chase balls and Frisbees, and a jog in the park will put both of you in a better frame of mind. Obedience work requires a firm hand, for

American Staffordshire Terrier

the terrier will test you to the limit of your patience. He is bullyish and aggressive and likes to be the boss. Fox Terriers can be particularly difficult—not because they are more temperamental than other dogs, but because they are small and cute and therefore apt to be spoiled.

Terriers are wonderful family dogs, and also make good pets for working people as long as they are well exercised and trained. Because they take a lot of punishment, they are excellent companions for small children. Even the smallest breeds are extremely strong, both physically and temperamentally. Terrier aggressiveness tends to take the form of confidence rather than of nastiness, and this toughness has made the terrier a helpful adjunct in the treatment of severely disturbed children; he is so aggressively affectionate and persistent in the face of rejection that he will continue to make advances until he gets a response. He will jump up and lick the child's face and hands until the child pats him, and there is at least one case on record where a Fox Terrier broke through the defenses of an autistic child and made treatment possible.

Terriers have healthy appetites. They also like to eat at the table while you eat, which can easily develop into the bad habit of begging. You can avoid this by concentrating on "down/stay" or "go to your place" during mealtimes (see Chapter 9). Although shedding is not much of a problem, grooming is an arduous job, especially in the case of the longhaired breeds—the Airedale, the Fox Terrier and the Bedlington—who require elaborate scissoring and shaping. Some terriers are plucked, a time-consuming task that means going over the coat by hand and removing clumps of dead hair. Among the easy groomers are the American Staffordshire, the Border Terrier, the Smooth Fox, the Manchester, the Staffordshire Bull, and the Bull Terrier, who require only a daily brushing and a monthly bath. Terriers are enthusiastic travelers, but since the typical terrier jumps around a lot, strict obedience must be enforced in the car to prevent unfortunate accidents.

In general, terriers have not been overbred. The Wirehaired Fox is, however, extremely popular, and for this reason may have suffered more than the others. Be on the lookout for nervous temperaments, but don't expect any terrier to be passive or shy. A puppy should be active, playful, confident and outgoing.

The terrier has an average to long life span—twelve to thirteen years for the small terriers is not considered exceptional.

GROUP V: TOYS

Affenpinscher	Papillon
Brussels Griffon	Pekingese
Chihuahua	Pomeranian
English Toy Spaniel	Poodle (Toy)
Italian Greyhound	Pug
Japanese Spaniel	Shih Tzu
Maltese	Silky Terrier
Manchester Terrier (Toy)	Yorkshire Terrier
Miniature Pinscher	

Toys range from sensitive, nervous types to responsive and even aggressive ones, although aggressiveness usually has more to do with environment and handling than with heredity. Some, like the Yorkie and Chihuahua, show a tendency to be dog fighters and have little regard for the enemy's size.

The toy adapts to country life, the only risk being that he might get lost in the shrubbery. And of course he is the perfect apartment dweller: he can get all the exercise he needs by racing several times around the perimeter of the living room. In fact, his greatest advantage is that he can live almost anywhere, including a great many places where canines are not ordinarily allowed. He fits conveniently in a lap, a pocket or a small apartment, and makes it easy to ignore the fact that he is there. Volume and intensity of voice, however, bear little relationship to size. If the toy feels insulted by excessive confinement—which in his case may mean being kept in a very small room behind a closed door—his barking and whining can build to such a pitch that an entire apartment building finds him objectionable. The moral of this is, if you don't want to move, don't take him for granted.

Toys sit and sleep on the furniture more than other dogs, not because they are by nature ill-behaved, but because it is pleasant and convenient for the owner to have them there. This is a matter of individual choice, but safety factors are worth considering. A fall out of bed, for example, could easily injure a small dog. The worst problems occur because owners tend to spoil toys. They can easily be carried just about anywhere, and often are. If they are customarily treated this way, they will be difficult to board or even to leave alone in the house for an afternoon without whining and howling. Begging and other feeding problems develop when the owner becomes overly concerned about the fact that his little three-pound dog is eager to eat only a few ounces of food a day, which is really all he needs for sustenance. Housebreaking problems, which exist automatically because small dogs have very small bladders, are aggravated by erratic eating and drinking patterns. Many people also believe that toy dogs do not need to be obedience-trained. Nothing could be farther from the truth. The absence of training combined with consistent spoiling will produce an obnoxious, yappy, perhaps even aggressive little beast who is appreciated by no one except the owner, who somehow remains oblivious to the dog's faults. Precisely this kind of dog and this kind of owner have given toys a bad name.

Toys mature earlier than other dogs and must therefore be trained at an early age. The two toughest customers are the Chihuahua and the Yorkshire Terrier, who make up for their diminutiveness with a stubborn streak several miles long. The Maltese and the Yorkie are especially difficult to house-train. You must decide early whether to housebreak or to paper-train, and stick to your decision for the remainder of the dog's life. Even so, you can expect an occasional accident.

Toy dogs are excellent companions for the elderly and for working couples, but in the latter case they must be paper-trained and taught to be left alone for long periods of time when they are still quite young. If the dog is overly pampered, you will have difficulty

Princess, the Margolis' Maltese

introducing him to children. In general, the toy is not a good pet for the very young (two- to five-year-olds). He is too delicate to withstand any abuse.

Long, silky-coated toys like the Maltese and the Yorkie require extensive grooming—daily brushing to prevent mats from forming in their coats, and wrapping before shows to prevent the delicate hairs from breaking (see Chapter 10). Shorthaired toys like the Pug and the Chihuahua need little or no grooming. Medical problems run the gamut, with patellar luxation (slipping kneecap) at the top of the list of genetic ills. This may result in severely malformed legs, but if caught early it can be corrected before the damage is severe (see Chapter 8). Certain breeds, such as the Yorkie, have suffered from overbreeding, so you must be careful where you buy.

One of the greatest advantages to owning a toy is that you can travel anywhere with him. Car travel is easy, for the little toy uses scarcely any space. He is also the only dog small enough to fit under your seat in an airplane, although it should be noted that Pugs and Pekes have respiratory troubles and their owners are advised to take them for short air trips only. Kenneling is also fine as long as the dog is accustomed to it at an early stage.

Although toys are fragile because of their size, they tend to live longer than larger dogs, with an average life span of about fifteen years.

GROUP VI: NON-SPORTING DOGS

Bichon Frise	Keeshond
Boston Terrier	Lhasa Apso
Bulldog	Poodle
Chow Chow	Schipperke
Dalmatian	Tibetan Terrier
French Bulldog	

This group, consisting of breeds that are essentially unrelated, has a diverse range of temperaments. The Dalmatian can be nervous; the Chow can be an aggressive bully; the Keeshond and Lhasa can be stubborn; the Poodle tends to be responsive and outgoing; the Bishon Frise tends to be shy. The Bulldog, originally bred for courage, strength and aggressiveness, has since been turned into the sweetest and most peaceful of all animals.

Most breeds in this group adapt to both city and country, although the Dalmatian is somewhat difficult in the city because of his nervousness. The normal problems of chewing and jumping must

Two Lhasa Apsos and a Shih Tzu

Dalmatian

be corrected when the dogs are young. As a whole, non-sporting dogs require an average amount of exercise, with the Dalmatian needing a little more than that to help reduce the excess energy he might otherwise expend destructively around the house.

Most of these breeds are responsive to training, especially the present number one favorite, the Poodle, both standard and smaller sizes. The Chow, the Dalmatian, the Lhasa and the Bulldog are a little on the stubborn side and need firm handling.

The non-sporting breeds in general love children and can withstand children's roughhousing. The Poodle, the Dalmatian and the Boston Terrier are three of the greatest child-lovers in the canine kingdom. The Chow, too, loves children, but he has an inborn protective instinct and bears watching with strangers. All non-sporting breeds are good for working people, and all except the Chow and the Dalmatian are good for the elderly (the Chow being too stubborn and the Dalmatian too lively for the elderly to handle).

The Bichon Frise, the Chow, the Keeshond, the Lhasa and the Poodle require extensive coat care. The worst medical problems belong to the Bulldog and the Boston Bull, who have respiratory difficulties because of their flat faces. Otherwise, these dogs are not particularly fragile, either physically or temperamentally, and none has suffered extensively from bad breeding. They are good travelers and kennel well.

They have an average life span of ten to thirteen years.

RULE 2:   KNOW THE BREED.

Breeding is the process of specialization. Each breed has been developed by the careful selection for and strengthening of certain genetic characteristics. The Bulldog, for instance, was bred with a flat face so that he could hang on to a bull. Although he does this better than the Greyhound, the Greyhound can run faster than the Bulldog. Terriers were bred to be aggressive, hounds to be phlegmatic. The Bloodhound was bred for tracking. He does this better than a Borzoi, but the Borzoi has better eyes.

Each dog of a specific breed has particular abilities that make him easier to train to certain kinds of tasks. For each special quality, however, he may have a corresponding deficiency. Because of his flat nose, the Bulldog has respiratory problems. The Greyhound, with his long muscles and narrow frame, has less physical strength than the Mastiff. The Bloodhound has a well-developed nose, but he sees poorly. You need to know these kinds of facts before choosing a breed.

For each breed you are considering, we suggest you make out a breed sheet based on the following questions. Sources of information are books, breeders, trainers and veterinarians.

HISTORY
1. What is the past history of the breed?
2. How did the breed originate, and what was its purpose?

TEMPERAMENT
1. What is the breed temperament?

RECENT HISTORY
1. Is the breed popular?
2. Has the breed been overbred?
3. Have temperament problems or physical genetic defects become prevalent?

LIVING CONDITIONS
1. Is the breed likely to adapt to the living conditions that you are going to provide for him?
2. How much space does he need?
3. How much exercise does he need?

TRAINING
1. Is he difficult to train?
2. When should training start?
3. Is he difficult to housebreak?

GROOMING
1. Is he difficult or easy to groom?

MEDICAL
1. Is he a "tough" breed, disease-resistant and easy to keep fit? Or is he a weakling, subject to respiratory, infectious or genetic diseases?

SAMPLE BREED SHEET

Breed: American Cocker Spaniel

History: Originally developed as a hunting dog.

Temperament: Affectionate, can be high-strung, aggressive; tends to fight other dogs.

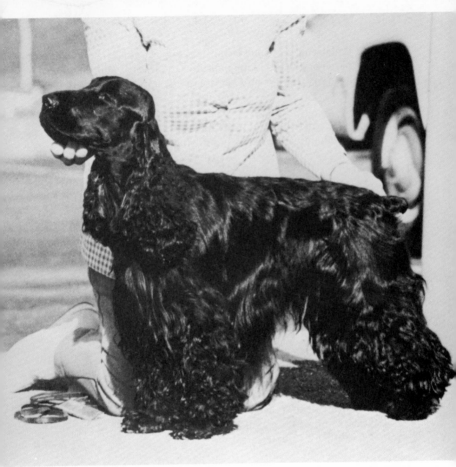

American Cocker Spaniel

Recent History: Indiscriminate breeding has made the cocker both
physically and temperamentally sensitive.

Living Conditions:

Does not always adapt well to apartment life. Does not like
being confined; tends to chew and jump on the furniture; needs
plenty of running exercise. In the suburbs and the country he
likes to dig. He is a good family dog if properly bred—if not, he
may snap at children. Is okay for working people if he receives
enough exercise, and is fine for the elderly. He is an excellent
traveler and adapts well to a kennel. Has a good appetite but is
economical to feed because of his size.

Grooming:

For the house dog, a thorough daily brushing is recommended, and an occasional clipping to keep his coat from getting shaggy. Shedding can be a problem, although not a serious one. For the show animal, grooming is a serious affair. The dog's coat must be clipped and styled, brushing and fussing sometimes continuing up to the moment before he enters the ring.

Medical:

The breed is prone to

CHRONIC SEBORRHEA (especially goldens):   Crusty, scaly lesions, particularly around ears, eyes, along the back, tail and abdomen. May be lifelong.

EAR PROBLEMS: Common because of long, floppy ear flaps.

PYODERMA AROUND THE MOUTH: Moisture in the lip fold provides an excellent medium for infection. The skin in this area is red with a foul-smelling discharge. Responds well to antibiotics and cleansing procedures.

BENIGN SKIN GROWTHS

ACANTHOSIS NIGRICANS (common in blacks):   The skin of the underarms, hind legs and flanks becomes dark and thick, with crusty skin folds and loss of hair. The condition can begin in a mild form as early as six months of age and gets progressively worse. The cause is not known. Treatment is usually topical.

MALIGNANT MELANOMA (in blacks):   Malignant skin tumor arising from melanin-producing cells. Males are more often affected. Tumors around the mouth and toes tend to be highly malignant and spread early.

ECTROPIAN AND ENTROPIAN EYELIDS: Eyelids that turn out or in against the eye, causing chronic tearing.

DISC DISEASE: High incidence, although not as common as in Dachshunds.

OBESITY

GENETIC DISEASES: Possibly acanthosis nigricans and seborrhea.

NORMAL PRACTICES: Tails are docked when the pups are three to four days old—highly recommended procedure. Dewclaws on hind and forelegs may be removed, but dogs with dewclaws are not faulted at AKC shows.

LIFE SPAN: Unless the dog has one of the serious and chronic diseases mentioned above, he tends to live from twelve to fifteen years.

RULE 3:   KNOW THE BREEDER.

If you have followed our advice up to now, you have gone to shows, investigated the different classifications and breeds of dogs, and, we hope, narrowed your choice to *one* of them. Where do you go to get it?

Every thoroughbred dog has a breeder. The more you know about this person, the better off you are. For this reason, we recommend that you go directly to him. Pet shops and shelters are alternative solutions, particularly if you have decided on a mixed breed. The ways to select these will be discussed later.

The Breeder

Most dedicated breeders are not in the *business* of breeding dogs. They do it for the fun of it. They make their profit from grooming, boarding, training, and selling food and equipment. Breeding, if it is properly done, rarely results in profit, and sometimes in loss.

A breeder with a small kennel may turn his operation into a family affair, so that the puppies are around children from the start, everyone cares for them, and they are likely to get the kind of attention that helps them develop healthy personalities. They are also likely to have adapted to the kind of home environment that you will provide.

The breeder offers other advantages as well:

1. You get a better dog than you usually get from a pet shop, for the same or a lower price.

2. You can see the puppy's dam and sometimes his sire and even his grandparents. It should be noted, however, that many owners ship their bitches elsewhere to be bred.

There are also disadvantages to buying from a breeder:

1. Most breeders are not as conveniently located as pet shops. But many people are willing to travel hundreds of miles to purchase a superior animal.

2. Breeders usually give only a forty-eight-hour guarantee. Theoretically, their puppies leave the kennel in excellent mental and physical condition. In most states, however, pet shops are required by law to give a two-week guarantee, which extends beyond the incubation period of the distemper virus. For this reason, a forty-eight-hour guarantee is a disadvantage.

Bargains in buying from a breeder:

1. Breeders sell what they call "pet-quality" puppies for a lower price than those designated "show potential" or "show quality." This doesn't mean that these dogs won't develop into show-quality animals, but merely that the breeder thinks they won't. As we have said, it is very hard to tell whether or not a puppy will be a show-quality animal until he is six months old. Pet-quality puppies belong to show-quality litters and have been bred from show stock. Many an ugly duckling has grown up to be a champion.

2. Breeders sell puppies with major faults at a greatly reduced price. Some of these faults—for example, an overshot or undershot jaw—can cause medical problems. Others, such as a sickle tail, disqualify a dog from Westminster but have no effect on his general health. Such puppies make excellent pets.

3. Breeders sometimes let you take a puppy on what are known as breeder's terms. This means you pay nothing for the dog, but you must sign a contract with the breeder, and it is up to him to state his conditions. The breeder offers this arrangement for two reasons: because he wants to own the dog and because he has an interest in seeing that it is raised in a good home, which he has decided yours is. You become personally liable for the dog even though the breeder still legally owns it. If the dog is injured because of your negligence—or what is decided to be your negligence—you must reimburse the breeder for the dog's potential value and price.

Selecting a Breeder   Unfortunately, there are breeders who in various ways misrepresent their puppies and themselves. How do you avoid buying from one of these?

1. If possible, get a recommendation from a friend or someone you trust. Then write to the American Kennel Club to find out whether the breeder has a good reputation. The Kennel Club keeps files of derogatory information and is willing to supply you with such reports. Many breeders will give you a list of customers. You can contact some of these people to find out if they have been satisfied.

2. Examine the breeder's facilities. If his runs and pens are neat and clean, if there is no perceptible "doggy odor," if the cages are spacious and not crammed together into one small area, if the general environment is appealing, and if the breeder takes pride and pleasure in showing you around, then chances are his dogs are sound. Make sure that he keeps separate pens or runs in which he can isolate sick animals.

3. Look for a breeder who sells only one or two breeds. If he deals with a large number of breeds, he may be running a factory.

Pet Shops

It is true that many pet shops are excellent stores reflecting the attitudes of the proprietors, who are humane and caring individuals. This sort of shop is an excellent place to go when you live far away from the breeder and have no way of getting there.

One must not, however, overlook the possible disadvantages. Some pet shops purchase their dogs from puppy mills, wholesale dog factories where dogs are kept in cages and denied human companionship and exercise, and where the bitches are forced to mate every time they go into heat, which means that they are always in bad shape, usually malnourished and sometimes sick. They are often infested with worms, a condition transferred to the pups through the placenta. Genetic faults are not screened out. As a result, the puppies are born sick and faulty. Often ill from traveling, the mill puppy arrives at the pet shop when he is only four or five weeks old; because he has been taken from his mother too soon, he may have psychological problems right from the start.* For the next several weeks he lives in a pen. Is it any wonder that he becomes aggressive or shy?

The pet shop is more likely than the breeder to sell diseased animals. Pet shops don't sell sick animals because they want to. It's just the nature of the business. When a puppy is shipped he's under stress and may come down with shipping fever.

The pet shop offers lower-quality animals than the breeder, who has devoted years of attention to his breed, and usually sells pups at prices equal to those of the breeder. The shop owner is a middleman. If he is buying directly from the breeder, he has to pay the breeder's price and then cover his own overhead and make a profit. If he buys from a mill, there is an additional middleman called a broker. The more hands the dog passes through, the higher the price you must pay for him. If a mill breeder sells a dog to a pet shop for $100, the shop owner may mark up the price three times, and if there's a broker involved, he'll also take a cut. In this case, if you're paying $300 for a dog at a pet shop, you can't possibly be getting an animal of the same quality you would get if you bought from a reputable breeder at the same price.

* The Animal Welfare Act of 1976–77 has made it illegal to ship puppies by air who are less than eight weeks old. This may help alleviate the puppy-mill situation.

However, pet shops often put puppies on sale, either because they are overstocked or because they want to move puppies out of the store before they become "kennelized" or too old to sell. Many of these puppies make excellent pets.

Be sure to ask to be shown around. The dogs should be clean and well taken care of. Cleanliness is vital when you are dealing with even a small turnover of animals, because it is a major factor in the prevention of disease. If the shop owner has nothing to hide he'll be proud to show you what's behind his window cases and equipment displays. By the way, glass-enclosed cages are deceptive. They are not very porous and do not allow odors to escape.

Ask where the dogs came from. A good pet shop is willing to disclose its sources. Many purchase their dogs from home breeders.

Be on the lookout for overcrowding. A good pet shop doesn't overstock. If the shop has fifteen cages, then it should stock fifteen dogs, one per cage, unless the dogs are very tiny. Small cages should be no less than 24 inches wide and 24 inches deep. The store should have reserve cages for the dogs as they grow bigger. If the store is very large and has as many as fifty cages, then it must have a large enough staff to keep the dogs clean, healthy and well exercised. A small shop with limited stock and enthusiastic personnel is more likely to meet high standards than any of the large chain stores is.

A pet shop that offers other dog-related services, such as grooming, makes most of its money this way, and will not urge you to buy a lot of unnecessary and expensive equipment. Initially you should spend no more than $12 to $14 on accessories, not including the puppy gate, which costs around $25.

Buy only from a shop that offers a two-week health guarantee against distemper and other infectious or communicable diseases. *Never buy from a shop that claims its eight-week-old pups have received all their shots.* This may sound like a bargain, but it's a medical impossibility. Distemper shots come in a three-part series, and the puppy doesn't receive his final inoculation until he is twelve to sixteen weeks old.

Shelters

When you want to adopt a dog and save it from being destroyed, you go to a shelter, where you will find every size, shape and variety of mutt as well as an occasional purebred or two. Most shelters in this country are fine places staffed by enthusiastic animal lovers. The worst problems occur because of lack of space and funds.

Because many of these shelters also serve as pounds, they are required to accept all stray animals regardless of condition, and therefore, in spite of veterinary care and vaccination programs, are unable to prevent the arrival and departure of diseased animals from their premises. To make up for this fact, however, most offer two-week medical guarantees.

Before picking out a dog, ask for a tour of the premises. Cages should be clean and not overcrowded. Some shelters deal with the space problem by keeping dogs in colony kennels, which means that there may be as many as twenty animals per cage. Because this situation is conducive to the spread of disease, we do not recommend adopting a dog from a colony kennel.

We know many many owners who have adopted dogs from shelters and lived happily ever after. Shelters often do more than sweep the streets. Private, nonprofit shelters may have specific criteria for accepting animals. They may require that the animals be examined by a veterinarian before they are allowed on the premises. Sometimes they are able to interview the former owner. Bide-a-Wee in New York City, for example, keeps a record of the dog's history attached to his cage. You can find out whether or not the dog is good with children, whether he gets along with cats or with other dogs, whether he needs a backyard, whether he can be left alone all day, where he came from, who cared for him, and why he was given up.

Many shelters will take the time and trouble to interview prospective owners because they are concerned about whether you and your pet will be able to develop a lasting friendship. Naturally they don't want dogs to come back. Sometimes they may even offer obedience classes for you and your dog, the average price for such classes ranging from $30 to $50.

RULE 4.   KNOW THE DOG.

Now forget everything we have said so far—not because it's worthless information, but because it's all academic when you find yourself facing an actual litter, a six-month-old hound, or a five-year-old bitch to whom, for some unfathomable reason, you have taken a fancy. If you have studied the breed, the breeder, the shop or the shelter, you are a step ahead. But the truth is, even if you know nothing about the dog, the history of his breed, or his previous life style, *you can learn all you need to know within half an hour or less*—just by using your eyes, ears and instincts, and by performing a few simple tests. The particular puppy, his physical condition and his individual personality are much more important than his breed, his breeder, or any bad things that may have happened to him.

Differences between individual animals, even between puppies from the same litter, can be profound. One puppy may be a bully, another shy, another responsive and affectionate. No breed book can prepare you for this. We have therefore narrowed down your final selection process to two essential steps. First, you must determine whether the dog is healthy. Second, you must give him a personality test.

Choosing a Healthy Dog

If you're careful, you can detect the signs of disease before you take a dog from his kennel. A medical checklist can be found below.

MEDICAL CHECKLIST

SYMPTOM	POSSIBLE ILLNESS
Heavy discharge of mucus from eyes or nose	Respiratory infection, conjunctivitis, distemper
Potbelly	Worms
Listlessness	Worms, distemper
Diarrhea in the cage	Worms, distemper
Cough (To check for a cough, rub the throat gently with your finger; this triggers the cough reflex if excess mucus is present in the trachea. Also, place your ear against the dog's chest and listen for the sound of the ocean; if present, this also indicates excess mucus.)	Kennel cough, roundworms, distemper
Sores on skin or patches of hair missing	Skin disease, heavy infestation of parasites

SYMPTOM	POSSIBLE ILLNESS
Dog fails to respond when you clap your hands or whistle	Deafness
Dog fails to respond when you move your hands in front of his face	Blindness
Foul odor emanating from ears	Ear infection
Twitching	Nervous disorder, distemper

Whether you purchase your dog at a shelter, a pet shop, or from a breeder, insist on a medical guarantee. Then have the dog examined by a veterinarian within forty-eight hours of purchase. Make sure the seller gives you the medical papers that provide a complete record of inoculations administered and medications given while the dog was under his auspices. Show this to the veterinarian so that he can get a clearer idea of what additional shots and medications may be necessary.

Testing for Personality

Temperament divides into two categories. The first includes the traits that a dog is bred for. A Weimaraner is bred for his hunting instinct, soft mouth, endurance and strength. A German Shepherd is bred for intelligence, adaptability, trainability and the watchdog instinct. All breeds have mental characteristics bred into them and retain these characteristics as part of their standard. The true business of the professional breeder is to breed with the appropriate mental as well as physical characteristics in mind.

The second part of temperament is what we call the dog's personality. It's all the things inside his head that determine his behavior. A large part of it is genetic, predetermined, inherited from his parents and grandparents. The rest is molded within the first weeks of his life and depends on the kind and quality of socialization he receives, the pleasantness or unpleasantness of his environment. By the time the puppy is twelve weeks old, his personality is immutable. His behavior can be modified with the proper training, but his basic personality is fixed for life.

The genetic factors that determine a dog's personality are handed down from preceding generations; nothing can alter his genes. Socialization and environmental factors, however, make a great deal of difference. When a dog is properly socialized, he spends the first seven weeks of his life with his mother and his litter mates, learning how to get along with other dogs and benefiting from his mother's nurturing and from the security and warmth of her body. If he is taken from his mother too soon, his temperament may be unalterably damaged. As we have said, the period for the dog's socialization with human beings is from his seventh to his twelfth week of life. During this period it is absolutely essential that he be handled by people. If he is played with and cuddled, he has an excellent chance of becoming a loving and affectionate pet. If he is ignored or treated harshly, he will learn very quickly not to trust human beings.

The puppy's environment also affects him. If he is kept exclusively in a kennel or a cage during the first twelve weeks of his life, he may be shy and withdrawn when he enters the outside world. If, on the other hand, he is brought to a home where he can enjoy constant contact with people and possibly even with other animals while he is still under three months old, and if he has his own sleeping quarters with a soft blanket, rawhide toys and all the other creature comforts that he needs, he will almost certainly be a cheerful and affectionate dog.

A dog's personality falls into one of six basic types. A *responsive* dog is happy, outgoing, loving, alert, curious and willing to please. A *nervous* dog has excess energy and is constantly pacing and panting. He is easily distracted and difficult to train because he can't concentrate and doesn't pay attention. His nervousness is usually the result of a genetic mismatch. A *shy* dog is a frightened dog. He is quiet, timid and withdrawn. He may hide under the furniture, or he may be afraid of strange noises. His shyness is usually the result of a combination of genetics and mishandling. The *sedate* dog is quiet, inactive and easygoing. He is not overly enthusiastic and due to his natural lethargy is somewhat resistant to training. But once trained, he is easy to control. An *aggressive* dog is a dog that bites, snarls, growls and threatens. His aggressive nature may be the result of genetics, mishandling, improper socialization with litter mates, premature separation from his mother, or a combination of two or more of these factors. The *stubborn* dog, sometimes misrepresented as spiteful, is obstinate and determined, often willing to give up his own comfort to prove a point. If you order him *down*, he will lie down slowly, keeping his belly suspended above the ground. He will do this with great decorum, sometimes posing with his forelegs crossed aristocratically. Far from being spiteful, the stubborn dog is usually friendly and outgoing, and once you get him trained and working, he makes a splendid pet. His stubbornness is invariably the result of genetics.

Which of these six basic personality types suits you best depends largely on your own personality and what you want of a dog. The *responsive* dog is easy to train and adapts well to family life. He loves to romp with the children and barks at strangers. The *nervous* dog is difficult to train and difficult to handle, but if you are willing to work hard with him and if you have an acre or two where he can run off his excess energy, then by all means consider him. His friendly, grateful nature makes him a superb pet. The *shy* dog appeals to more sensitive natures. He requires the gentlest of handling, but it is a great pleasure when you finally draw him out. The *sedate* dog is perfect for elderly people. He needs little exercise and, once trained, handles with elegance and ease. The *stubborn* dog makes a good hunter because he has the persistence to endure in the field.

An *aggressive* puppy must be corrected and controlled. If his problems are genetic, he will be extremely difficult to work with. He needs extensive obedience training—twice as much as a responsive dog—and even then there's no guarantee that he will work out. If he's young, you have the age factor on your side. An older dog—say, a 70- or 80-pound German Shepherd—has 1,200 pounds of pressure in his jaws and could be so lethal that even a professional may not want to deal with him. If a professional does attempt to train him, his methods will be severe, almost harsh at times. He has no choice. An aggressive dog is a potential killer.

We have devised a series of tests that can be administered to any dog between seven weeks and twelve years of age to help you determine the dog's personality. They can be performed anywhere, with a minimum of equipment: a set of keys; a corrective collar (choke) for an older dog, a nylon slip collar for a puppy; a six-foot leather leash; and a shake-can made from an empty soda can with pennies inside. It should be noted that several of them do not reveal a stubborn personality.

1. PICK THE DOG UP.

This test is particularly suited to puppies, but you can perform it on an older dog if you are able to lift him. The purpose is to determine

ALL PHOTOS BY FRANCINE MEISLER

whether the dog trusts you. Pick him up and cradle him like a baby, belly up, feet in the air. First, hold him level. Then very slowly tilt him so that his head is down. Gently place your hand under his throat to see how he reacts. This is an extremely vulnerable position for a dog, but you will be surprised at how many will lie in your arms without a whimper.

RESULTS

PERSONALITY	BEHAVIOR
Responsive/Sedate	Will just lie in your arms, look at you, lick your hand. If you snuggle your face against him, he will lick you.
Nervous	Won't lie still. He will whine, wiggle, jump out of your arms.
Shy	Will be too frightened to move at all. His expression will be terrified, his eyes will bulge out; he may scream or try to bite.
Aggressive	Will snarl, curl his lips, try to go after you, try to bite.

NOTE: If a dog shows any signs of aggression and is more than a few weeks old, do not perform the above test on him.

FRANCINE MEISLER

2. USE YOUR VOICE.

Try making the high-pitched whimper that a dog makes. Talk to the dog as you would to a baby. If your voice is too loud, harsh, gruff or low-pitched, the dog may become frightened. If you know the dog's name, use it. "Hi, pal, hi, Ginger . . . Hi ya, pal . . . Hi, honey . . . Come on, girl . . . How are ya doing? . . . Come on, Ginger."

Call the dog to you, clap your hands, call again. The sound of clapping may or may not cause the dog to hesitate.

RESULTS

PERSONALITY	BEHAVIOR
Responsive/Nervous	Will run to you, be happy to see you, jump on you, lick you.
Shy	May come slowly; may be apprehensive when you clap your hands.
Sedate	May not come at all, or may come so slowly you're bored by the time he gets there.
Stubborn	May come—or may decide to do something else.
Aggressive	May come unless aggressiveness is a defense against timidity.

3.   WHISTLE.

Whistle to see if you can get the dog's attention. Sometimes, even if he is at a distance, he will stop whatever he is doing and come to you.

RESULTS

PERSONALITY	BEHAVIOR
Responsive/Nervous	Will come to you.
Sedate	May come slowly.
Stubborn	May not pay any attention to you at all, or he may look up, show curiosity, and then continue his own more interesting activities.
Shy	May show apprehension; may come slowly.
Aggressive	If you suspect aggressive personality, don't test.

4.   THROW THE KEYS.

Throw the keys in front of you. The purpose of this test is to see how the dog responds to noise and what he does after he discovers the cause of it.

RESULTS

PERSONALITY	BEHAVIOR
Responsive	He is always alert and curious. He will stop what he is doing, turn around, look at the keys, go over to them, and smell them. He may even pick them up in his mouth and play with them.
Nervous	May be so distracted that he won't even notice the keys. Or he may go to them quickly, run around them, and then retreat.

PERSONALITY	BEHAVIOR
Shy	Will back away from the keys, go slowly toward them, jump back, then cautiously approach again.
Sedate	May slowly approach the keys and check them out. He may pick them up in his mouth and pounce on them.
Aggressive	An aggressive older dog may bark at the keys, growl, curl his lips. Make sure he is on a leash.

5. RATTLE THE SHAKE-CAN.

The purpose of the shake-can is to create a noise louder than that of the keys. The can is particularly effective on grass or any other soft surface that will absorb the sound of keys. Do not throw the can directly at the dog because it will frighten him. Shake the can behind your back and drop it to the side; watch the dog to see how he responds.

RESULTS

PERSONALITY	BEHAVIOR
Responsive	Will look at the can, go to it, pick it up in his mouth, play with it, or bring it back to you.
Nervous	Will get very excited, pick the can up, throw it around, race around with it. Or he may be distracted and not pay any attention to it at all.
Shy	Will back away from the can and show you that he is frightened.
Sedate	May get up slowly and go over to the can. Or he may remain totally unimpressed.
Aggressive	PUPPY ONLY. Will bark at the can, snarl at it, growl at it, go after it, bite it.

NOTE: Do not give this test to an aggressive older dog.

6.   TAKE THE DOG OUTSIDE.

The object of this test is to see how the puppy reacts to the outside
environment. Is he curious about the different sights, smells and
sounds? Does he pace around, looking and looking? Does he stand
transfixed?

RESULTS

PERSONALITY	BEHAVIOR
Responsive	Will be curious. His body will be straight, his stance erect. He will be proud and unafraid of his surroundings. He will look around, sniff, pounce playfully on a leaf.
Nervous	Will constantly pace, looking and sniffing, looking and sniffing.
Shy	Will probably not walk at all. He will be frightened, may try to run back to the warmth and security to which he is accustomed.
Sedate	May just walk around slowly checking things out. Nothing fazes him.
Aggressive/Stubborn	Test does not reveal these personalities.

7.   TEST THE DOG WITH COLLAR AND LEASH.

The purpose of this test is to put pressure on the dog, to force him
to respond in a certain way. Place the collar around the dog's neck
and attach the leash (see Chapter 9 for the correct way to do this).
Walk with the dog to see what he does. He may pull slightly at the
leash. Don't use excessive force to hold him back.

RESULTS

PERSONALITY	BEHAVIOR
Responsive	Will follow you, stop; you call him—"Come on, boy"—and he will follow you again. He may paw at the leash, but will not attack it aggressively.
Nervous	Will be distracted, go to the end of the leash and correct himself, come back to you, then get distracted again.
Shy	May stop, dig his paws in and not move, or may fall on his back and behave a little aggressively, whine and scream.
Sedate	May tolerate the leash or simply resist it, but he won't show much energy one way or the other.
Aggressive	May bite at the leash, jump toward it, go after it, growl.
Stubborn	May fight the leash, jump up, shake his head. Shows resistance but not fear.

8. TEST THE DOG WITH FOOD.

The purpose of this test is to see how the dog reacts to food. With a young puppy the test is simple. You show him the food and see how he responds to it. Is he a voracious eater? Does he come to you, follow you? Does he care about the food at all?

For an older dog, the test is performed while he is wearing a collar and leash. Offer him a piece of food but say nothing. Do not encourage him to go to the food. Most dogs will automatically go to it. When the dog reaches out for it, jerk him and say, "No." Praise him immediately: "Good boy." Hold the food out again and proceed as before. Eventually the dog will stop reaching for the food.

RESULTS

PERSONALITY	BEHAVIOR
Responsive	May be "trained" after three or four jerks not to take the food.

PERSONALITY	BEHAVIOR
Nervous/Stubborn	May require many jerks.
Shy	May turn his head and back away after a single correction.
Sedate	May not go for the food at all. If he does, he will give up very quickly.

NOTE: Do not perform the above test on an aggressive dog.

These eight simple tests will give you a reliable insight into the personality of any dog and help you to distinguish between personality problems and puppy problems. A puppy that jumps on you and on the furniture, chews and nips playfully, wets the rug and barks when you confine him is not a dog with a personality problem. He is a normal, healthy, happy puppy, and if he is treated lovingly and trained properly he will develop into an affectionate, well-behaved pet. A dog between seven and twelve weeks old who screams or snarls when you pick him up, growls, bites or attacks has an aggressive nature. No puppy should snarl and growl at you; no puppy should go after you. Too many people think that puppies will grow out of these problems, but no dog outgrows his personality.

BOTH PHOTOS BY FRANCINE MEISLER

An aggressive dog can be controlled with obedience training if he is trained when he is small enough and young enough not to cause damage in the process. But if you buy an aggressive puppy and don't train him, sooner or later you will have a lawsuit on your hands. The aggressive puppy must be trained in the home, with his people around him, by a professional trainer who has the experience, the skill and the knowledge to deal with this kind of problem.

A Postscript about Purebreds

Whether you buy from a pet shop or breeder, there are three additional essential steps you must take:

1. *Be prepared.* Learn the breed standard and understand the various terms that are used to describe the animal, his conformation and his different qualities. A good shopkeeper or breeder will respond to this kind of accuracy, will be willing to give you additional information, and will also tell you if the dog has serious faults.

2. *Ask about AKC registration papers.* If you do not receive them at the time of sale, obtain a firm promise that they will be mailed to you within two weeks. If they are not, write to the American Kennel Club, 51 Madison Avenue, New York, New York 10010.

3. If your dog will grow up to weigh more than forty pounds, make sure that he has been bred from OFA-certified stock. (OFA stands for Orthopedic Foundation for Animals, an organization dedicated to the elimination of hip dysplasia in dogs.) This is not a perfect guarantee, but it is the best you can get against hip dysplasia. (See Chapter 8 for more details about this disorder.)

3

BRINGING YOUR DOG HOME

Whether you are buying a puppy or a full-grown dog, bringing him home is like bringing home a baby. In both cases, you can take care of most of the details in advance, and there are certain things that you should be sure to have on hand.

A pet shop offers an apparently endless variety of dog equipment, but many of the items are useless and a few are downright harmful. All that you really need are:

Bowls

You should have two bowls, one for water and one for food. If you are getting a Spaniel or a Basset or any long-eared dog, buy a bowl especially made to prevent the dog's ears from falling in the food. A special kind of dish called a cocker bowl has sides that slant inward from a wide bottom. Because the sides slant inward, the ears tend to dangle outside the bowl.

The best kind of bowl to buy is one made of weighted vinyl plastic. A puppy can't overturn it, and because vinyl is soft, he can chew on it without injuring himself. Ceramic bowls are heavy enough to prevent the puppy from overturning them, but they break easily. Also, some types of ceramic have been known to cause lead poisoning.

A Brush

If you are buying a puppy, get a soft brush with natural bristles that will be gentle to his skin. He will enjoy the feel of it and will learn that grooming can be a pleasurable experience. If you are buying an older dog, your choice will depend on the type of coat he has.

1. *Longhaired* (a dog with a long, silky coat, such as an Afghan or Maltese): A pin brush with a long wooden handle and blunted metal pins set in a soft cushion for bristles is the best choice.

2. *Medium, wiry hair* (a Poodle or Fox Terrier type of coat): Buy a slicker brush with angulated wire bristles about ⅜ inch long. This kind of brush is particularly good for smoothing out tangles.

3. *Medium, soft* (like a German Shepherd's coat): Buy a hound mitt. It will fit over either your hand or a rectangular piece of wood (if you want to use it as a slicker brush). One side of the mitt has wire bristles; the other side is a polishing cloth made of velvet or soft corduroy.

4. *Shorthaired* (Whippet or Weimaraner): A small, rectangular brush made of solid rubber with nub-like rubber bristles is ideal. A hound mitt is an acceptable alternative, but be careful not to scratch a shorthaired's sensitive skin.

Shampoo

A mild, all-purpose dog shampoo is suitable for a puppy or an older dog who is indoors most of the time. If the dog shows any sign of skin problems, consult your veterinarian. If you buy an older dog and intend to keep him outdoors, buy a flea-and-tick shampoo (unless you decide to use some other method of parasite control).

Toys

Since most puppies and many of the larger breeds need to chew, it's wise to supply your dog with toys to teethe on. The best toys to buy are rawhide bones, which are usually easily digested if the dog chews them up. Very occasionally, rawhide will irritate the gastrointestinal tract, so if your dog develops diarrhea, consult your veterinarian. In this case, a hard nylon bone is an acceptable substitute. Avoid soft rubber toys and toys with squeakies. The dog may chew up the rubber and swallow the squeakies. Avoid all painted toys (they can cause lead poisoning) and wooden toys (these can splinter and injure the dog's intestinal tract).

Food

Find out what your dog's previous diet has been and buy enough of whatever he's been eating to last for several days. This doesn't mean that you'll have to stick to this same diet forever, but you should give the dog what he's used to for a few days, at least until he has adjusted to all the other changes you are imposing on him. We have a lot of ideas about how dogs should be fed, so you might consult the next chapter of this book. Also, during your initial visit to the veterinarian, speak to him about feeding your dog. If you decide to change your dog's diet, do it gradually so as not to upset him.

Vitamins and Minerals

Never supplement your dog's diet without first consulting your veterinarian. Most commercial dog foods are so sound nutritionally that it could be dangerous to supplement them. Excessive amounts of vitamins are toxic, and minerals like calcium and phosphorus must be kept in the correct balance.

Collar

The type of collar you want depends on the size of the dog. A puppy should have a rolled leather or nylon collar about three inches larger than his neck. If the collar is too tight, it will choke the dog, and if it is too loose, the dog may put it in his mouth and choke himself on it.

For an older dog, get a metal chain-link corrective collar. If the dog is long-coated and has had some obedience training or is docile by nature, substitute a rolled leather or nylon slip-collar, which will cause less damage to the hair around his neck.

Leash

A six-foot leather leash is the right length for training purposes and will be soft against your hands. Canvas and nylon leashes are also acceptable but are rough and uncomfortable to hold. If you get a young puppy, you can snap the leash on the puppy's collar and let him drag it around the house so that he can get used to the weight of it. (Only do this when you are home or not so busy that you can't keep your eye on the puppy.)

Medical Supplies

We suggest you keep these together in one place where you can always find them when you need them. Augment the list below with any items or medicines recommended by your veterinarian.

RX FOR DOGS
● Child's rectal thermometer
● Petroleum jelly
● Hydrogen peroxide (for cuts and wounds, not for ears)
● Gauze and adhesive tape (1 inch wide)
● Cotton balls
● Cotton swabs (for ears)
● Kaopectate or Pepto-Bismol (or both)
● Aspirin
● Flea powder or spray (not both)
● Blanket
● One flat board (large enough to use as a stretcher, if you should ever need it)

Bed

Don't buy one. Fancy wicker beds are bad for three reasons: they are expensive, unnecessary and dangerous because the puppy will chew them. For a puppy, either build a small wooden box with sides low enough to allow him to climb out of it easily or get a cardboard box from the grocery store. Cardboard has two advantages: it is less bother for you and more digestible if the puppy decides to chew it. Line the box with blankets made of fabric with a tight weave so the puppy doesn't get his feet caught. Soft cotton baby blankets are perfect. The box provides security and protection from drafts and should be used until the puppy is four months old. After that you can place the blankets directly on the floor or on top of an old sponge-rubber cushion. Don't pad the bed with anything that has feathers in it. If the dog's bird-dog instincts get the best of him and he decides to chew, you'll have a real mess on your hands.

For the older dog, a folded blanket or a piece of carpet placed in a corner or in some other secure spot is comfortable and convenient. The bedding should be soft enough to protect the dog's elbows from the hard floor. This will prevent the hair from wearing away from his sharp edges and keep the skin from developing thick, ugly calluses.

Puppy Gate

This is a necessary item for both the puppy and the older dog if you intend to confine him in one specific area of the house. It eliminates the practice of closing the door. Some dogs whine and cry behind closed doors because they feel frightened and trapped; with a puppy gate, the dog can see out into the rest of the household and is less likely to feel dejected or afraid. A proper puppy gate is made of wire mesh with a wooden frame and comes in various sizes. Be sure to get one high enough to prevent your dog from leaping over it. Do not use a child's gate, even if you happen to have one lying around the house. A child's gate is made of wood that accordions together for storage. A puppy can easily crawl through the holes in this type of gate. Besides, while children, mercifully, teethe on hard rubber, puppies are inclined to teethe on anything in sight, and a dog will chew right through this type of gate in no time. Not only is the object of confining the dog completely lost, but the dog is very likely to end up with splinters of wood in his intestines—which might require an immediate trip to the veterinarian, emergency surgery and so on. You get the idea.

Sleeping Quarters

One major decision to make before you bring the dog home is where he will sleep. He needs his own area within the household, away from the rest of the family. Then if he has housebreaking lapses or throws up in the middle of the night, he won't disturb anyone's rest.

Many people make the mistake of taking their dogs into their own bedroom at night. This is a bad idea for several reasons. The dog may become so attached to you that it will be impossible to leave him alone without his howling. He won't sleep anywhere without you, which means he won't adjust to a kennel if you go on vacation. If you take him with you, you won't be able to leave him alone for a minute. The same strictures apply to letting the dog sleep in a child's bedroom.

The kitchen, bathroom or hall all make good sleeping quarters. The basement, which many people choose because it's easier to clean up after a dog there than it is in any other room in the house, is less desirable. The basement is apt to be cold and dungeon-like and to make the dog feel dejected. Also, if he is not expected to learn clean habits in the basement, he may think that he is not expected to learn them anywhere.

An outdoor bed is perfectly acceptable if you have a kennel, a run or a comfortable enclosed area that provides warmth and shelter. A dog can live outdoors most of his life with no ill effects to his psyche. Just be sure that he receives the daily affection and attention he needs, whether he is living indoors or out.

Never tie the dog up.* If you do, he will whine or bark, scream or chew. Worst of all, he can hang himself. A dog can panic when he is tied, work himself into a frenzy, run in circles, get tangled up in the rope or around the tree or stake, and choke himself to death. While we are on the subject of choking, *always* remove the dog's corrective collar before you leave him alone, because the collar can get caught on something and the dog can strangle.

The Trip Home

The chances are that your new puppy has never been in a car before. Try to make his first experience a good one. If you're buying an older dog, find out if he has traveled by car before; if he has, ask whether he enjoyed traveling and what ground rules his former master set down. If he is especially shy, he may approach the car with fear and trembling, quiver and quake with emotion, get sick during the trip and try to leap into your lap for protection. As his new master, your job is to change all this. Most dogs love car rides once they get used to the idea.

Whether you're getting a dog or a puppy, follow these rules when you go to pick him up:

1.   Take at least one other person with you. If you're driving and

---

* The exception to this rule is the sled dog. Sled dogs are often kenneled together and kept on chains.

the dog suddenly jumps in your lap or attacks the gearshift, you may find yourself in the middle of a very bad accident.

2. If the dog is full grown, make sure that he hasn't been fed for at least ten hours before the trip; if he's a puppy, for at least five hours. If the dog is empty, he's less likely to vomit. And if he's hungry when you get him home, you can feed him, which gives him a good introduction to his new quarters.

3. Let the dog get used to your car before you start. Let him sit in it for five minutes or so, in both the back and the front. Let him climb in and out of the car. After he is used to it, turn the motor on. After a few minutes drive twenty feet or so and stop. Try to make the car ride fun for the dog. If he is an older animal and cringes or pulls back on the leash as you approach the car, hold him close to you, stroke him and talk to him while he inspects it.

4. Put a puppy in a cardboard box small enough to fit in a lap and lined with towels or a blanket. Then if the puppy gets sick, he will throw up in the box, and if the puppy is nervous, whoever is with you can put his hand in the box and pat him. With an older dog it's often better to have him and your companion sit in the back seat.

5. Don't wear good clothes.

6. Take along lots of paper towels.

A Word about Car Sickness   Any animal is subject to motion sickness, just as people are. It's probably hereditary and is especially prevalent among animals with an acute sense of balance. Tension increases the problem by causing an acidic stomach; if the dog becomes extremely frightened, he may even get diarrhea. Motion sickness is caused by the rocking movement of the car, especially in stop-and-go traffic, and usually occurs when the dog has a full stomach.

The best ways to prevent motion sickness are not feeding him before the trip, driving smoothly and making him feel as comfortable and secure as possible. Do *not* give him tranquilizers unless they are prescribed by a veterinarian.

If after all these precautions the dog still gets sick, there's nothing to do but clean up and congratulate yourself on having chosen an animal with a well-developed sense of balance. You will have some advance warning. The first thing a dog does when he gets sick is to start panting and salivating. He may try to run away from you, which is the worst thing he can do. If he goes to the floor of the car, he will get sicker because there's more of a rocking sensation on the floor and the air is stuffy. If he's big, try to keep him next to you. If he's a puppy or very small, keep him in the box on your lap. If it's a very hot day, keep the window open, and provide him with a few ice cubes to lick. Don't give him large quantities of water; they will only make him vomit.

Introducing Your Dog to Your House

Bring the dog inside the house and immediately confine him to the area that will be his home. Let him explore. If he's a well-tempered dog, he will be curious and start sniffing around.

● *The Puppy*   Tell the rest of the family not to say or do anything negative to him. He's a baby and is new to this environment, so he has to be treated lovingly. Every member of the household should be allowed to touch him, hold him and talk to him, but gently. Don't rush at him. Let him get used to his new surroundings.

Introduce a puppy gently and slowly to his new surroundings.

BILL WARD

● **The Older Dog**   If you know the history of the dog, you may
not have any problem. If he has a good disposition and has been
with a family before, he may adapt to his new people right away. If
he's shy or frightened, let him feel his way. Too many people react
to the dog's personality in terms of what they think he *should* be
like, not in terms of what he is like. It's a scary experience for any
creature to be switched from one environment to another, and it may
take a while for a dog to settle down.

As soon as the dog has relaxed and got used to his surroundings,
let him explore the rest of the house. If he's a puppy, you'll certainly
have to keep an eye on him to make sure that he doesn't relieve
himself on your rug, but the older dog, too, must be watched,
especially if he's nervous. If he's already housebroken, he's unlikely
to make a mistake, but if he is not, you'll have to keep tabs on him
until he learns the rules.

After a little while, return him to his area of confinement and give
him something to eat. Before you bed him down at night, make sure
he is thoroughly exercised. For the puppy, this means a lot of
affection and play before bedtime; for the older dog, a run outdoors.
Exercise will help him sleep the first night.

The First Night

Leave the light on and the door open so that the dog doesn't feel
frightened. (Remember, you bought a puppy gate so the dog can look
out into the rest of the house.) Be sure he has his toys, his bed and
a bowl full of water.

● **The Puppy**   If he whines, try giving him a late-night snack.
There is always the chance that he is hungry, and he isn't housebroken
yet anyway. You might also put a hot-water bottle in his bed to keep
him warm. He's used to sleeping with his mother and litter mates,
so he's bound to feel a little cold and lonely. Sometimes a ticking
clock will help him relax. If you try all these things and the puppy
still whines, let him. Don't take him in your room or in bed with
you. He'll get used to his new home in a day or two, and the whining
will stop.

● **The Older Dog**   If he has a very responsive and adaptable
personality, he may just curl up on his bed and go to sleep. Or he
may behave like a puppy and whine. If it's a low whine, it's probably

just because the situation is new to him, and eventually he should go to sleep. Give him a little affection, then leave him and hope for the best. If he's had any obedience training, say "no" firmly. It may take him a couple of nights to get used to the situation.

If he sleeps outside, the chances of whining or even howling are vastly increased because he feels more isolated from the rest of the family. As long as he is just whining softly, you have nothing to worry about. If he starts to bark or howl, he will disturb the neighbors. All you can do in this case is correct him, explain to the neighbors, and hope for the best. Don't expect to get much sleep for the first couple of nights, but if you are determined that the dog sleep outside, keep him there until he gets used to it. It usually takes only a few nights.

The Next Day

1. Take the dog to a veterinarian (see Chapter 7).
2. Get a license. If you adopt a dog from a shelter, you won't be allowed to take him until you have bought a license. Otherwise, you'll have to see about getting one yourself. Call your local humane society immediately and the people there will tell you what to do.

Establishing a Routine

For both your own and the dog's sake you should establish a routine for your life together as soon as possible. Decide when you will feed him, walk him and put him to bed so that he will know what to expect. Make a set of rules for him and stick to them. Don't allow him on the couch one day and forbid him to get on it the next. Remember, he wants to please you, but it's hard for him to do the right thing if he doesn't know what that is.

Puppy Problems

Every member of the household should understand that all puppies do wrong things. They chew, jump, nip, get into the garbage, beg at the table. All these things are to be expected. The problem is how to go about correcting such behavior.

● **Chewing** Puppies chew to relieve the pain and itching of their gums while they are teething. An old washcloth soaked in cold water and frozen will help numb the gums and ease the pain. Every two hours or so give the puppy a new cloth, and refreeze the thawed cloth. Ice cubes are also fun for puppies to chew on, but they melt more quickly than the cloths, which will last for a couple of hours. Rawhide toys are also excellent. If you rub them with bacon fat, the dog will be attracted by the smell and will automatically favor these toys over the furniture. Or you can fill the hollow of a large cooked marrow bone with bologna. The idea is not to react to the problem but to distract the puppy by giving him something that's all right for him to chew.

Never give him steak or chicken bones (these splinter and may get caught in his intestines), your old pillow, your old sock or your old shoe. If you give him something old of yours, he will also chew on your newer models because he will recognize the smell and like it. If you correct the chewing problem while the dog is a puppy, you won't have trouble with it later on.

● **Jumping** All puppies jump. If the dog continues to jump as he gets older, it is generally because the owner has encouraged such behavior. In any case, the habit of jumping can easily be corrected. Let the puppy wear his leash around the house, and when he jumps, give him a firm correction and say "no." Never knee him in the chest or step on his back toes; such practices are barbaric.

● **Mouthing** This is almost always owner-induced. Most men like to play with a dog by boxing the dog's head with their hands, teasing the dog, or putting their hands in the dog's mouth. Mouthing begins when the dog learns to play by putting his mouth on your arms and hands. Eventually it becomes a biting problem: the dog decides he likes to put his mouth on you, his mouth gets bigger, he applies a little pressure with his jaws, and his teeth start to hurt your hand. You can stop this with a leash and collar and a firm "no." Or you can take a soda can full of pennies, shake it and say "no" when the dog starts to mouth. Or you can shoot a water pistol in the dog's mouth.

● **Begging** This is *always* owner-induced. It becomes a habit because when the dog begs, he gets food. If you don't want your dog to beg, don't feed him from the table—and don't let anyone else do it either. If the dog starts to go near the table, give him a quick correction with the word "no," or a shake of the penny-can with the word "no," or a blast with the water pistol. Once he is obedience-trained, you can give him a "down/stay," and he'll rest peacefully while you're eating your dinner.

● *Getting into the Garbage* This is something all dogs love to do. To a dog, garbage is something that smells good and tastes even better. Don't let the dog get too set in this habit before you change his ideas about it, because garbage is full of soft bones, meat strings and other items that can cause medical emergencies. As long as you remember that the garbage is dangerous, you won't allow your dog to get into it. Give him a firm correction with leash and collar and a firm "no." You can also use either the shake-can or a squirt gun.

● *Spoiling* This is not the same thing as loving. You can't love a dog too much. People end up spoiling a dog because they think that spoiling is a sign of love. Spoiling is feeding the dog from the table and thus teaching him to beg; being inconsistent about rules; allowing the dog to jump on you and not on your visitors; changing your mind about whether the dog can sit on the furniture. The trouble with all these things is that the owner ends up not loving the dog at all and treating him very badly. The dog gets punished when he begs at the table and gets thrown outdoors whenever there is company. Or he ends up at the pound. It's best not to spoil the dog in the first place, but if he begins to acquire bad habits, be sure to correct them immediately—the sooner the better.

Correction

When you correct a puppy, remember that he isn't being bad; he just hasn't learned any better. Your job is not to punish him but to teach him. And you must understand the dog's personality before you correct him. If he is responsive, he needs only a moderate amount of correction. If he is shy and sensitive, you should be gentle. If he is stubborn, you can be firm. But if you come on too strong and punish too hard, you ruin the dog's personality.

If you've never owned a dog before, it will be difficult at first, because you are learning at the same time he is. You are bound to feel frustrated and helpless. But think of it this way: buying the right equipment doesn't make you a cook. What good are the right utensils if you don't know how to use them properly? You have to read a book or get somebody to teach you. You can't get mad at the equipment if it doesn't work, and you can't get mad at the dog if he doesn't listen. You have to find out how to *make* him listen. And you shouldn't be embarrassed about looking for help.

Bassets and a Wirehaired Dachshund share a meal at the Gaines Dog Research Center. (*Photograph by Evelyn M. Shafer; courtesy of the Gaines Dog Research Center*)

THE INNER DOG: PROPER FEEDING

There are six basic types of dog food: canned, dry, semi-moist, homemade, frozen and dietary supplements. Choosing among them depends on a number of factors including cost, availability, nutritional content and taste. Some of these are more important than others, but you have to reckon with all of them if you intend to make the best possible choice. Every dog is different. So is every owner. We can give you facts and figures and a few recommendations, but it's up to you to weigh this information.

Canned Foods

As a rule, canned foods contain more fat than the dry and semi-moist. This is because it is easier to preserve fat in a can. Additional fat, which increases both calories and taste appeal, can be a plus or a minus, depending on the dog's condition, metabolism and temperament and on the amount of exercise he receives. The fact that the fat contains cholesterol has no bearing on the dog's health. Dogs *do* get heart disease, but cholesterol is not a contributing factor.

Sometimes canned foods contain slightly more protein than dry or semi-moist products, or protein that is of a higher biological value, which means simply that the dog can utilize more of it more efficiently. All other things being equal, additional protein or protein value can do the dog only good.

High-quality canned food tends to be more expensive than dry food of the same quality.

Dry Foods

This comes in several forms, the traditional one being the biscuit, which can be served whole as a meal to dogs who like that kind of thing. There are also dry meals, kibbles or expanded pellets. The expanded foods are puffed full of air, and some dogs prefer the texture to that of meal. Expanded foods may also be coated with fat, which increases their palatability.

Dry foods cost less per pound than semi-moist or canned foods and provide the same quality of nutrition (sometimes better). They are easy to measure and convenient to buy in bulk and store. While they may have a lower fat content, small additions of inexpensive vegetable oils can make up for this fact.

Many dogs find dry food unpalatable. This can be counteracted by supplementing the food with canned food or vegetable oils, or by moistening it, which releases its odor. Moistening the food has the additional advantage of decreasing the dog's need for his water bowl.

A few words of caution: Moistening the food hastens spoilage. Too much moistening may destroy the texture of the food by creating a soft and unpleasant mush. Moisture on the shelf invites the growth of mold and bacteria. Feed bags must be protected from rats and roaches.

Semi-Moist Foods

The greatest advantage of semi-moist foods is their high palatability, which makes them acceptable to finicky eaters, including a dog with little appetite. Their greatest disadvantage is that they often increase the dog's thirst, which is a problem during the housebreaking process. They are almost as expensive as canned foods.

Homemade Foods

A perfectly good, well-balanced nutritious meal for your dog can be made in your own kitchen. Select foods with the appropriate calorie count and nutritional components combined in the proper ratio; with the help of your veterinarian, select the vitamin and mineral supplements that will keep your dog healthy and sound. This of course requires considerable time and effort, and it may also turn your dog into a finicky eater, particularly if you want to travel with him or leave him in a kennel.

Frozen Foods

After they are thawed, frozen foods must be used immediately, since they tend to spoil rapidly; and they are not always available. Don't get your dog too used to them. A sudden switch could cause digestive—not to speak of emotional—upset.

Supplements

It's impossible to open a dog magazine and not find at least one advertisement for a dietary supplement. The dog owner is led to believe that unless he pours great quantities of vitamins, minerals, meats, proteins and the like down his dog's throat, the poor creature will not survive. Our best advice, as we have said, is to add supplements, especially vitamins and minerals, only on the advice of your veterinarian.

● *Protein* Cooked eggs, lean cooked meat, cottage cheese and milk if it does not cause diarrhea are all good for a dog and are recommended especially for the growing puppy, the pregnant and lactating bitch, the working dog, the hunting dog, the sick dog and the malnourished dog.

● *Fat or Oil* This may be added to the dog's food in the form of meat fat, bacon drippings or vegetable oils. Since many dogs find bacon fat hard to digest, we prefer vegetable oils (corn, olive, safflower, or peanut). Corn oil is particularly high in linoleic acid, an essential nutrient for the dog. It is recommended for the working dog, hunting dog, malnourished dog, or dog in poor coat.

● *Table Scraps* In limited amounts, table scraps mixed with a balanced commercial food may increase the commercial food's protein content and palatability without otherwise harming its contents. The scraps should be chopped fine and mixed in well to prevent the dog from removing them with his tongue and leaving the rest behind.

● **Biscuits and Treats**   Biscuits are touted as teeth cleaners, but we prefer rawhide bones, partly because the dogs works at them longer, and partly because biscuits are high in carbohydrates and may provide additional, unwanted calories. Some biscuits are offered as training treats, and this practice we disagree with altogether.

● **Bones**   Large cartilaginous knuckle bones, well cooked, are good for the teeth. Small bones the dog can chew up should never be fed.

Water

Almost 70 percent of a dog's body weight is made up of water. If he loses 10 percent or more, he will die. For this reason, a dog needs plenty of clean fresh water. However, when he is on a housebreaking schedule, you will have to regulate his water intake in order to train him. This produces no ill effects if he is normal and healthy, and he drinks plenty of water when he has it. We haven't yet trained a dog who died of thirst.

Although it is possible to feed a dog one type of food exclusively, we prefer a combination of one-quarter canned food mixed with three-quarters moistened dry food. Read the labels and look for the following:

● A statement as to whether the food is complete and balanced. All commercial foods that *are* will say so. This means that the food contains all the right nutrients (except water) in the right proportions to each other, and the dog needs nothing else.

● The name and address of the manufacturer. This means that he's not afraid of questions.

● A list of ingredients. Meat, meat meal and meat by-products should be near the top.

Additional Considerations

Availability   Sudden changes in diet often cause gastrointestinal upsets, so, particularly if you and the dog travel a lot, it is important to be sure you can get the food the dog is used to.

Nutrition   Many people think that dogs are exclusively meat eaters. But even the wild dog and the wolf eat vegetables by consuming the viscera of any animals they kill and redigesting the contents of their prey's stomach.

Your dog eats first to satisfy his caloric needs and second to build and maintain his condition. He needs calories to provide him with energy, and within those calories he needs proteins, fats and carbohydrates in the correct proportions. In addition, he needs vitamins and minerals. If you took a handful of meat, a handful of cereal and a handful of vegetables and tossed them together, you would probably provide him with all the right ingredients. But unless the ratio was right, his diet would still not give him the nourishment he needs.

Protein   Some proteins are better for dogs than others. The protein in a whole egg is considered 100 percent efficient in a dog's body, which means that he utilizes all of it. Muscle and organ meats are second best, followed by the proteins in cereal grains, which have a range of good to poor.

Carbohydrates   These provide the dog with a cheap, efficient source of energy. If his diet does not contain enough carbohydrates, his body will start using up fat, and if there is no fat present, it will start using up the available protein, which he needs for other things. Grains and legumes are the best sources of carbohydrates, but for the dog to use them efficiently they must be cooked.

Fats   Fats provide energy, supply the dog's body with certain essential fatty acids and help to transport the fat-soluble vitamins A, D, E and K. The most important fatty acid is linoleic acid, so fats high in this are essential to the dog's diet. Pork fat and vegetable oils are both excellent sources. Beef fat and butterfat are relatively poor sources.

Vitamins and Minerals   These maintain a complex relationship in the dog's body, and an excess of one can actually cause serious depletion of others, disrupting the entire network and upsetting the body chemistry. Calcium and phosphorus are the minerals needed in the largest quantity in the dog's diet, but they must be supplied in the ratio of 1.2 parts calcium to 1 part phosphorus for optimum bone and tooth formation.

These chemicals also have an intimate relationship with vitamin D, which is essential for bone growth, growth in general and reproduction. Vitamin A is necessary for good eyes, skin, teeth, bones and kidneys. Vitamin E helps restore damaged tissues; K helps the blood clot. The B vitamins are necessary for the skin, the nervous system, the production of blood cells, appetite, digestion and the circulatory system. The dog also needs vitamin C, but it need not be supplied in his diet. A normal, healthy dog manufactures his own.

Many foods contain these vitamins to a greater or lesser degree, including organ and muscle meats, fat, milk, yeast, cereal grains and vegetables. Most commercial foods also provide the necessary vitamins and minerals.

The Taste Factor

Some companies use "flavor enhancers" and promote the idea that taste is the most vital element of a dog's food. But most dogs will gulp down just about anything that remotely resembles food—and some things that don't. The only dog that may possibly starve

"No dog will starve itself," although this Wheaten Terrier is pretending to.

himself to death is the Siberian Husky; this is rare and usually the fault of the owner, who has allowed the dog to develop peculiar eating habits.

We urge you to remember that highly palatable foods increase the likelihood of obesity, since they make the dog more likely to eat to please his palate rather than to provide for his caloric needs. Only if the dog is sick, is undernourished or shows a decrease in normal appetite are highly palatable foods recommended—on a temporary basis.

The Puppy

A puppy requires approximately twice as much nutrition per pound of body weight as an adult dog. The major manufacturers of dog food all provide puppy chow designed to satisfy these special requirements in canned, semi-moist and dry forms. Since dry chow may cause diarrhea in a puppy under three months old, we recommend mixing it with one-quarter canned food. Stay off semi-moist food if you want to avoid housebreaking problems. Small quantities of cottage cheese, cooked eggs or cooked lean meat mixed with the food make a good protein supplement once a day. Vitamin and mineral supplements should be added only on the advice of a veterinarian.

It's almost impossible to overfeed a growing puppy, as long as you don't stuff him. He knows how much he wants. And he should be fed often while he is small: but if you try to push food down his throat, it will only come out the other end in any number of undesirable places.

1. From weaning to twelve weeks, a model schedule might be 7:30 A.M. 12:00 noon, 4:30 P.M. and 8:30 P.M.

2. From twelve weeks to six months, feedings may be reduced to three a day and the late feeding should be pushed up to about 4:30 or 5:00 in the afternoon to accommodate housebreaking; the dog should be watered for the last time at 7:30 at night. This way, if you walk him for the last time at 11:00 or 12:00, there's a chance he'll be able to hold through the night. *Caution:* Some breeds, like the Yorkshire Terrier, tend to be hypoglycemic. A light snack at about 7:30 P.M. may help. If the puppy still shows signs of stress, give him his late feeding at 8:30 and hope for the best.

3. From six months to a year the schedule should be two meals a day, one at 7:30 A.M. and one at 5:30 P.M.

NOTE: Self-feeding is fine for all puppies who live in a kennel, a run, or outside.

The Adult Dog

As the dog reaches maturity, he must be gradually changed to a regular dog diet. Dried puppy feed is no longer appropriate, as it supplies a caloric and nutritional density that far exceeds his needs. You will probably know this because his appetite will automatically lessen without any symptoms of disease.

There are many commercial foods available and some specially prepared formulas that provide adequate nutrients in a concentrated form, so that the dog produces a smaller stool. These last may cost more per pound but are fed in smaller amounts, so ultimately the cost may be about the same.

In general it is wiser to feed the dog less rather than more; he should always be eager to empty his bowl. Historically, the dog ate every two or three days in the wild. Because his stomach is large in comparison to the rest of his intestinal tract, he can eat a large quantity of food and retain it over a long period of time. This doesn't mean that you should feed your dog every other day, but one meal a day is adequate for most dogs by the time they are a year old. It can be served at any time, but we suggest the morning. It takes twelve hours for the food to travel from the inside out, which means that the dog will be completely empty after you walk him for the last time at night. Keep water available at all times unless the dog has a housebreaking problem.

The Old Dog

Old age has a debilitating effect on the dog's body, so it's wise to provide the old dog with smaller quantities of higher-quality protein and less fat. Some commercial foods for the older dog already do this and provide supplementary vitamins and minerals. Concentrated formulas may be best because the dog will have to chew less food. If his teeth are worn down, try a softer diet.

The Lap Dog

The lap dog poses special feeding problems: because he eats so little, his owner can afford to feed him expensive cuts of meat, ice cream and liver. Toy breeds are often taught to eat soft diets, and as a result they never have any abrasion against their teeth. Since they tend not to chew on bones or rawhide the way larger dogs do, this increases the buildup of tartar on the teeth, the erosion of gums and the chance of dental problems later in life—which are greater anyway in the small dog for genetic reasons.

Almost all small dogs are overfed. A two- or three-pound dog needs only a couple of ounces of food a day, but to his master, this looks like a pitifully small amount. The large dog wolfs his food. The small dog picks at his, which only increases his owner's apprehension. Thus begins the pattern. "Tempt me, tempt me," says the little tyrant. And he is hand-fed to obesity.

If you leave the dog alone, he'll probably be sensible. And the small dog *does* need more calories per pound of body weight than the larger dog.

The Large Dog

During his puppyhood, the large dog needs a diet that promotes growth and provides adequate building materials. Unlike the small and moderate-sized dog, he requires more of what's good for him, and great care must be taken to see that he gets it. Between birth and one year of age, he will grow from a couple of pounds to perhaps 120 pounds, which is human size. But it takes a human being thirteen or more years to get there.

The modern maxim "Biggest is best" leads the owner of the large dog to try to make his pet achieve maximum growth. Actually, the size of the dog is genetically controlled, so supplying the dog with excessive amounts of supplements, including high doses of vitamins and minerals, may actually prove detrimental to his growth as well as to his health. If you push food and supplements into the dog too fast, he may gain too much muscle and weight for his bone structure to support.

The giant breed may not reach his full size and weight until he is a year and a half to two years old. During that growing period, he needs both canned and dry foods, supplemented with the proteins we recommended for all puppies. By the end of the growing period, he may have cost you hundreds of dollars. But cheer up, there is relief in sight. Once he has attained his adult size, you can gradually switch him over to an all-dry diet. How much will still be a problem, however. Some of these breeds, such as the St. Bernard, tend to be lazy and put on weight. Make sure yours gets plenty of exercise, and watch the calories if he lies around a lot.

Big dogs are also subject to gastric torsion, otherwise known as bloat. Its cause is unknown, but researchers have found that it occurs most frequently after a big meal followed by a large drink of water and heavy exercise. An ounce of prevention is worth a pound of cure. Divide the dog's daily portion into two meals and feed him morning and evening. Restrict his water intake and exercise for about an hour after eating.

The Intermediate-Sized Dog

Dogs weighing between 40 and 80 pounds seem to be less prone to the ills of the very large and very small, perhaps because their owners feel more secure when size is not at issue and are therefore more sensible about their pets.

The Pregnant and Lactating Bitch

Start her off on a good diet when she's a puppy, and half the battle is won. When she is about halfway through her pregnancy, her nutritional requirements double. She should be eating a complete and balanced diet, but she'll need about twice as much of it. Some companies advise the owner to start feeding the bitch dried puppy feed, which supplies additional calories and protein. This is an alternative to doubling the quantity, and later on the puppies can eat from the same bowl. Natural protein supplements are a good idea, and check with your veterinarian about extra calcium-phosphorus and vitamins.

While she is lactating, the bitch's nutritional needs may triple. She should be given either extra food or protein supplements. Be sure she has plenty of water for milk production. When the puppies are about three weeks old, she will begin to wean them. At this time, you should begin gradually to feed the bitch less. This will help decrease her milk supply and will aid in the weaning process.

Schedule   Sometimes the swelling uterus makes it uncomfortable for a pregnant bitch to eat large quantities at a time; in this case, divide her daily food into two or three portions. Do not restrict water.

The Fat Dog

Examine your dog. If you feel more than a thin layer of fat over his ribs, he's probably obese. Obesity does not make dogs jolly. It makes them more lethargic, less active and less healthy. If they carry around too much excess weight, it's an effort for them to move at all. Obesity also puts a strain on the dog's cardiovascular system, just as it does on the human's, and on muscles and tendons. The strain on muscles and tendons is particularly harmful to older dogs, who may be developing arthritis. Obesity also results in complications at birth for the pregnant bitch.

The first thing you should do about a fat dog is to eliminate all snacks. Some owners notice that their dogs are gaining weight and don't understand why. "I only give him a can of food every two days," they say. But that's not counting the biscuits he gets for playing dead (which is the easiest thing for him to play when he's fat), the scoop of ice cream for being a "good boy," and the cheese, crackers, apples and cookies he steals from the kids.

If you plan to put your dog on a really firm diet, speak to your veterinarian about it. He may prescribe special food that contains fewer calories than any you can buy at the store; he may also recommend vitamin and mineral supplements. Supermarket diet foods for dogs reduce the caloric intake by about 20 percent without reducing the nutritional quality. For those who insist that "food is love," there are several excellent books of recipes for homemade diets, but we honestly feel it is better for you to get off your indulgence kick altogether. Food is not love when a dog is overweight. Strictly speaking, you are shortening your dog's life span.

If your dog is only slightly overweight, there are a number of simple ways to thin him down. In addition to cutting out snacks, you can reduce the fat in his diet by reducing the quantity of canned food he is eating. If he is eating only canned food, gradually switch him over to dry, which has a lower fat content. It has the additional advantage of being slightly less palatable, so he may be inclined to eat less of it anyway.

Above all, resign yourself to feeding him less even though he whimpers and whines about it. Fat dogs always look hungry; after all, that's how they got fat in the first place.

Incidentally, spaying normally does not affect the bitch's metabolism, but the castrated male tends to gain weight. Watch him.

·   ·   ·

The Undernourished Dog

Today this is a rare problem except in the case of dogs who have been in pet shops for a long time. The typical symptoms of malnutrition are a dry, dull coat, listlessness, thinness along the back, or a potbelly. If the dog has a vitamin D or calcium deficiency, his toes may splay.* Usually this can be corrected with the proper nutrition and exercise. *Pica*, a craving to eat foreign matter like dirt or plaster, is another common symptom of malnutrition.

A skinny dog should be put on a high-protein diet of one-quarter canned food mixed with three-quarters moistened dry. Small supplements of fat will raise his caloric intake without harming the balance of his diet. You may also have to tempt his appetite with highly palatable foods. He should be encouraged to eat as much as he wants twice a day until he is in good condition, and then the amounts should gradually be reduced until he is eating a normal diet.

The Sick Dog

Sometimes malnourishment is part of an illness. In this case, it makes little sense to try to correct dietary deficiencies without curing the disease. If a dog has a bad case of worms, feeding him an excellent diet may be almost equivalent to feeding him nothing at all. On the other hand, some diseases, such as distemper, require a regimen of hand-feeding in conjunction with medication. In this case, the owner has the difficult job of getting nourishment into the dog regardless of his decreased appetite. A dog with diabetes may have a huge appetite and eat voraciously, losing weight all the while because his body is unable to utilize the calories. This condition can be treated only with injections.

Dogs with heart, kidney and gastrointestinal ailments are sometimes fed special diets, but, as with all sick dogs, these should be prescribed by a veterinarian. If the ailment is chronic, the owner may be expected to keep his dog on a special diet for the rest of the dog's life.

The Dog Who Has Been Wrongly Fed

Sometimes a dog begins to show symptoms of disease because his

* This may also occur if the dog is raised on hard surfaces, such as concrete, even if he is eating an excellent diet.

diet is wrong. Dogs fed an all-meat diet, for instance, utilize protein poorly because they lack carbohydrates and also develop calcium deficiencies. Not only is meat deficient in calcium, it is high in phosphorus, and with an overload of phosphorus, the calcium that is present will not be absorbed.

A calcium deficiency causes the growth plates of the dog's bones to enlarge (you can feel this at each section of the ribs). The animal will become splay-footed, down in the carpus (wrist), have weak bones and be subject to spontaneous fractures. The problem for the owner is that a deficiency of vitamin E or phosphorus looks very much like a deficiency of calcium. Therefore, unless you know the cause of the dog's illness, it's very unwise to dose him with supplements.

Very occasionally, a dog will show a vitamin deficiency, like the puppy who is not exposed to enough sunlight and is unable to manufacture vitamin D. In this day and age, however, with the complete and balanced commercial foods that are available, a condition called hypervitaminosis (which is caused by overdosing) is far more common. Symptoms are a lack of appetite, nausea, diarrhea, and in extreme cases, dehydration and death.

Hypervitaminosis A is caused by either dosing the dog with large capsules of that vitamin or feeding him huge supplements of liver. It most often occurs in very small dogs who get addicted to liver and refuse to eat anything else. Vitamin A builds up to a toxic level, and eventually bone lesions occur. The dog suffers a lot of pain, goes lame and exhibits general dullness and lack of appetite. Tests will reveal high levels of vitamin A in the blood. If the lesions have progressed too far, the disease is not reversible.

Three conditions come from feeding the dog certain foods raw that provide valuable nutrients when cooked. A thiamine deficiency develops when the dog eats too much raw fish. A more common condition results from the popular belief that raw eggs improve the condition of a dog's coat. Nothing could be farther from the truth. Excessive amounts of raw egg white destroy the dog's ability to utilize biotin. The first symptom of a biotin deficiency is dermatitis—with subsequent damage to the dog's coat.

There are many myths about raw meat. Some people believe it makes the dog more aggressive; others think that it accustoms him to the scent and taste of blood, which makes him a better hunter. Neither notion is true. Dogs like the taste of raw meat and are able to digest it, but it can sometimes introduce a protozoan disease called toxoplasmosis. The symptoms of this disease include fever, loss of weight and appetite, irritability, depression, coughing and lack of muscular coordination. It can sometimes result in meningitis in the dog.

These are all instances where prevention is far easier than the cure. The following precautions should be observed:

1. Feed the dog a balanced diet. Never feed just meat. Never feed just liver.

2. Add vitamin and mineral supplements only on the advice of a vet. And *absolutely never* feed your dog human vitamin capsules. The average adult human being weighs well over a hundred pounds and can absorb medicines and vitamins in quantities that are toxic to a dog.

3. Don't feed raw fish, raw eggs or raw meat.

The Dog in Poor Coat

A poor coat is symptomatic of many of the most common ailments. For this reason, it's important to have a veterinarian diagnose the cause. Sometimes when the owner bathes his dog too frequently, the dog's skin dries out and his coat becomes lackluster. Long-haired breeds are particularly susceptible because the natural oils in their skin have a longer route to travel. In this case, extensive brushing helps by stimulating the oil glands, improving the circulation and getting the skin to work. Small supplements of oil—particularly corn oil, which is high in linoleic acid—may also be added to the diet.

The Inside Dog

The dog kept primarily inside the house has a lower caloric requirement. Feed him a little less than is recommended on the dog-food package and avoid semi-moist foods, which tend to cause housebreaking problems.

The Outside Dog

Extremes of hot and cold weather all speed up the dog's metabolism and require dietary adjustment. In extremely hot or cold temperatures, the need for calories may actually double.

·   ·   ·

Other Considerations

Breed and temperament have a considerable amount to do with the dog's dietary needs, metabolic rate and appetite. The nervous, high-strung dog needs more calories just to keep alive than the sedate dog, who spends much of the day resting. Some dogs put on weight more easily than others. Some breeds are more discriminating as to flavor, texture and palatability. Studies of "taste preferences" have shown miniature poodles are fussier than Labrador Retrievers, and Labs are fussier than Beagles, who are raised in packs where the competition for food may help to explain their typically voracious appetites.

Changing the Dog from One Diet to Another

Sudden changes in diet cause gastric disturbance and diarrhea. Also, dogs are creatures of habit. They sometimes won't accept a new food if it appears all at once. A change in diet should be accomplished gradually over the period of about a week. Each day increase the amount of new food, and decrease the amount of old. This is a sound method for all dogs and is particularly important for hunting or working dogs, who require significant changes at certain times of the year.

5

HOUSEBREAKING AND PAPER TRAINING

It would be very nice if your dog never had to relieve himself at all. It would eliminate some of the major anxieties of dog ownership. You wouldn't have to worry about the carpets, the lawn or the street. As it is, you and the dog have to face the problem as early on in your relationship as possible and do something about it.

Fortunately, the instinct for cleanliness comes naturally to the dog and goes all the way back to his wild ancestor, the wolf. The wolf mother cleans up after her infant cubs, just as the dog mother does. As the mother licks the pup, she provides the stimulus for elimination, which follows soon after and is promptly removed by the mother's tongue. When the wolf cub is only a few weeks old, he learns to eliminate away from the den, just as the puppy learns to eliminate away from his sleeping quarters. Neither wolf nor dog likes to live in close proximity to his own waste. If you, as a dog owner, take advantage of the dog's natural inclination for cleanliness, you will be able to house-train him easily and quickly.

You have two choices: *housebreaking* and *paper training*. These are not to be confused with each other, for they are as different as day and night. *Housebreaking* is teaching your dog to relieve himself away from his premises. It does not mean that if he lives in the bathroom, he will be allowed to relieve himself in the living room. It means outside the house only, whether it be in the backyard, on the front lawn, at the curb or in the street. *Paper training* is teaching the dog to relieve himself on a piece of paper in a certain area in the house. It does not mean that the dog has sixteen pieces of paper in sixteen different locations. It means there is one location where he is expected to defecate and urinate.

The first step is to decide whether you are going to housebreak or paper-train your dog. Once you have made that decision, it is hard to change it. Most house-training problems occur because the owner is not firm about what he wants in the first place, and the dog is confused. This is particularly likely to happen in the following instances:

1. The veterinarian will not allow you to air your dog until he receives his final DHL vaccination at twelve to sixteen weeks of age.

2. In areas of the country where the weather is cold, a seven- or eight-week-old puppy cannot be expected to brave zero-degree weather and must be kept indoors either until he is bigger and stronger or until the weather is warmer.

You cannot afford to let the puppy make a mess of the entire house, so you must keep him confined in a small area most of the time and cover that area with papers. It is easy for him to get the idea that he is expected to go on papers. But if this particular puppy is going to grow into a fifty-pound dog, you don't want him to learn that going on paper is what you expect him to do. Therefore *never praise him for going on paper* and *never correct him* for *not* going on paper. If he automatically selects a favorite spot, the best thing for you to do is to take no notice of it one way or the other. Later when you earnestly praise him for relieving himself in the gutter, he will realize that this is a far, far better thing to do.

Whether you decide to housebreak or paper-train is a matter of common sense. Housebreaking is a universal choice in the sense that *any* dog—regardless of his size, sex or breed—can be housebroken. It also has the aesthetic advantage of keeping the mess and smell outdoors where both can be absorbed by the environment. But if you work eight hours a day in an office and have to get to and from it to reach your dog, or if you are elderly, you may find it difficult to adapt your life to a small dog with a tiny bladder who needs to be walked rather frequently. You can of course hire someone to walk your dog for you once or twice a day, but to expect that dog not to relieve himself for ten or more hours is really cruel. Paper training has the advantage of confining the very small mess of a very small dog to a very small area of the house, where you can clean up easily and where the dog can relieve himself if you are gone all day or if your activities are restricted.

Our use of "he" in the preceding paragraph is somewhat misleading. We do not really recommend paper training male dogs at all. The male learns to lift his leg when he is six months to a year old, and if he is allowed to spray on the walls of the bathroom or kitchen, your entire house may soon smell like a public urinal. It is possible to devise a method of protecting your walls with paper or plastic, but if you consider the amount of time it takes to clean the plastic or tape the paper, it is probably not worth the effort. We recommend paper training for females only.

It is also not particularly handy to paper-train a dog that will achieve an adult weight of more than fifteen pounds. You can, of course, paper-train a Great Dane, but you will have to deal with the rather awesome consequences. For one thing, your house would have to be extremely well ventilated. And for another, a Great Dane would probably go through newspapers faster than you could read them—unless you read so many papers that you don't have the time to train a dog in the first place.

Paper training has yet another disadvantage. It is easy for a dog to learn the difference between the house and the great outdoors. In housebreaking, the dog learns that *inside* the house is off-limits. In paper training, the dog has to learn to distinguish between different places that are all inside. Most of these places are *wrong*. In fact, there is only one that is *right*. But the distinction is a fine one, and the dog may feel she has a right to quibble about it. For this reason it takes longer to paper-train than to housebreak.

Housebreaking

Housebreaking should begin when the dog is seven to eight weeks old. At this age it's easy to establish a puppy's behavior patterns. However, a dog is never too old to be housebroken unless he has medical problems.

Housebreaking is a five-part program including *scheduling*, which is when you feed, water and walk the dog; *diet*, which is what you feed the dog and how much of it you feed him; *odor neutralization*, which means how to get rid of the smell; *confinement*, which means where you keep the dog and how you restrict him; and *correction*, which means how you confront the dog with his mistakes.

The key of this whole process is to make all five things work in conjunction with one another. You can't do *one* and expect the dog to get housebroken. The whole process usually takes two to three weeks, but in exceptional cases it can be accomplished in a single day.

The Schedule   If the dog lives outside, a schedule is not necessary, but if he's living in the house, it is absolutely essential. Suppose you put food and water down all day. The dog eats and drinks whenever he wants, and relieves himself whenever he wants—which is exactly what you *don't* want. If the dog is fed, watered and walked at certain times of the day, he will acquire a sense of when you expect him to relieve himself. He will learn to hold for longer and longer periods of time. You would be foolish to expect him ever to hold for as long as twelve hours, but on the other hand, you can't plan to stay home and walk the dog every two hours for the next ten years, either. A good schedule falls in between these two extremes. You train the dog to relieve himself a certain number of times each day at the appropriate times and in the appropriate places. You don't have to guess when the dog needs to go out because, practically speaking, you are teaching him to adjust his internal schedule to your external one. This is a useful, humane and civilized method of dealing with the call of nature.

When you establish a schedule, you should consider the following:

1.   A correct schedule is based on the dog's age. The younger the dog, the more often he must be fed. Because he is growing, the puppy needs more food per pound of body weight, and because he is small, he can't possibly eat enough at one feeding to sustain him for an entire day. Consequently, he also has to be walked more frequently than the older dog.

2.   The smaller the dog, the more frequently he must be walked. A tiny toy with tiny insides cannot be expected to hold as long as an Irish Wolfhound.

3.   The first walk in the morning depends on when you walked the dog the last time the night before. If you walked him at 3:00 A.M., there's no good reason to walk him at 6:00 A.M. But if you walked him at 11:00 P.M., there's a good reason to walk him at 7:00 A.M.

4.   The first thing you do when you get up in the morning is to relieve yourself. Life is no different for a dog. It's fair to assume that you'll take your human prerogative and relieve yourself first, but you should walk the dog immediately thereafter. It is not fair to assume that you'll have the time to take a shower, brush your teeth, shave and eat breakfast first. Once the dog is trained, of course, the schedule becomes less rigid.

5. You must not give your dog access to the toilet bowls in your house. He may inadvertently swallow disinfectant along with the water, and drinking from them will throw him off his housebreaking schedule. When you give him water, he will want to urinate right away. Thus you must give him water only at certain times of the day.

6. You must not give the dog table scraps, dog biscuits or other treats whenever you feel like it. Again, this interrupts the schedule.

7. Above all, you must set the schedule and force yourself to stick to it. The dog will feel better, and so will you.

Model schedules are as follows:

PUPPY, THREE TO SIX MONTHS OF AGE (THREE FEEDINGS REQUIRED)

7:00	Walk
7:30	Feed, water and walk
11:30	Feed, water and walk
4:30	Feed, water and walk
7:30	Water and walk
11:00	Walk

There are occasions—when it's very hot, for example, or when the puppy has exercised heavily—when the puppy should be watered and walked in between these scheduled times. This is left up to the owner's discretion. If the puppy whines at night from hunger, feed him at 6:00 P.M. rather than at 4:30. A puppy *less than three months old* should have a night feeding at 7:30 or 8:30.

SIX MONTHS TO A YEAR (TWO FEEDINGS REQUIRED)

7:00	Walk
7:30	Feed, water and walk
12:30	If someone is home, water and walk
4:30	Feed, water and walk
7:30	Water and walk
11:00	Walk

You are eliminating the midday meal. You still want to feed the dog no later than 4:30 or 5:00 in hopes that most of the food will have enough time to pass through his system before his final walk at 11:00. If you feed him later than 4:30 or 5:00, you will have to walk him later than 11:00.

A YEAR AND OLDER (ONE FEEDING REQUIRED)

7:00	Walk if possible, but not so important
7:30	Feed, water and walk
12:30	If someone is home, water and walk (optional)
4:30	Water and walk
7:30	Water and walk
11:00	Walk

Feed in the morning, since it takes twelve hours for food to pass through the dog's system. The mature dog can hold for eight to ten hours if necessary. Once he is going on schedule, he should be given water all the time.

The Working Person   If you are the proud owner of a three- to six-month-old puppy and you also happen to work for eight or nine hours a day, you still have to manage to adhere to the above schedule or some close facsimile. The puppy must be fed three times a day, and he must be walked. You either have to do the job yourself or hire someone else to do it—perhaps a dog-walking service or a local child.

Diet   The best diet for a puppy in the housebreaking process is composed of one part canned food combined with three parts moistened-down meal. A total diet of dry or canned food may cause a loose stool, which will make the housebreaking process more difficult. Semi-moist food is coated with a chemical that will make the puppy drink too much water; consequently housebreaking will be impossible.

The proper amount of food is just as important as the proper kind. If you feed the puppy an excessive amount, he will need to relieve himself more often than you will like. If you feed him too little, he will start to chew the house down. Actually it's difficult to overfeed him, but if he starts to leave food in his bowl or to defecate excessively, these are strong indications that he's eating too much. Most overfeeding occurs when extra food and supplements are pushed on the puppy by an anxious owner.

Neutralizing the Odor   If you had a dog before, make sure that the house is totally free of odor before you bring a new puppy home. Every time the dog relieves himself where you don't want him to, clean the spot with an odor-neutralizing product so the dog won't return to it.

It is vital that you get rid of all odor. A dog can smell one part urine to about a million parts water. Regular household products like ammonia will not do the job, and deodorants will mask the smell for you, but not for your dog.

Confinement   Most people make the mistake of giving a dog the run of the house, so he goes wherever he wants. He doesn't feel any restriction at all. The purpose of confinement is to give him a feeling that he's in a certain area, and if he wets or defecates in this area, he has to stay there. Most dogs do not like this. Whenever you leave the dog alone in the house, you should confine* him to one room— a large bathroom, kitchen, hallway. If he also eats and sleeps here, it will soon feel like home to him, and he won't want to mess in it.

Correction   Correction is not the same as punishment. Punishing a dog for something you haven't taught him is cruel. Correcting a dog for something you're in the process of teaching him is quite different. If the dog is running around loose in the house and starts to have an accident, say the word "no" firmly, pick him up, and take him outside immediately and show him where to go. Praise him enthusiastically when he is finished. Praise is important because it gives the dog the idea that he's pleasing you, which is what he wants to do.

Another technique is to take an empty soda can, put fifteen or twenty pennies in it, and tape up the hole. When the dog starts to have an accident, shake the can and say "no." The sound will startle him, and you can rush him outside.

The proper correction is always based on the dog's personality. If you own a shy dog and scream "no" at him, he will wet out of fear, and you have defeated the whole purpose of housebreaking him.

Responsive dog:	a firm "no." Do not be overbearing.
Nervous dog:	a firmer "no." No shake-can.
Shy dog:	a gentle "no." No shake-can.
Sedate dog:	a gentle "no." No shake-can.
Stubborn dog:	a firm "no" and a shake-can.
Aggressive dog:	a firm "no" and a shake-can

Here are two cardinal sins to avoid while you are housebreaking a dog:

1.   Never hit him with your hands or with a rolled-up newspaper,

* Use a puppy gate (see p. 61).

point your finger at him or accuse him with statements like "What did you do?" or "Bad dog!" A simple "no" is all that is needed, and hands are for affection, not punishment and humiliation. If you hit the dog, slap him or strike him with a newspaper, he will very quickly get the idea that hands are dangerous and to be avoided. This is how you make a dog hand-shy.

2. Never rub a dog's nose in the mess that he has made. You wouldn't like it, and neither does he. Besides, he has an infinitely more sensitive nose than you do.

Your job is to figure out why the dog is having accidents and then do something about it. Ask yourself whether you are applying the five basic techniques correctly. Are you missing something? Is the dog ill? Does he have worms? Are you giving him too much water? Don't let yourself make so many mistakes with the dog at this very basic level that you impair his personality—turn him into a fear-wetter or a fear-biter. These problems are far more serious than a mess on the rug, and far harder to correct.

Common Housebreaking Problems

1. Feeding too late at night. Always remember it takes twelve hours for food to pass through a mature dog, and only six to eight for food to pass through a puppy.

2. A continuous supply of water. Water is always a touchy subject, because a dog needs water a lot more than he needs food. Dogs can survive many days without food, but they can't live without water. You don't want to discourage a puppy from drinking water on a hot day, particularly if your home is not air conditioned. The dog should have as much water as he wants, as long as you get him out. Don't exercise the dog late at night so that he gets thirsty before bedtime. And unless it is absolutely necessary, don't give him water past 7:30 at night.

3. Failure to adhere to the schedule, feeding the wrong food or too much food, failure to eliminate the odor of an accident, and improper confinement—all common mistakes.

4. Excessive wetting. Sometimes if the dog is overly excited and/or has a nervous or overactive personality, he will wet the moment you walk in the door. This is not a housebreaking problem, and the dog should not be corrected for it. The solution is to be as calm and easygoing with the animal as possible. Don't overexcite him by encouraging him to jump up. Talk softly and stroke him gently to try to quiet him down. If you overexcite him by your voice or by rough or aggressive handling, you will only make the problem worse.

5. Paper training when the dog is a puppy. Sometimes the owner paper-trains the puppy for too long a period of time, and ever after that, whenever paper is brought into the house, the dog relieves himself on it. If you must put a dog on paper temporarily, don't make a big deal out of it; don't praise or correct him.

Paper Training

Paper training works like this:

1.   As soon as you get the dog into the house, choose an area where you will confine her and layer that area with paper, two to four sheets thick. Wherever the dog relieves herself in that area, she goes on paper. She has no choice. Paper the area in this way for a week to ten days.

2.   Choose a specific spot where you want the dog to go. Every time she soils, remove the used paper and put fresh paper down. Put a sheet of paper soiled with urine under the fresh paper in the spot where you want the dog to go. She will smell her urine and return to that spot to relieve herself. Naturally, you will praise her extravagantly whenever she does.

3.   After a week to ten days, begin to decrease the papered area, working from the outside inward to the chosen spot until eventually it is the only papered area left. This should take from three to five days. If the dog regresses, you must increase the amount of paper and then gradually decrease it again.

4.   After the dog is trained to one spot, she may be let loose in the house. If she makes a mistake at any time, you must confine her again to the single area where you started.

Scheduling   It is not necessary to schedule food and water while you are paper-training the dog, but it is better if you do so. The schedule gives you the opportunity to become involved with your dog, and gives the dog the opportunity to learn something. You can praise her, and you won't have to clean up the papers so often; the dog will learn to hold, so eventually she will go only three times a day.

Diet   Diet is less important in paper training than it is in house-breaking, because the dog has constant access to her toilet.

Odor Neutralization   It is the same as with housebreaking. Every time the dog has an accident, you must clean the area with an odor neutralizer, whether she has relieved herself off the paper or in the wrong place, on a paper.

Confinement and Correction   Confinement and correction are also the same as in housebreaking.

Disposing of the Papers   If you paper-train your dog, you have the problem of disposing of the papers. Especially in the beginning you must make an effort to dispose of the soiled papers immediately, and this will eliminate the problem of coprophagy, which is when the dog eats its own feces. Dogs tend to do this because they are bored, because the feces smell like food, and, we think, in the case of hunting dogs, because they like to carry things in their mouths. If you leave the dog's stool around, the likelihood that she will get into this habit is greatly increased. It's also best to get the papers out of the house so that the smell will not linger; this requires either a trip to the incinerator (in an apartment house) or to the garbage can outside.

Why Dogs Make Mistakes

Dogs don't think like human beings. They don't understand *why* certain things must be done in a certain way, but if they are properly educated, they will know simply that things *must* be done in a certain way. We don't believe there is any such thing as a spiteful dog. People think a dog is spiteful when he has accidents while his owner is away, but this is simply because he knows that his owner is not there and thus thinks he will avoid his owner's displeasure. He goes on the carpet because his urine disappears into the carpet—out of sight, out of mind, so to speak. Your dog wants to please you. And he wants to avoid your displeasure. Those are his two strongest motives in house-training and in any other kind of training. But while he is in the learning process, he is going to make mistakes and have accidents. That is only natural.

6

A DAILY HEALTH
EXAMINATION

Some dogs seem to come with good genes that automatically make them healthy. The healthiest breeds are those that are least popular and therefore have suffered least at the hands of unscrupulous breeders; and those that structurally resemble the wolf, a creature made to adapt to difficult conditions in the wild. Dogs that have been bred for mutations—pushed-in faces, short noses, undershot jaws and narrow hips—are particularly prone to medical problems. Take the Bulldog. According to veterinarian Susan McLellan, the present Bulldog would die out without man to care for him. Because Bulldogs have been bred for big heads and narrow hips, the big-headed puppies often won't fit through the birth canal and the bitch needs help to deliver. Because flat faces are considered desirable, the Bulldog has breathing problems and drools. He also has eye problems and skin problems because of the folds in his face. He often has arthritis of the hips.

Most dogs have far fewer genetic problems, but all of them are subject to health problems. We believe that if you learn how to give your dog a daily examination, you will be able to catch most of these before they become serious, and the serious ones before they become fatal. This does not mean that you will know how to administer medical care on your own, but rather that you will recognize when your dog should see a veterinarian. Initially, the exam may take you as much as half an hour, but after about a week, you'll get the hang of it and it will become a 10- or 15-minute part of your daily grooming routine.

The Ear

Lift up the ear flap and look in the ear canal. In the shorthaired breeds, you can see this easily, but in longhaired breeds, hair in the ear may obscure it. If you have any doubts, take a little mineral oil and slick the hair down so that you can tell for sure whether there is any wax in the canal.

If the ear has dark wax in it, clean it out gently with mineral or baby oil on a cotton swab. You can go fairly deep into the ear without hitting the eardrum. Because the ear canal is deep and L-shaped, it is difficult to get past the angle at the bottom and puncture the eardrum.

Do not use castor oil, which is irritating, or alcohol, which is drying. Some groomers recommend hydrogen peroxide, but it bubbles, and the sound and feel of the bubbles may frighten the dog so much that he won't let you clean his ears again.

What to Look For   Redness, swelling, or any discharge, especially a pussy one. Some dogs have chronic ear problems, and you'll find infections rather frequently. An infection requires ointment, which only a veterinarian can prescribe.

● *Otitis* is another name for inflammation of the ear canal. It's easily detectable if you compare the ears because often only one is inflamed. If the dog constantly scratches at his ear, shakes his head, or feels pain when you touch his ear, it is probably a sign of otitis.

● *Ear mites* are especially common in puppies and strays. The ear mite is a roundish, tank-shaped bug with legs that move a great deal. He belongs to the spider family, but he looks like a miniature tick. The ear mite can't live off the dog's body, is transmitted by contact from one dog to another, and migrates from the dog's head or body until he arrives at the ear, where he likes to set up housekeeping. The ear mite is common in all breeds of dogs, and since he causes a lot of itching, he's fairly easy to detect, even though he's too small to see with the naked eye. A lot of scratching at the ear and inflammation in the ear canal may indicate his presence. The ear mite is easy to get rid of, but you probably won't be able to do it yourself. The mite lays its eggs in the dog's ear, these eggs hatch and the mites will return unless the vet dispenses eardrops that contain an insecticide.

● *Growths* in the ear are fairly common. Many of these are benign and not dangerous, but any growth should be examined by a vet, especially if it starts to enlarge.

● *Deafness* is relatively common in older dogs, just as it is in older people. In younger dogs, it can result from chronic ear infections with secondary infection of the interior part of the ear, and sometimes from injuries to the ear. Congenital deafness is rare in animals, but it can and does occur and is inherited.

● *Vestibular problems* occur when the balance mechanism in the inner ear is injured or infected. Symptoms are a tilting head and a loss of coordination, which typically result in the inability to stand and walk correctly. It is fairly rare.

The ear flap should be felt for any unusual swelling or scabbiness. This is especially important for longhaired, long-eared breeds whose hair obscures the ear.

● *Aural hematoma* or swelling occurs in the ear flap when the dog is constantly shaking his head because he has an ear infection. The shaking breaks the blood vessel within the ear flap; since the blood has nowhere else to go, a swelling develops. The ear must be drained surgically under anesthesia, then sutured so that it won't fill up with blood again.

● *Wounds* occur frequently in the ear flap, especially from dog bites Since the ear is a vascular area, a cut or bite will bleed profusely. Very long-eared breeds, like the Basset, have ears that drag on the ground and can easily get stepped on. (They also get dirty, but most people recognize this fact and wash them frequently.) You may try applying a cold pack to the ear to constrict the blood vessels and stop the bleeding.

● *Mats* are commonly mistaken for tumors. Sometimes when the owner feels behind the ear, he'll notice a thick knot of hair that throws him into a panic. This, of course, is a job for the scissors, and not the vet. But be careful; it's easy to cut the skin and not just the mat.

Ear Cropping   This is not something you will examine for, but while we are on the subject of ears, we might as well discuss the pros and cons of cropping. It is against the law in England and in some states in the United States. Where cropping is illegal, it is against AKC regulations to show a cropped dog. But in many cases, the breed standard calls for cropping, and if you own one of these breeds and intend to show him, you will probably have to get his ears cropped whether you like the idea or not.

Cropping is an expensive surgical procedure, costing anywhere from $40 to $100, depending on who does it, what part of the country you're in, and whether there are any complications afterwards. Different breeds are cropped at different ages. The operation itself is not painful if it is done under general anesthesia, but during the healing period the ears are sore and itchy because there are stitches. These are removed a week to ten days after the operation, but the ears must be taped for several weeks to make sure that they stand correctly. It is certainly not comfortable for the dog, and when people begin to realize how lengthy and difficult the procedure is, they often wish they had left the dog alone. It is supposed to improve the looks of some breeds, particularly Dobermans, Great Danes and Schnauzers.

If your dog is simply a pet, there's no reason to have his ears cropped. It's simply a matter of style. In fact, if you decide to go ahead with the operation, you must resign yourself to three or four weeks of constantly caring for those ears. Even at that, you can't be sure they will stand properly.

The Eye

Get a good penlight, which will provide a fairly strong, focal source of light, and shine it directly into the eye. Look for the haw, the third eyelid, which corresponds to the pink tissue in the corner of the human eye. The haw is quite large in dogs, particularly in breeds like the St. Bernard. Because it is so large, the veterinarian can sometimes pull it over an injured eye and suture it so that it serves as a bandage.

Pull the eyelids up. If the white looks white and clear, the eye is normal. In short-nosed breeds there may be two or three prominent blood vessels running through the white. This is not abnormal. Look at the cornea itself. If you see cloudiness deep in the eye, you are seeing an increased opacity of the lens that occurs quite naturally as part of the aging process and does not impair the dog's vision. More than a slight cloudiness, however, may indicate a cataract and should be checked by a veterinarian. Any sudden change in color is also important and should get immediate attention. If the cornea has a milky appearance, it could be serious.

Some breeds—the Yorkie, the Poodle, the Maltese, the Shih Tzu, the Lhasa Apso—have a constant discharge from their eyes. Clean under the eyes every day to prevent this discharge from caking up.

Dogs with a lot of hair in their eyes are harder to examine. Some don't like having the hair pulled back. Others don't seem to be bothered by this or even by having their hair tied up in ribbons or clipped with barrettes. There's nothing wrong with adopting this as a permanent hair style as long as the dog doesn't object to it. The dog will not go blind from the sun; the dog with hair over his eyes is no more sensitive to the sun than any other dog is.

What to Look For   Discharge, excessive tearing, inflammation, redness, irritation, sudden change in color, or a bloodshot eye. If the dog keeps one of his eyes closed, it often means that there is some damage to the cornea and he's in pain. The dog may rub at the eye, which means there's something really bothering him. Look for a persistent protruding haw or differences between the eyes. If the cornea is cloudy or has white spots on it, take the dog to a veterinarian.

● *Conjunctivitis* is an inflammation of the conjunctiva, the tissue that lines the lids, and it has a plethora of causes. Dust and dirt blown into the eye frequently cause an infection, especially in the city, where the dog stands only about two feet above the pavement. Breeds with prominent eyes are more prone to infection.

● *Injury* is a common problem with short-nosed breeds. Their eyes are extremely prominent and prone to damage. In fact, if a lot of pressure is exerted against the side of the head, the eye will pop out of its socket. Take the dog immediately to the veterinarian, who may be able to save the eye by pulling back the lids and helping the eye back inside the socket. Do not attempt to do this yourself.

Eyelid cuts should also be treated by a veterinarian. With improper healing, the eyelid may not completely cover the eye, which therefore will suffer from an absence in lubrication, or the eyelid may subsequently turn in, causing irritation.

● *Cherry eye* is caused by infection in the lymph gland of the haw. It looks like a big red blob sticking in the corner of the eye.

● *Cataracts* can destroy the lens and cause blindness. They appear as a deep cloudiness or white color which indicates a thickening of the lens. As they become progressively more mature, the whiteness increases.

The Nose

Compare the nostrils. The dog can get a blade of grass up the nares area and then have discharge from one side or the other. This is especially common in California and other areas with foxtails, seed-head that grows on wild grasses. It sticks to the hair, and because it has a sharp end it is likely to penetrate.

Short-nosed breeds like the Bulldog and Pekingese have more breathing and respiratory problems than other dogs. A certain amount of snoring and noise is not unusual, but excessive vomiting of mucus or serious difficulty in breathing may require medical attention.

What to Look For   Discharge from the nose and inflamed, raw areas in the folds of the skin around the nose in short-nosed breeds; lip-fold pyoderma in the fleshy-lipped breeds (for example, Cocker Spaniels and St. Bernards).

● *Stenotic nares* occurs in the short-nosed breeds when the nose fold is improperly formed and does not allow air to pass through. This condition contributes to respiratory ailments and may need surgical correction. Listen for extreme snoring and respiratory difficulty.

● *Nosebleeds* are rather rare in dogs: a bloody nose can be caused by a traumatic injury, or it can occur when something gets stuck in the nasal area. Regular human nose drops (Neo-Synephrine) or spray and cold packs against the nose may help stop the bleeding. If the dog paws at his nose, have the veterinarian check for the presence of a foreign object.

The Mouth

Some dogs are shy about having their heads touched, which makes it hard to examine the mouth. If you sit on the floor with the dog, you will find it easier. Pull the lips up gently and examine the molars way in the back of the mouth. You needn't open the mouth if this makes the dog uncomfortable; the lips are·very loose, and if you pull them up and away from the teeth, you will be able to see all the way into the back of the mouth, where decay and tartar accumulation is often the greatest.

Good dental care should start early, when the dog is no more than two or three years old. Smaller dogs and toy breeds are particularly subject to dental problems, but they can be prevented with good care, regular scalings by the veterinarian, and brushing (if the dog will allow it).

What to Look For   Red, irritated gums; bad breath; growths; foreign objects; tartar; discoloration of the teeth; bloody discharge from the mouth. Really bad teeth may become loose and bleed.

The color of a dog's gums and tongue are a good indication whether there is something wrong. Look for a bluish tinge (except in the case of a Chow, who has a black mouth; with him, you must pull down the lower eyelid and look at the conjunctival sac, which should be very pink).

● *Warts* are very common in young dogs and are often transmitted from one puppy to another. Usually they regress spontaneously. They don't often return to the same exact spot, but they may come back in another area. If there are a lot of them in a place where the dog is likely to bite into them, they may have to be removed.

● *Foreign objects* like bones can get stuck in the mouth between the teeth. Sometimes the bone gets wedged up in back behind the molars and across the roof of the mouth. Usually the dog starts pawing at his mouth, but there have been cases in which foreign bodies remained for weeks in the back of the mouth without the owner noticing.

● *A ruptured salivary gland* under the tongue causes a lot of swelling. It looks like a growth under the tongue, but it is not. Usually it is on one side only, so one side of the tongue looks different from the other. The dog seems uncomfortable and starts making motions with his mouth.

● *Distemper teeth* is a permanent discoloration or pitting of the teeth that occurs as a result of the dog's having distemper or some other infectious disease during the period in the dog's puppyhood when the teeth are being formed.

● *Decalcification of the teeth* comes from malnutrition, because the dog is not receiving enough vitamin D, or because the ratio of calcium to phosphorus in his diet is wrong, or because one of these minerals is deficient or absent. It can also occur if the dog has a severe infestation of worms. It appears as a discoloration or mottling of the teeth.

Teething   This is not a condition you need to check for, but you will surely notice it. Puppies begin to sprout "milk teeth" soon after they are born. The dog has 42 permanent teeth, which begin to erupt when he is about fourteen weeks old. Therefore the puppy teethes twice—and more or less continuously—from the time he is about four weeks old until he is nearly six months old!

The Skin

Run your hands backward and forward over the dog's entire body so that you can feel any scabs, lumps or swellings beneath the hair-coat. Sometimes a thorough brushing will reveal abnormalities. Skin ailments are one of the dog's most common problems, especially in the summer, when the animal spends a great deal of time outdoors and becomes subject to skin parasites and summer eczemas.

If you notice that your dog is working at his skin in one particular area that appears to be red or inflamed, clip the hair away, wash the skin with a mild soap and water, and apply a soothing skin cream. Apply a cortisone skin cream if you have one, or Vaseline to lubricate and soothe the area. Sometimes a little aspirin will reduce the itching. Mild antihistamines, such as Dristan, may also be administered. Since antihistamines have a strong depressive effect on dogs, do not exceed the following dosages.

Small (Chihuahua to 19 pounds)	⅛ tablet
Medium (20–25 pounds)	¼ tablet
Large (50–80 pounds)	½ tablet
Extra large (80–100 pounds)	½–¾ tablet
Giant (101–150 pounds, etc.)	1 tablet

What to Look For   Hair loss, often from continued scratching. On the long- or silky-haired breeds, you may notice an area where the hair is an inch short and matted. Look also for red or raw patches, pustules, crusty, flaky debris, dandruff-like flakes, a dull coat. Examine the axilla (armpit), the abdomen, and the areas above the tail, around the back of the neck, in the ear and between the toes for fleas and ticks. Parasites love these warm, soft areas where the skin is thin and tender and it's easy to suck blood. People who live in or visit the country should check their animals for ticks every day.

● *Ticks* are insidious little beasts because the dog may give no indication that they are there. Generally they cause only an irritation of the skin. Occasionally, if the infestation is particularly severe in a puppy, he can become anemic from excessive blood loss. Ticks can cause a disease called tick paralysis, but this is rare. The cure is simple. Remove the ticks.

The worst danger from ticks is Rocky Mountain spotted fever, but this occurs in human beings, not dogs. The brown dog tick carries this disease, and since he has a white spot on his back, he's fairly easy to recognize. If you are removing that kind of tick from a dog, never squeeze it so that the blood gets on your hands.

The best way to remove a tick is with tweezers. Grasp the tick firmly and pull it gently out. If the tick seems too firmly entrenched, put a little alcohol on the tweezers. A firm, steady action with the tweezers is most likely to remove the head, but if the head somehow gets separated from the body, it will not cause serious problems. The area may be inflamed for a longer period of time, but eventually the skin will throw this off and heal itself.

• *Fleas* are the intermediary hosts for tapeworm, but they are most annoying because they make the dog scratch, which can lead to serious skin problems. In short- or light-haired dogs, fleas are pretty easy to detect. In long- or dark-haired dogs, you have to look on the abdomen, in the armpit and around the ears.

Flea and tick collars are the most common method of protection from fleas. They contain an insecticide which exudes a vapor that coats the animal's whole body. It can be toxic, so check your dog frequently around the neck to make sure that his skin is not reacting. The collar is most effective against fleas, but some collars will kill ticks, too, especially if the tick is exposed to the insecticide for a long enough period of time.

Powders and shampoos are also effective, but read the directions carefully. The most effective treatment for a heavy infestation is the dip, which is usually a much stronger insecticide. It is a good idea to let the veterinarian do this for you.

Too much insecticide can cause muscle twitching and even convulsions. For this reason, it is unwise to combine two or more methods of parasite control. In other words, *don't* use a collar in conjunction with a spray or powder to give double protection. You may end up poisoning your dog.

Go easy with insecticides on pregnant bitches. Too many drugs and chemicals during pregnancy can be toxic. The dog absorbs insecticides through her skin, and if a pregnant bitch receives a large dose, it may affect the fetuses adversely. Consult with your veterinarian about proper dosages.

• *Eczema* may be nonspecific, which simply means that the vet is unable to determine the cause of it. A "hot spot" is one example of nonspecific eczema. The dog becomes attracted to a certain area on his skin where he feels or thinks he feels an itch. He begins to scratch. This causes an infection, which causes the dog to bite and scratch even more.

• *Chronic seborrhea* is excessive scaliness. The skin is irritated, red and raw at various points on the body, particularly on the abdomen. The cause is not known, but it is thought to be a hereditary defect in the skin's metabolism. The problem often starts when the dog is a year or two old. He develops an itchy, flaky coat, and his skin gets infected easily. The condition can be treated with medications and ointments, but it cannot be cured.

● *Allergies* are common in dogs. A dog develops a skin rash because he is allergic to some substance in his environment, such as grass, pollen or a wool rug. Sometimes he is actually allergic to fleas. Desensitizations to allergens can sometimes be accomplished by injections of the substance to which the animal has a strong reaction, but no veterinarian will guarantee success. Of course you would never cure a flea allergy by injecting the dog with fleas. The remedy here is to deflea the dog, which will rid him of the problem.

● *Sarcoptic mange*, unlike other types of mange, can be transmitted to humans. It is caused by a microscopic mite that burrows into the skin and is most common in stray dogs and puppies that have been exposed to a large number of different animals. In the early stages of the disease, it's difficult to diagnose, even by a veterinarian, and may go unnoticed. Once the disease has progressed for a month or two, it becomes more obvious. Symptoms are scratching, hair loss, rashes and redness. Often the tips of the ears will be crusted. In human beings, it usually appears as a red, itchy skin rash. Sarcoptic mange is easy to cure with a very strong insecticide dip. Human beings, of course, must see their own physicians for treatment.

● *Demodectic mange*, which cannot be transmitted to humans or other dogs, is much easier to detect than sarcoptic mange but very difficult to cure. The mite that causes it is often found on perfectly normal animals and does not usually cause disease. For this reason, researchers have come to believe that dogs that suffer from this complaint have a genetic lack of resistance. It is particularly common in Dachshunds and Boston Terriers. The mite is found in the hair follicle, and the animal develops bald patches, which in severe cases spread over the entire body, leaving the skin raw and red—which accounts for the popular name for this affliction, "red mange." If the mange is limited to small patches, typically on the head, around the eyes and on the legs, it can be controlled and successfully treated, but if the disease worsens in spite of all treatment, the dog may not be able to live very comfortably or very long.

● *Hormonal hair loss* occurs when there is a hormonal imbalance in the body. This type of hair loss typically occurs in bilaterally symmetrical patterns along the sides, above the tail, on the back of the legs, or on the underside and abdomen. If you hold the dog so that you can see both sides of him equally well, you will see that the hair loss is the same on both sides of his body. The condition commonly occurs in older male dogs with testicular tumors, in which case it is produced by the excessive estrogen secreted by the tumor, and it can be cured by castration. Other causes are harder to determine. Some dogs go entirely bald but appear to be perfectly normal and healthy otherwise.

• *Pyoderma* is a pus-producing staphylococcus infection of the skin. Some dogs are subject to chronic pyoderma, which is very hard to cure. For some reason the skin gets reinfected, especially the skin of the feet, and the dog chews at it, making it worse. Big sores and lesions develop. It occurs most frequently in dogs with a lot of folds in the skin, such as Bassets, Bulldogs and Pugs. You can prevent it from happening in the first place by washing these folds with antibacterial soaps and keeping the crevices dry. If an infection develops, the veterinarian will have to do a culture-sensitivity study to determine which antibiotic will most effectively attack the organism.

Abscesses   Usually the owner won't notice an abscess until it breaks and drains. Clip away matted hair and clean the wound with hydrogen peroxide. Apply hot packs to draw out the infection, and if the area seems particularly itchy, you may apply a local anesthetic cream like Lubricaine. *Do not use local anesthetics over a long period of time*, as they tend to irritate the skin. If the area drains a lot of pus, take the dog to the veterinarian.

Small Skin Lesions   A cut on the footpad may bleed profusely, although the dog won't bleed to death from such a wound. To bandage, pack clean cloth or gauze pads over the wound, and wrap strips of gauze around the pack. Wrap the gauze with tape. *Do not bandage too tightly, and if you are in doubt, err on the loose side.* Otherwise you could cut off the blood supply to the area. When you bandage, apply even pressure from the tip of the toes to the top of the bandage, creating a firm but not tight bandage, sufficient to control the bleeding until you can get the dog to the veterinarian.

The Feet

Gently lift the paws one at a time and examine each for abnormalities. The nails should be clipped so that they just touch the ground: The toes should not splay, and in most breeds, the carpus (wrist) and pastern (the bone below the wrist) should be straight and at a right angle to the ground.

What to Look For   Mats between the toes, burs, foreign objects, inflammation, cut pads, long nails. Watch the dog in motion to determine whether he limps.

The Tail

Most people don't think of the tail as a potential source of medical problems, but it, too, should be examined daily. If the tail has a tight curl in it, check the curl to see that a skin infection is not in the process of developing. Feel along the bones to make sure that they are all in place. Check the hair and skin underneath it.

What to Look For   Mats, burs, skin infections, hair loss, sores, broken bones. If the dog seems to feel pain in the tail, he may be suffering from a sprain or fracture.

The Anal Glands

The anal glands are really an outgrowth of the skin, even though they are situated on either side of the rectum and are closely associated with it. The anal gland is a scent gland used by most wild animals to mark territory, but in the domestic dog, it no longer serves any real purpose. The glands are positioned (one at four o'clock, one at eight o'clock) underneath the skin next to the rectum. The gland itself is round with a narrow neck that empties out near the rectum, usually when the animal defecates. Because the neck is so narrow, it can easily get clogged.

The glandular tissue keeps producing scent all the time, so if the neck of the gland gets plugged up, the gland will fill with its own secretion and rupture underneath the skin because there's nowhere else for the liquid to go. If this happens, an abscess will form underneath the skin. The gland itself, because it is simply an outgrowth of the skin, has bacteria in it and can also become infected, which may cause a bloody secretion. If the gland becomes a constant source of problems for the dog, the veterinarian may recommend its removal. The dog suffers no ill effects from this operation.

Some people have heard so much about the anal glands that they become obsessive about them, constantly expressing them as a routine part of their grooming procedures. This is usually not necessary. The majority of dogs never have a problem with the glands. Sometimes the secretion is dry and pasty instead of liquid (as it's supposed to be), and it has to be loosened with fluids and flushed out.

What to Look For   Soreness and inflammation in the anal area, a reluctance to defecate, constant licking and biting around the rear. If the dog slides his rear along the floor, this indicates that something is causing irritation and the veterinarian should have a look.

The Daily Exam

If the preceding pages look long and difficult, then you may use the chart opposite as a checklist of items to look for.

Dr. Susan McLellan and her Whippet demonstrate how to examine a dog's skin.

STEPHEN PROCUNIAR

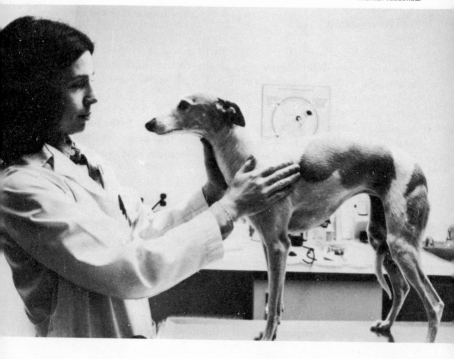

DAILY EXAMINATION CHART

PART OF THE BODY	SYMPTOM
Ear	Examine the ear canal, and remove any excess hair and accumulation of wax. The ear will probably not need cleaning more than once a week. Look for redness, swelling, discharge. Look for swelling and scabbiness along the ear flap.
Eye	Shine a penlight directly into the eye. Look for discharge, excessive tearing, inflammation, swelling, differences between the eyes, squinting. Examine the cornea for cloudiness or spots.
Nose	Look for discharge, inflamed, raw areas in the skin, ulcers, discoloration, crustiness. Compare nostrils. Listen for respiratory difficulty.
Mouth	Lift the lips and look at the rear molars. Look for red, irritated gums, growths, foreign objects, swelling of the tongue, tartar, discoloration of the teeth, bloody discharge, bluish tinge to gums and tongue. Note any foul odor.
Skin	Run your hands back and forth through fur. Look for hair loss, abnormally short hair, mats, redness and pustules on the skin, crusty, flaky debris, dandruff, a dull coat. Examine armpit, abdomen, behind ears for ticks and fleas. Check beneath flea collar for possible reaction to insecticide.
Feet	Check toenails. Make sure that toes do not splay, and that the dog is not down in the carpus or pastern. Look for mats, burs, foreign objects between toes, inflammation, cut pads, limping.
Tail	Feel along tail. Check for mats, burs, skin infection, hair loss, sores, broken bones.
Anal glands	Look for soreness, inflammation in the anal area. Note if dog is reluctant to defecate or slides along the ground.

7

YOU, YOUR DOG AND THE VETERINARIAN

The best way to find a veterinarian is to ask a friend who has a dog and is satisfied with the care and treatment he has received. If you don't have a friend to rely on, don't get a recommendation from whomever sold you the dog. The breeder or pet shop has a veterinarian who has a vested interest in keeping that business. Although he may be perfectly honest with you about the condition of the dog, his point of view is almost necessarily slanted. You will do better to research the situation yourself.

Here's what to look for:

1. The veterinary facilities should be clean and well equipped. If the office is dirty, it tells you something about the veterinarian. If he's going to allow it to be dirty in front where you can see it, heaven knows what's going on in the back.

2. Ask the veterinarian whether he can be reached in an emergency late at night, on holidays and over the weekend. If he can be reached only during office hours, go to someone else. Most medical emergencies don't occur during office hours.

3. Look for a plaque on the wall saying that the veterinarian is a member of the state or national veterinary association.

4. Look for a plaque saying that his hospital has been approved by the American Animal Hospital Association or by the state hospital inspection program. This means the facility has been inspected and has had to meet certain criteria.

5. Look for that elusive quality called bedside manner. This doesn't mean that the veterinarian has to get down on the floor and play with the dog, but he should have a friendly personality. A good doctor does more than inspect the dog's machinery and prescribe medicine. He should be willing to answer all your questions and to communicate on an open and friendly basis, just to make sure he gets all the facts straight—and gets them straight to you.

6. Ask if he schedules patients by appointment. If you live in a rural area, this may not be necessary, but if you live in the busy city or suburbs, you'll want to know that you aren't going to be sitting in the waiting room for an hour and a half. Not only is this inconvenient to you, it may be dangerous to your dog. If there's another dog in the waiting room that's vomiting, coughing or running a high fever, that dog ought to be isolated in an examination room, something the doctor can't do if his office is jammed with twenty-five patients. If the veterinarian schedules his clients fifteen minutes apart, that is more than adequate. It will take approximately five minutes for the veterinarian to examine the dog, and he'll have ten minutes left to talk to you.

7. Don't shop around for price. You want someone who is good and who does the job. If you find a veterinarian who charges much less than anyone else in the area, he's probably cutting corners. There may be a difference in the type of exam he gives before he inoculates the dog. The vaccine he uses may be less effective. The anesthesia he uses may be more dangerous. He may not glove and gown before he performs surgery.

The one exception to this rule may be—and we say *may* be—the shelter clinic. Some of the humane shelters are able to provide a high quality of care at a low cost in modern, clean facilities.

Ask around. See if you can find out something about the reputation of the clinic in your locale. Pay a visit and inspect the premises yourself.

8. In some offices the veterinarian has one or more assistants who perform many of the jobs that he used to do by himself. These individuals are called veterinary technicians. They have completed a course of instruction at a two-year college, and have been taught how to assist the veterinarian in a number of ways. Their presence is usually a good sign.

9. Be suspicious if the veterinarian has a big display in the corner where he's selling leashes, vitamins or cure-alls. Most veterinarians will sell you vitamins only after examining your dog and determining whether or not he ought to have them.

10. Be wary of guarantees of success of medical treatment or surgery. This usually indicates somebody who's not being honest.

11. Be wary of claims of exclusive knowledge unless you are dealing with a board-certified ophthalmologist, a board-certified surgeon, etc.—a bona fide specialist who has the diplomas to prove it. A sure sign of quackery is the person without any specialized degree who claims he can perform a miracle with some bizarre technique, special equipment or knowledge that no other veterinarian is privy to.

You should never leave the whole job of diagnosis and treatment up to the veterinarian. While the patient is the dog, you are the dog's mouthpiece. Be prepared to give complete and accurate information about diet, scheduling, environment. If your dog is sick, watch him carefully so you can answer the following questions:

1. When did he eat last, and how much?

2. Has he vomited, and what did the vomit look like?

3. Did he have diarrhea? What did the stool look like? Was it bloody?

4. How much water has he been drinking?

5. Have you noticed any change in his water consumption?

6. Is he lethargic?

7. Does he cough in the middle of the night?

If you don't know all the answers, admit it; don't try to fabricate.

When to Take Your Dog to the Veterinarian

You've been on the road now for two weeks, and everything has been fine. Then one morning you wake up to the sound of your dog gagging in the corner. A half an hour later he has diarrhea in the middle of the rug. You clean up the dog—and the room—as best you can, walk the dog in the hope that he'll empty himself, and settle down with the Yellow Pages.

You call around until you get someone to answer the phone. And you go there. It's an unfortunate situation, but in this case, there's no other way to handle it. If you enter the veterinarian's office and find it distasteful in any way, you're probably better off going back out on the street and starting over again. Of course if you have a severe emergency, you'll have to cross your fingers and hope for the best.

This situation is one of the worst that can happen. In most cases,

Dr. Susan McLellan and the kennels in the back of her clinic, which owners of prospective patients may examine.

you'll have your own veterinarian to call on. But never wait until an emergency develops to line up one if you can help it. Before you move from one area to another, get a health certificate from your present veterinarian listing all the dog's inoculations and when they were given. If the dog has any chronic or uncommon aliment, ask the doctor for a copy of the dog's medical records, or a description of the ailment and what he has done about it. As soon as you have relocated, find a new veterinarian immediately.

The Initial Visit

You are the proud owner of a new dog. You have found a veterinarian, made an appointment and given him the health papers that came with the dog. You are standing in the examination room, holding your dog on the table. Now's the time to ask questions:

1. Ask about any health problem that bothers you.
2. Ask about health problems that are specific to the breed of dog you own.

3. Ask about regular vaccinations and scheduled checkups.

Follow-up Visits

A normal, healthy dog who lives a relatively peaceful and uneventful life may not need an examination more than once a year when he receives his DHL booster and rabies shot. Dogs with chronic ailments must be attended to on a more frequent basis, the scheduling to be determined by the veterinarian. Pre-breeding visits for both dog and bitch are recommended, and the pregnant bitch should be placed immediately under veterinary surveillance.

When Your Dog Is Sick

In the old days it was easy. All we had to do was feel the dog's nose, and we'd know whether he was sick or well. Today we know that the dog's nose reflects the conditions of his environment. If he sleeps outside where it is cold and damp, his nose will also be cold and wet. These days, however, he's more inclined to select the living-room couch—at least when you're not looking. And like the couch, his nose will be warm and dry. The only way you can tell whether the dog has a fever is by taking his temperature.

The dog's body, like the human body, has ways of expressing the fact that things are going wrong. These ways are called symptoms. The chart on pages 116 and 117 provides a list of the most common symptoms with a brief commentary on each. We have not included "fever" on the chart because this is a symptom that you won't notice unless you specifically look for it, but fever is nevertheless a very important sign. Normal temperature ranges between 100° and 103° F., but the high end of the scale is normal only if the dog has been active. A temperature below 100° and above 103° F. indicates disease, and should be reported to the veterinarian immediately.

How to Take Your Dog's Temperature

Two-People Technique   Place the dog in a standing position. One person presses the dog against him and holds the dog's head to prevent him from turning around and putting his mouth on the second person. The second person lifts the dog's tail and inserts a rectal thermometer, lubricated with petroleum jelly, gently into the anus. Don't let go of the thermometer, or the dog will squeeze it out. Hold it in place for about one minute.

One-Person Technique   This is more difficult and recommended only for smaller dogs. Slip your arm around the dog and under his abdomen so that his head and forelegs stick out behind your back. This requires some trust on your part, but more on his. Hold the dog firmly so he can't turn around. Insert a rectal thermometer as above, and hold it in place for one minute.

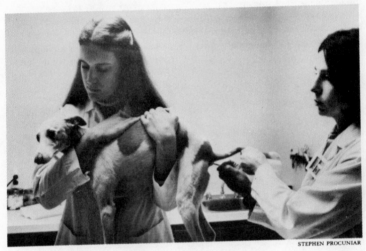

STEPHEN PROCUNIAR

Two-person method of taking a dog's temperature.

One-person method of taking a dog's temperature.   STEPHEN PROCUNIAR

TAKE YOUR DOG TO THE VET IF HE SHOWS:

SYMPTOM	COMMENT
Sudden weight gain or loss	Indicates disease; a potbellied appearance does not mean the dog is fat, but is usually accompanied by emaciation and malnutrition.
Increased drinking, urination; blood in urine	Indicates disease.
Straining to urinate or defecate	Indicates disease or blockage.
Lack of appetite; abnormally great appetite	A ravenous appetite in a puppy is normal; in an older dog, it indicates disease, especially if it reflects a sudden change in eating habits.
Abnormal stools	Transient diarrhea, chronic diarrhea, abnormally light or dark stool, bloody stool—all indicate disease.
Vomiting	Occasional vomiting is insignificant; persistent vomiting indicates disease. Examine vomit to determine (1) How much is there? and (2) What does it look like? Is it white? Is there milky froth? Is it foamy? Yellow? Blood-streaked?
Discharge from eyes, nose, ears	Some dogs have chronic discharge; heavy, persistent, crusty discharge indicates disease.
Abnormal swelling	In any part of the body this indicates disease.
Coughing	Persistent cough indicates disease, especially if it occurs at night and gets worse instead of better.
Inability to sustain exercise	An older dog will not exercise like a puppy, but if he's used to running and suddenly stops running, this indicates disease.
Discharge from vagina or rectum	Indicates infection or disease.

SYMPTOM	COMMENT
Biting at self	Indicates disease.
Bad odor	From any part of body, especially ears and mouth, indicates infection or disease.
Limp	Standing or walking with one limb raised or carried indicates injury or disease. Some dogs will fake a limp, so be careful.
Cow-hocked or bowlegged	Appearance indicates orthopedic problems.
Difficulty going up sets of stairs; jumping; getting up or lying down	Indicates disease.
Poor color or jaundice	Indicates disease; poor color could mean an emergency. See p. 215.

The Lying-Down Technique   If the dog is very sick, you can take his temperature while he is lying down. Again, it is best to have a second person hold his head.

Lying-down temperature-taking technique.

STEPHEN PROCUNIAR

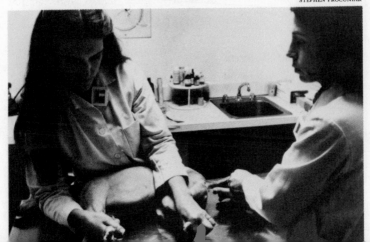

Giving Your Dog Medicine

When you take your dog to the doctor, he may prescribe medication. Your job is to get that medicine where it belongs—not down the front of your best shirt but inside the dog.

Giving a Liquid   Do not open the dog's jaws and pour medicine down the back of his throat. At worst he will choke to death. At best he will spit medicine all over you. The dog's lips are very soft and flexible. If you pull his lips away from his teeth, the side of his mouth will form a pocket into which you can pour the medicine from a spoon or liquid measure. The liquid will run down the back of his tongue and into his gullet before he has the opportunity to express contempt.

Giving a Pill   Crushing tablets between two spoons and mixing the powder with the dog's food is an acceptable method if the dog is not too sick to eat, and if the smell of the medicine doesn't make him lose his appetite. The following technique generally proves far more effective with either a tablet or a capsule: Slip your thumb in the tiny pocket behind the dog's canine teeth, and he will automatically open his mouth. If this does not work, pressure on the hinge of the jaw will sometimes force the issue. Push the pill with your fingers as far back down the center of his tongue as you can, halfway down his throat if that is necessary to keep him from spitting the pill out. He doesn't have the same gag reflex a human has, so he won't choke, and if he does start to choke, don't believe him. Remove your hand, close the jaws and hold them shut while, with your other hand, you stroke the dog's throat. When he tries to lick the tip of his nose with his tongue, this means he has swallowed. The faster you do this, the better, since the element of surprise often makes him swallow whether he wants to or not.

Health Insurance for Pets

At the present time, there is no nationwide health insurance plan for pets. The best to be had is Medi-pet, offered by National Petcare, Inc., in Los Altos, California. As yet it is available only in the San Francisco area. It costs $68 a year per pet and entitles the animal to veterinary services at clinics affiliated with the plan. It covers medical and surgical costs, booster shots, blood donations, prescrip-

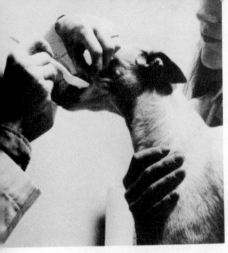

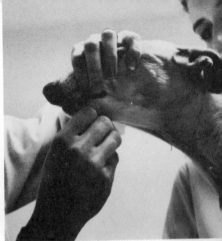

ABOVE: Administering liquid medicine so that the dog will not choke.

ABOVE RIGHT: To give a dog a pill, slip your thumb in the tiny pocket behind his canine teeth.

RIGHT: He will automatically open his mouth.

BELOW LEFT: Push the pill as far back on his tongue as you can.

BELOW RIGHT: Close his jaws and hold them shut while you stroke his throat to make him swallow.

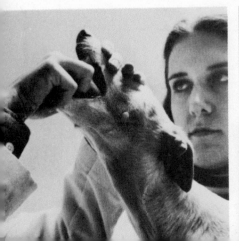

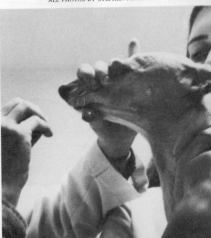

tion drugs, unlimited veterinary visits and routine examinations. It does *not* cover cosmetic surgery, puppy shots, special boarding and nursing care, spaying and pregnancy-related problems and congenital conditions pre-dating coverage.

8

A CATALOG OF COMMON CANINE ILLNESSES

We include this chapter to amplify the previous one. Suppose you notice that your dog is limping. You take him to the veterinarian, who prescribes medicine and sends you home accompanied by a big word like "osteochondritis dissecans." He has put the fear of God in you, and we are here to take it back out. You can turn to the part of this chapter that talks about osteochondritis dissecans, find out what it is and its symptoms and remedy. We have included only the most common complaints—in order to keep the book small enough to fit on your shelf.

Muscle and Bone Complaints

● *Hip dysplasia* affects just about any breed that weighs forty pounds or more when it reaches maturity. It also affects the smaller breeds, but less frequently. Hip dysplasia is arthritis of the hips, meaning that the hip joint is initially unstable, and the angle at which the hip enters the pelvis is not right. Bones grow, and the head of the hipbone and its socket must exert the proper pressure on each other for the bones to form correctly. Otherwise the bones will not form a firm joint but will shift around, causing damage to the cartilage and ligaments around the joint. This is followed by pain and swelling and finally outgrowths of bone in response to the inflammation. The condition gets worse and worse until finally it is a full-blown arthritis.

Hip dysplasia is graded from 1 to 4, with a grade 4 dysplasia representing the worst possible condition, where the joint is practically nonexistent. Although the grading represents a difference in prognosis, it does not reflect the amount of pain that the dog suffers. In other words, you may have a puppy who suffers severe pain although an X-ray of his hips shows only a grade 1 dysplasia, or a severely dysplastic animal who suffers no pain. Some animals with grade 4 dysplasia show in the ring without a limp. (It is of course senseless to show an animal that has a trait like this, because the reason for showing is to breed the dog for characteristics you want to pass on to the next generation, but some breeders get away with it.)

The Cause   More than one factor is involved. It is generally believed that hip dysplasia is transmitted genetically from parents to offspring, but a dog forced to grow too fast, one who puts a lot of muscle and weight on his bones before his skeleton can support it, tends to get dysplasia more quickly than other dogs.

There is no such thing as an absolute guarantee against hip dysplasia. The closest you can get is OFA (Orthopedic Foundation for Animals) certification, which means that the parents have been X-rayed and found free of it. If the grandparents, too, were OFA certified, you have an even better chance of getting a hip-sound pup.

The dysplastic dog may begin to show signs of the disease when he is nine or ten months old, or sometimes as early as four or five months if his condition is severe. But a dog may have perfect hips when he is ten months or even a year old and still develop the condition later on, which is why the OFA will not certify a dog until he is at least eighteen months.

You need not bother with X-rays if you get the dog for a pet and do not intend to breed him, and if he shows no symptoms. It is an expensive procedure. It has to be done under anesthesia, and often multiple plates have to be taken if the positioning is incorrect. The X-rays must be nearly perfect for the OFA to accept them for certification.

Symptoms   Hip dysplasia usually affects both hips, although in some cases the condition is worse in one hip than in the other, which is why the dog may appear to be lame on only one side.. He has difficulty lying down and getting up and appears to go lame after extensive exercise. If one leg is worse than the other, he may limp and carry the bad leg. If both legs are equally bad, he develops a stilted gait like a rabbit hopping. A dog with hip dysplasia also tends to be cow-hocked.

Treatment   Seven or eight years ago, when hip dysplasia first became something everybody talked about, once the owner received a positive diagnosis, he began to feel that his dog was doomed. Actually, this is rarely true. The great majority of cases are successfully treated.

Most dogs with hip dysplasia have a problem around nine to eleven months of age when they are getting big and have a lot of weight to support before their bones and muscles are completely formed. The joint gets sore from the constant instability and the dog begins to suffer. If you control his exercise, keep him on the lean side, and medicate him for the pain, he will usually pass through this stage. Once he becomes an adult, even though the condition is still present, he may never actually suffer from it again.

Medication   The vet may prescribe aspirin or other painkillers or occasionally, for a really severe problem, cortisone, but this last is usually not administered over long periods of time. In the very young dog cortisone may interfere with bone maturation; it tends to cause weight gain, excessive drinking and urination, and if it is used for months at a time, it may harm the adrenal gland.

Surgery   Several types of surgery are performed on the dysplastic dog. One involves severing the pectineal muscle on the inside of the thigh right below the hip. Perhaps in response to strain on the hip, this muscle becomes tight and inflamed, so by cutting the muscle, you lessen the tension on the joint and relieve the pain. Before you consider this operation, however, you should consider the fact that it does nothing to correct the dysplasia and there is no guarantee it will be successful. But if it is done properly, the animal will suffer no ill effects from it.

A *femoral head osteotomy* is usually performed on the giant breeds at a young age before the bones are completely formed. In this operation, the angle of insertion of the head of the femur is changed. It is a sophisticated procedure and must be performed by a doctor with special orthopedic training and equipment.

A third surgical procedure, called a femoral head resection, is performed on mature dogs as a salvage procedure. The femoral head (ball of the ball-and-socket joint) is removed completely, and a muscular joint is allowed to form post-surgically. This removes the painful bone-on-bone contact and works well on dogs up to about sixty to seventy pounds. Dogs over this size are apt to put too much weight on the subsequent muscular joint that forms and usually do not do as well post-surgically. For the same reason, it is usually done only on one side. It can be performed by an experienced veterinarian.

A fourth type of surgery is replacement of the joint by prosthesis, which can be done on the young or mature dog. This is still largely an experimental procedure and must be performed by a specialist.

● *Elbow dysplasia* is a condition totally separate from hip dysplasia. The cause is not known. The projection at the end of the forearm breaks off, so that you have a loose piece of bone in the joint instead of a smooth articulation. It occurs most frequently in the young dog, six to eight months old, and is most common in the German Shepherd.

Symptoms   Lameness, soreness around the elbow, lameness on one of the front legs. It usually but not always occurs on both sides.

Treatment   Controlled diet and exercise, medication and surgery.

● *Osteochondritis dissecans* occurs in the shoulder when the edge of the shoulder blade hits the cartilage of the humerus and breaks it.

The Cause   There seems to be a hereditary predisposition to the disease, mainly among the large breeds that grow very fast, at an early age, before the cartilage and bones are fused and firm. When the dog runs hard, the edge of the scapula strikes and injures the soft cartilage of the humerus.

Symptoms   A unilateral limping in the front leg, with a tendency to take rather short steps, or a bilateral limping if both sides are affected, resulting in a short, stilted gait. The owner may notice a limp on and off for a week or two.

Treatment   A minor cartilage fracture can be relieved and healed with rest. Sometimes a pain-relieving medication is prescribed. Sometimes surgery is required to remove the chips of cartilage and curette the damaged area so that it has a chance to heal smoothly. If surgery is performed before a lot of arthritis forms in the joint, the results are often excellent, and the joint is restored to normal.

● *Patellar luxation* is the skeletal scourge of the smaller breeds, especially the Toy Poodle, Yorkie and Chihuahua. For some reason or another, in some of these toy breeds, the tibia or shinbone curves too far to the inside, so the whole pull of the muscle along the leg is crooked; the kneecap is pulled over to the inside of the leg, and the entire leg becomes bowed and bent. In extreme cases, the leg looks as if it were twisted. More frequently, the dog's kneecap keeps popping in and out of place, the ligaments are stretched and the leg is apt to be injured.

The Cause   This condition is definitely hereditary, but is hard to control because of a multiple gene factor. Fifty to 75 percent of Toy Poodles and Yorkies have patellar luxation to some degree.

Symptoms   This is strictly a back-leg problem; the front leg has no kneecap. Typically the dog will run on three legs with one in the air. It is not uncommon for the dog to be lame in both legs, but this makes the problem harder to detect because the dog does not limp.

Treatment   If patellar luxation is not severe, the dog can be treated with medication. The condition is easy to diagnose, and surgery is usually successful if the dog is operated on before the deformity has become extreme and there is a lot of arthritis in the knee. The surgeon does a remodeling job, so that the dog gets the proper muscle pull straight down his leg.

● *Disc disease* occurs in the middle-aged dog when there is a calcification of the intervertebral discs. The intervertebral disc normally acts as a shock absorber between the vertebrae. If it calcifies, it collapses and sits in position like a little rock. If enough pressure is exerted on the disc, it may rupture toward the spinal cord. In some cases it can destroy the spinal cord, leaving the animal permanently paralyzed, but in most cases there is only a slight rupturing or inflammation around the disc, resulting in less serious neurologic problems. The degree of severity is determined by the amount of damage done to the spinal cord.

The Cause   This condition is probably hereditary, and seems to occur most often in dogs like the Dachshund with a long back, although Cocker Spaniels and Miniature Poodles are also frequently affected.

Symptoms   Back pain, difficulty in climbing stairs, difficulty getting up and lying down, partial loss of the function of the legs, complete paralysis.

Treatment   If the animal shows pain without neurologic symptoms, the vet will prescribe medication. If the condition seems to recur a number of times in a number of separate discs, he may recommend surgery. The procedure is called *disc fenestration* and requires an orthopedic specialist. He cuts into the side and removes the calcified material. All the discs in one area of the spine may be fenestrated. In the case of a sudden paralysis, the surgeon may opt to perform a *laminectomy*, an emergency procedure in which the top of the spinal canal is lifted off and the spinal cord itself is examined. When the doctor finds the disc material, he removes it, hoping to relieve the paralysis. If the spinal cord is badly damaged, nothing can be done.

●   *Cruciate ligament rupture* usually occurs in the older dog with a weak ligament. The dog makes a fast turn or slips, and the ligament holding his tibia and femur together ruptures. The condition occurs in both large and small breeds, typically in the overweight dog or the hunting dog. It can occur as the result of an automobile accident, but this is rare.

The Cause   Injury as a result of stress on weak ligament.

Symptoms   Pain; limping; loose, unstable joint.

Treatment   The ligament is usually surgically repaired, especially if the rupture is complete, leaving a very unstable knee. Surgery is not 100 percent effective, but the prognosis is good.

●   *Arthritis* can occur in any breed of dog, usually in an older animal with a predisposing cause such as patellar luxation or cruciate ligament rupture. Hip dysplasia is a form of arthritis where the swelling and inflammation are secondary to the condition of an unstable joint. Occasionally a dog will get rheumatoid arthritis, where the joints swell and the rheumatoid factor is present in the blood.

The Cause   Unstable joint, injury or rheumatoid factor.

Symptoms   Pain, swelling of the joint, limping.

Treatment   Medication or surgery to correct the underlying cause.

The Respiratory System

One particular canine respiratory phenomenon may cause the owner a great deal of anxiety. This is called the reverse sneeze. The dog gets a postnasal drip and a tickle in his throat. In an effort to clear it, he will put his head down and make a loud snorting noise. It sounds as if he were choking to death. He'll humph and humph, and suddenly the explosion will occur. He licks his chops, and everything is all right. This is most likely to occur in a dusty or polluted environment when little particles in the air get into the dog's throat and nose and cause a tickling sensation.

● *Kennel cough* is particularly common in kennels and pet shops. It is highly contagious but usually not serious, typically running its course in two to three weeks, after which time the dog begins to develop immunity. It starts as a tracheal irritation and a cough, but infection may spread to the lungs, where it becomes pneumonia. Kennel cough is due not just to one infectious agent but to two or three in combination, making it difficult to vaccinate against the disease.

The Cause   A virus causes the initial insult, which is then complicated by a bacterial onslaught.

Symptoms   A harsh, persistent cough. The dog may go into a paroxysm of coughing, and then try to gag something up. Frequently people mistake the cause as a bone caught in the throat. The first one to two weeks are the worst, with the dog going into coughing spasms that may last as long as ten minutes. Toward the end of the second week, the cough will begin to taper off. Medical treatment is advised to relieve discomfort and prevent secondary bacterial infection.

Treatment   You may now have your dog vaccinated against kennel cough, but the vaccine works against only one viral agent and is therefore not 100 percent effective. But it helps limit the severity of the disease and is probably beneficial for animals subject to high exposure—for example, dogs that are shown or frequently boarded. The dog needs two doses of vaccine initially and a booster every six to twelve months. For the average owner, it is probably not worth the trouble, but it will in no way harm the dog.

Generally the dog is treated as an outpatient, partly because the vet does not want to harbor kennel cough in his clinic, and partly because the dog is usually not all that sick. The vet will prescribe rest, warmth and antibiotics to prevent secondary infection. The dog should be kept inside as much as possible so that he won't come in contact with other dogs and so that he won't overexercise.

● *Distemper* is a systemic disease involving the respiratory system, the intestinal tract, and sometimes the brain and nervous system. Typically the first signs of distemper are a purulent discharge, or discharge of pus, from the eyes and nose, coughing and respiratory difficulty. In the early stages it's very hard to distinguish between distemper and kennel cough, which is why we mention the disease here. See page 143 for a full description.

● *Bronchitis* occurs in animals just as it does in human beings, and it can be chronic. It is hard to distinguish from kennel cough, but the history of the disease usually differs in that it appears when the dog has not been exposed or boarded.

The Cause   It usually occurs in the older dog when the respiratory tract is somehow weakened so that an infection gets into the bronchial tree. It may be caused by high levels of pollution or by an allergy or by weakening of the respiratory tract due to another previous disease. It is not contagious.

Symptoms   A persistent cough that increases in frequency and duration.

Treatment   Medication will help keep the dog comfortable, but he may continue to cough and retain a low-grade infection.

● *Collapsing trachea* is a congenital problem of the toy breeds, typically Toy Poodles and Yorkies. For some reason the tracheal rings are not very stiff, and the trachea, instead of being round in shape, tends to flatten out. When the dog breathes in, there's an increase in pressure, and the trachea collapses. The condition worsens as the dog gets older and may ultimately prove fatal.

Cause   Genetic.

Symptoms   A loud honking noise accompanies breathing. The dog will slow down during exercise, particularly in hot weather, when he must pant to eliminate body heat.

Treatment   Medication, including bronchial dilators and anti-inflammatories. The young dog may live comfortably for a number of years and not require treatment until the disease becomes more severe.

● *Elongated soft palate* occurs in the short-nosed breeds because the head's structures are all shrunk together. Sometimes the soft palate will get sucked into the trachea and block the air passages. Over a number of years, this may result in secondary changes, including a collapsed larynx. In hot weather, the condition becomes extremely severe.

Cause   Genetic.

Symptoms   Increased snorting and breathing problems; possibly heat prostration in hot weather.

Treatment   The owner should protect the dog from hot weather and excessive exercise and be extremely cautious during car travel. In severe cases, surgery may be recommended.

The Heart

A cardiac problem can be detected only by a doctor. A full physical exam, chest X-rays and an electrocardiogram (EKG) are required for an accurate diagnosis. Smaller breeds, forty pounds and less, are more prone to heart problems than the larger breeds. Dogs with respiratory problems are also victims. Both dogs suffering from collapsing trachea and short-nosed breeds can develop secondary cardiac enlargement because of the strain on their breathing apparatus. Obesity, although it does not cause cardiac problems, complicates treatment by putting an extra burden on the heart.

● *Congenital heart disease* is relatively common in dogs, especially in the purebred dogs that have been line-bred and inbred. Frequently puppies purchased from pet shops have heart murmurs, which is one reason why it is so important to have the puppy examined by a veterinarian.

Cause   Genetic.

Symptoms   Coughing and an enlarged heart; sometimes an enlarged belly (ascites).

Treatment   Some congenital heart problems can be corrected with surgery, but the procedures are expensive.

● *Valvular heart disease* occurs in the older dog, when the valves thicken and no longer close as efficiently as they once did so that some of the blood leaks back. Eventually the heart muscle itself enlarges to compensate for the inefficiency of the pumping mechanism. Over a period of months, sometimes years, the compensation ceases to be adequate, blood backs up into the lungs, and the dog goes into heart failure. Prompt treatment of cardiac disease is therefore necessary before cardiac failure ensues. Cardiac symptoms can be treated, but the underlying condition cannot be cured.

Cause   The valves of the heart become thickened, distorted and scarred over the years, usually because of an inflammation of the valves resulting from a bacterial infection in some other part of the body.

Symptoms   The most common symptom is night coughing. The dog will be restless at night, wake up, cough and cough, fall back to sleep, then wake up and start coughing again. He coughs because when blood backs up into the lungs, fluid begins to accumulate in the alveoli and bronchi, actually blocking the air passages. Sometimes fluid even drips from the nose. He has a tremendous amount of difficulty breathing, tires easily and is sometimes reluctant to move because it's an effort just to get enough oxygen. He will sit very upright with his mouth open and look worried about the situation. (This is no joke—the animal actually looks concerned.)

Treatment   Medication—digitalis, bronchial dilators and diuretics—is usually combined with a low-salt diet. Some dogs survive only a few weeks under medication; others live for years. In most dogs medication brings a significant improvement.

● *Heartworm* was first discovered in 1847 by a physician who was dissecting a dog's heart and found large worms in it. This is one of the ugliest diseases a dog can get. The adult worm invades the aorta and pulmonary arteries, where it is bathed by nutrients in the blood and can grow to be as much as a foot in length. Worst of all, heartworm doesn't manifest itself until the disease is quite advanced. There are cases on record where the dog just keeled over with no prior signs of illness.

Cause   Heartworm is a scientific marvel that involves a delicate interrelationship between worm, mosquito and dog. It's a relationship that probably took eons to develop. This is how it works:

1.   A mosquito bites dog number one, who has heartworm and circulating microfilaria in his blood.

2.   The mosquito ingests the heartworm microfilaria, which incubates in his body for a period of two to three weeks; then the larvae migrate to the mosquito's salivary glands.

3.   The mosquito bites dog number two, injecting infective larvae into the dog's subcutaneous tissues.

4.   The infective larvae migrate subcutaneously through the dog's body to the major blood vessels of the heart. The migration stages last from two to four months.

5.   The larvae develop into adult worms in the heart and start discharging motile embryos called microfilaria into the dog's bloodstream. This stage takes another two months to develop.

There are several interesting facts about this nasty parasite. First, the larva has a homing instinct for the heart and rarely goes astray. Occasionally, however, this has happened. There's one case on record where the heartworm ended up in the dog's toe.

Second, the larva must be passed to the dog through the mosquito. You can take the infected blood of one dog and actually inject it into another dog and the second dog will not develop heartworms.

Third, in the initial stages of the disease, the microfilaria cannot be detected in the bloodstream. The disease has to reach step five, when the worm has actually developed to the adult stage in the dog's heart, before it can be diagnosed. For this reason, tests for heartworm should be performed every six months. Even then, they are not 100 percent accurate.

Heartworm does not affect human beings.

Symptoms   Microfilaria in the bloodstream; symptoms of congestive heart failure.

Treatment   The best cure for heartworm is prevention. In warm parts of the country where mosquitoes are a year-round affair, the dog should be on preventive heartworm medication every day of his life. In cooler parts of the country, the veterinarian will usually recommend that the dog be placed on preventive medication only during the mosquito season. If properly administered, preventive medication is 100 percent effective.

Once the dog actually has the disease, it is not necessarily hopeless, although the cure is not so easy. Arsenic compounds are injected intravenously in amounts calibrated to kill the worm and not the dog. These compounds are toxic to the liver, which must be tested and monitored while the dog is under treatment. If changes are detected, the medication must be stopped. The medication is extremely caustic and must be administered carefully. One drop outside the vein will cause tissue to slough off. Sometimes the worm is killed, breaks up and passes into the lungs, where it can cause pneumonia and severe, even fatal, illness.

The Liver

Liver disease is quite common in older animals and is usually caused by viral or bacterial infections, sometimes borne by the blood from primary infections located in other parts of the body.

Symptoms Gastrointestinal upset with vomiting and diarrhea, weight loss, general malaise, mental depression, yellowing of the skin and mucous membranes. If you pull up the eyelid, you will see yellow in the white part of the eye. The gums have a yellowish cast. On light-haired dogs, you can also see yellow pigment in the skin of the abdomen.

Treatment Antibiotics to cure the infection and help the liver along until it has the chance to heal itself. Hospitalization and intensive care are usually required.

The Pancreas

The pancreas is an enzyme-secreting organ of the body. It produces the digestive enzymes that go into the intestine, and it has a duct that delivers these enzymes into the intestinal tract. A lot of things can go wrong with the pancreas. The ducts can get blocked. There can be tumors. The pancreas can become inflamed and rupture, shooting enzymes into the abdomen and causing peritonitis. Sometimes the pancreas becomes so diseased and scarred that it can no longer produce the enzymes needed for digestion.

Symptoms Vomiting and diarrhea are the first signs. The dog's abdomen may be taut and painful. The disease can be acute, with a sudden onset of vomiting and diarrhea, or chronic, with constant diarrhea and vomiting.

Treatment Depends on the cause of the disease and its severity.

● *Diabetes:* The pancreas produces insulin, which breaks down glucose (blood sugar) in the bloodstream, which then delivers it as nourishment to the cells. If insulin is not present in great enough quantities in the body, the glucose will not reach the cells, which consequently become starved. This is the condition called diabetes mellitus (sugar diabetes). It can build to the point where the animal is actually starving to death.

The Cause Insulin-producing cells of the pancreas are destroyed.

Symptoms Excessive thirst and urination; sudden weight loss, which may be accompanied by a ravenous appetite; vomiting; diarrhea; severe depression. Excessive glucose in the blood and urine. The condition must be rectified at once, or the dog will not survive.

Treatment The dog is stabilized on insulin, which the owner is taught to inject at home. The shot is given with a tiny needle so as not to hurt the animal, and is injected subcutaneously, right underneath the skin. Diet and exercise must be carefully regulated.

The Gastrointestinal (GI) Tract

The GI tract includes the esophagus, stomach and intestines. Most dogs are very sensitive in this department—so sensitive, in fact, that vomiting and diarrhea are symptoms of more than half of all canine disease. Ninety-five percent of the time, both symptoms are due to something rather simple.

A large number of gastrointestinal problems can be avoided by preventing your dog from eating foreign matter, especially garbage.

Some dogs are really omnivorous, and these are the ones you have to watch out for.

● *Simple Diarrhea:* Sudden changes in diet can cause diarrhea. Milk causes diarrhea in puppies and some older dogs because they can't digest the lactate. Rich fatty foods and spicy foods, especially for older dogs, are also to be avoided.

Treatment   Occasional vomiting and mild diarrhea can be treated at home with Kaopectate or Pepto-Bismol. A German Shepherd will tolerate an amount equivalent to the dosage for an adult human being. A toy breed should be given only one teaspoonful. Repeat dosages every four to five hours.

Toy	1 teaspoon
Small Dog	1½ teaspoons
Medium (25–35 pounds)	2 teaspoons
Large (40–90 pounds)	1 tablespoon
Giant (90–150 pounds)	2 tablespoons

Put the dog on a bland diet, something low in fat and easy to digest. For small dogs, try a combination of strained baby food and cooked rice; for large dogs, mix one part cooked rice with one part chopped meat, parboiled to get the fat out of it. If vomiting and diarrhea persist, if the dog becomes depressed, or if there is blood in the vomit or diarrhea, see your veterinarian.

● *Worms* are probably the single most common ailment in the dog. Puppies are sometimes born with worms if the mother is infested. That's why it's a good idea to deworm your bitch *before* you intend to breed her, since deworming during pregnancy may cause damage to both her and the fetuses.

Many types of worms affect dogs. The most common are round-worm, hookworm, whipworm, tapeworm and Coccidia, the last being a type of protozoan and not really a worm at all.

Symptoms   Remarkably similar in all cases, which makes it necessary for the veterinarian to diagnose your dog before treating him. Roundworms and tapeworms are visible to the human eye, but just because your dog has one type of worm doesn't mean he isn't at the same time the victim of another. Symptoms are dull coat, potbellied appearance, poor nutrition, anemia, vomiting, diarrhea, bloody diarrhea, occasionally bloody vomit, coughing up of roundworms from the lungs, possibly a subnormal temperature. A stool specimen, perhaps even multiple specimens, are needed for precise diagnosis.

Treatment   For roundworms, hookworms and whipworms, the dog must be treated at least twice. You will see why if you examine the life cycles of these worms on pages 136 through 139. Medication eliminates only the adult stage of the worm. If the veterinarian administered a large enough dose to kill the larvae of the worm as well, he might also kill the dog. Thus he administers one treatment, waits two or three weeks and administers another to kill the fresh batch of adults that have developed from the larvae. The correct timing of the second treatment is important to ensure that it occurs after all the larvae have hatched but before they have laid new eggs.

The medications you can purchase at a pet store will attack roundworms only. The veterinarian alone can dispense drugs powerful enough to kill other types of worms.

When the veterinarian deworms your dog, he will probably want to keep him in his clinic where he can be on the lookout for side effects. For one thing, if the dog is given the medicine orally, there is always the chance that he may vomit up the drug, which means that he will need remedication. The veterinarian has to be able to estimate how much of the drug the dog has lost in order to redose him. For another, the dog may show systemic effects from deworming medication—tremors or convulsions, for example. The veterinarian will administer additional drugs to reverse these effects. Some drugs are safe enough to be given at home; your veterinarian will tell you what is best.

Coccidia   This is a protozoan that lives entirely in the intestinal tract. The oocyst (not a true egg) is swallowed by the dog, penetrates the intestinal wall and creates more oocysts, which are then passed on in the stool. This disease may be treated at home by administering sulfa compounds prescribed by the veterinarian. Coccidiosis usually responds well to medication and runs its course in about two weeks.

Tapeworm   All dogs may get tapeworm, but it is most common in the mature dog. The two most common tapeworms in the dog will not affect humans. *Diphyllobothrium lateum*, which occurs mostly in man, will only occasionally be found in dogs or other carnivores. *Echinococcus granulosus*, a tapeworm that infests both man and dog, is a problem in some countries but is very rare in the United States.

The dog acquires tapeworm by ingesting a flea or killing a rabbit.

ROUNDWORM LIFE CYCLE

Method of Infestation: Intrauterine; ingestion of eggs.

Victims: All dogs, especially puppies; older dogs somewhat immune.

Number of Treatments: Two; retreatment in two to three weeks to kill adults that have redeveloped from new larvae.

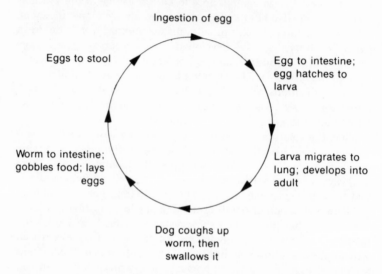

Ingestion of egg

Eggs to stool

Egg to intestine; egg hatches to larva

Worm to intestine; gobbles food; lays eggs

Larva migrates to lung; develops into adult

Dog coughs up worm, then swallows it

Symptoms: Dull coat, potbellied appearance, poor nutrition, worms sometimes visible in stool, worms coughed up from lungs; vomiting, diarrhea, subnormal temperature.

Public Health Hazard: People susceptible; usually children from direct contact with dog's stool.

Both are intermediary hosts, each for a different kind of tapeworm. Symptoms are usually mild gastrointestinal signs or the appearance of ricelike segments in the stool. Although the life cycle does not require more than one treatment, medication is sometimes less than 100 percent effective, so two treatments may be required.

● *Malabsorption syndrome* occurs when there are abnormalities in the mucosa or lining of the bowel. To the naked eye, the mucosa looks flat, but it really isn't. There are valleys and dips in it, which

WHIPWORM LIFE CYCLE

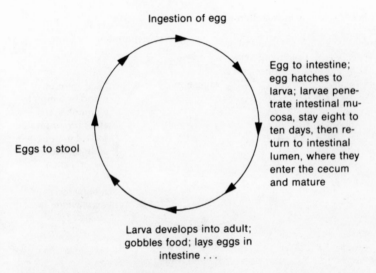

Ingestion of egg

Egg to intestine; egg hatches to larva; larvae penetrate intestinal mucosa, stay eight to ten days, then return to intestinal lumen, where they enter the cecum and mature

Eggs to stool

Larva develops into adult; gobbles food; lays eggs in intestine . . .

Method of Infestation: Intrauterine; ingestion.

Victims: All dogs

Number of Treatments: Two, sometimes three. A third treatment six to eight weeks later is advised because the whipworm lives in the cecum and is difficult to eradicate.

Symptoms: Dull coat, poor nutrition, vomiting, diarrhea, bloody diarrhea, anemia; worm eggs microscopic; adult worm invisible to human eye.

Not a public health hazard.

---

provide a tremendous surface area for food and fluid to be absorbed by the bowel. Abnormalities prevent the correct absorption of nutrients.

Cause Hereditary, occurring in certain lines of animals and appearing early, usually when the puppy is only a few months old.

Symptoms Chronic diarrhea. A biopsy will reveal abnormalities in the mucosa.

HOOKWORM LIFE CYCLE

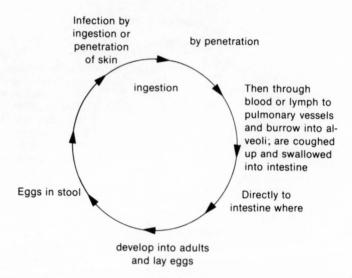

Method of Infestation: Intrauterine (larval migration is necessary for prenatal infection); ingestion; penetration through skin, especially of feet.

Victims: All dogs.

Number of Treatments: Two; second treatment two to three weeks later, depending on type of medication used.

Symptoms: Dull coat, poor nutrition, vomiting, diarrhea, bloody diarrhea, anemia; worm eggs microscopic; adult worm invisible to human eye.

Public Health Hazard: People susceptible to skin rash, not worms.

Treatment   Medication and special diet. It can be controlled but never cured.

● *Hemorrhagic gastroenteritis* is an emergency. It is especially common in Schnauzers, but also occurs frequently in the smaller breeds.

Cause   Not known.

Symptoms   Severe diarrhea. The stool is not just blood-streaked, but

TAPEWORM LIFE CYCLE

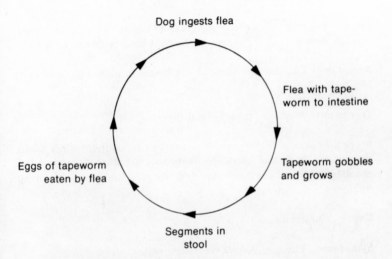

Dog ingests flea

Flea with tape-
worm to intestine

Tapeworm gobbles
and grows

Segments in
stool

Eggs of tapeworm
eaten by flea

Method of Infestation: Usually by ingesting a flea. One type of tapeworm lives in rabbits, and the dog gets it when he kills and eats a rabbit. There is always an intermediary host.

Victims: All dogs, but the adult dog is particularly susceptible.

Symptoms: Sometimes none. Mild gastrointestinal signs. Positive diagnosis made by examination of ricelike segments in the stool. Visible to the human eye.

Number of Treatments: One or two; medication is often less than 100 percent effective.

Not usually a public health hazard: Common canine tapeworms do not affect humans. See description for additional information.

---

almost entirely blood, resembling currant jelly. The dog will vomit, be very depressed and dehydrated, and go into shock.

Treatment See the veterinarian immediately. He will treat the condition with fluids, high doses of corticosteroids and antibiotics, and anti-shock therapy.

● *Colitis* is a much-overused diagnosis, but it sometimes occurs in older dogs. The feces are normally very fluid in the small intestine, but when they reach the large intestine (the colon), absorption of the fluid occurs. If the fluid is no longer correctly absorbed, the dog will have a chronic diarrhea.

Cause   For some reason the bowels can't handle food the way they used to. Stress or diet change can be contributory factors.

Symptoms   Chronic diarrhea; if the bowel is ulcerated, a bloody stool.

Treatment   Medication and bland diet.

● *Esophageal problems* occur sometimes in younger dogs when the vessels from the heart are incorrectly positioned around the esophagus, forming a vascular ring. As the dog grows, the ring tightens.

Cause   Congenital.

Symptoms   The dog vomits right after eating.

Treatment   Surgical intervention to correct the placement of the blood vessels.

● *Esophageal achalasia* is a condition in which the esophagus dilates. The cause is unknown, but there is evidence that the disease is inherited. It is common in young dogs but can also occur in adults. The main symptom is frequent vomiting, especially of undigested food.

The Urinary System

Inflammation of the bladder (cystitis) is common and not serious. It is caused by bacterial infection, a blow to the abdomen, or trauma—for example, from a car accident. A bacterial infection occurs when bacteria ascend to the bladder via the urethra. When the infection continues over a long period of time, laboratory cultures must be prepared to determine what organism is causing the infection, which is then treated with an antibiotic specific to that organism.

Kidney disease is far more serious, because it ultimately affects all the organs in the body. Kidney disease can be either acute or chronic. The former usually displays itself by vomiting and diarrhea. The dog will try to drink more water and will produce more urine in an effort to get more fluids through the kidney. With severe vomiting and diarrhea, he can't retain water and becomes dehydrated. The infection must be alleviated and the animal helped through this period of disease so that the kidney can heal and start functioning normally again.

If the infection is brought under control but a lot of damage has been done to the kidneys, the dog develops a more chronic kidney condition. In an older dog, this condition is not unusual. The dog may never show signs of acute illness, but he drinks more and urinates more. When it gets to the point where the kidneys can no longer handle waste products, he goes into terminal kidney failure. However with medication, increased fluids and low-protein diet, the dog can be stabilized for a rather long period of time.

● *Bladder stones* form in dogs just as they do in people. In the male dog, if a stone of the right size forms, it can pass into the urethra and block it, causing an acute emergency situation. The stone must either be forced back into the bladder or surgically removed.

Cause   Chronic cystitis or chronic infection of the bladder. Stones occur frequently in Dalmatians because this breed normally has an unusual amount of mineral in the urine.

Symptoms   Straining to urinate without passing urine, especially in a male dog. Straining in the female is usually just a sign of cystitis. Her urethra is much larger than the male's and therefore harder to block.

Treatment   Surgical removal, with medication post-surgically to make stone formation less likely.

● *Kidney stones* are less common and are treated in the same way.

● *Tumors* occur rarely in the kidney, more frequently in the urinary bladder. Symptoms are chronic blood in the urine and straining to urinate. The only cure is surgical removal.

● *Prostatic disease* occurs in the male dog. The prostate gland is connected with the bladder but is actually part of the reproductive system. If it becomes infected, the dog has what is called prostatic disease.

Cause The prostate has ducts that enter the urethra, putting this gland in close context with the urinary bladder. If the bladder becomes infected, bacteria can ascend through the prostate ducts and infect the gland. In older animals, the gland sometimes enlarges from hormonal causes.

Symptoms Swelling; bloody discharge from the penis independent of urination.

Treatment The prostate does not respond well to antibiotics. If enlargement is due to hormonal causes, the dog may be treated with estrogens to shrink the gland. Sometimes castration is indicated.

• *Adrenal malfunction* can affect the entire body. If the adrenal glands produce too much or too little hormone, the result is severe metabolic upset. The signs are gastrointestinal disturbances, hair loss and sometimes increased drinking and urination. *Hypoadrenalism* (too little hormone) is treated orally with hormones, which are balanced carefully by monitoring blood electrolytes. *Hyperadrenalism* (too much hormone) is treated by administering a drug to reduce adrenal function; sometimes surgery is indicated if the abnormal secretion is due to a tumor.

The Central Nervous System

This system includes the brain and the spine. Central nervous system disease may be caused by tumors, direct infection from a penetrating wound, or infectious disease.

The signs of central nervous disorder are changes in personality, paralysis of certain groups of muscles, dilation or constriction of the pupils of the eyes, constant or abnormal motion of the eyes, and difficulty in walking, sometimes expressed by a circling motion. Treatment depends on the cause of the disease.

Systemic Diseases

The body is more than just a sum of its parts. Somehow all the marvelous structures—organs, muscles, bones, nerves and skin— together make up a living being. But life begins in the cell, so it is not surprising that the worst battles for survival are fought there against deadly organisms smaller than the cell itself which have the capacity to destroy the entire system.

● *Distemper* has an incubation period of about ten days. It affects first the respiratory system, then the gastrointestinal system, and finally the central nervous system. It often progresses to encephalitis, which causes convulsions, chorea (quivering of certain muscles) and ultimately death. The survival rate is less than 5 percent. Even if the animal survives the first onslaught, there is often irreparable neurologic damage, which makes it pointless to save his life.

Cause   A virus.

Symptoms   Vomiting, diarrhea, pus from the eyes and nose, pneumonia, convulsions (typically, "chewing-gum convulsions," a term that is self-explanatory).

Treatment   The best cure is prevention—i.e., inoculation. Once contracted, the disease is treated with antibiotics, to prevent secondary infection, and intensive home care. Treatment is rarely effective.

● *Hepatitis* has an incubation period of five to nine days. It primarily attacks the liver but affects the other systems as well. It bears no relationship to human hepatitis.

Cause   A virus.

Symptoms   Fever; thirst; lack of appetite; hemorrhaging of the blood vessels, especially in the mouth; hemorrhagic gastroenteritis. Typically the fever will rise for twenty-four hours, then drop, after which death soon follows. Secondary symptoms are conjunctivitis and a cloudy bluish cornea called "hepatitis blue-eye," which may occur during convalescence and is incurable.

Treatment   Again, the best treatment is prevention by inoculation. The disease is difficult but not impossible to cure. It may be treated with serum injections, antibiotics to fight secondary infections, vitamin B complex, special diet and intensive-care nursing at home. The illness runs its course in four to six days, and can do a lot of permanent damage to the liver.

• *Leptospirosis* has an incubation period of five to fifteen days. It attacks the kidneys, with secondary systemic effects including a general malaise and gastrointestinal upset. It is carried by the urine of rats, cattle and other dogs who have had the disease. There is also the possibility that the dog will infect his owner, which makes this disease a public health hazard.

Cause   Bacteria. Farm dogs pick the disease up from cattle or rats. Sometimes an animal is a carrier and never exhibits symptoms himself.

Symptoms   Fever, malaise, vomiting, diarrhea, loss of appetite, painful walking, jaundice, cardiovascular collapse or kidney failure terminating in death.

Treatment   Once again, inoculation. The disease can be treated with antibiotics, since it is a bacterial infection, but the animal may suffer severe kidney damage nonetheless.

• *Rabies* has an incubation period of several weeks to months— hence the long quarantines required by such island countries as Britain. Rabies has pretty much been eliminated from the dog population of the United States by the excellent vaccination programs provided for domestic animals; nevertheless, rabies is always present in the wild-animal populations of the country, especially among foxes, skunks and other feral animals. It is a public health hazard.

Cause   A virus.

Symptoms   Personality change and neurologic problems. Rabies is also called hydrophobia (from the Greek *hydor*, meaning "water," and *phobos*, meaning "fear") because it paralyzes the muscles so that the animal is unable to swallow water. The image in people's minds is of a mad dog with saliva dripping out of his mouth, which is deceptive, since this commonly occurs when an animal chews and swallows a foreign object. Actual paralysis of the jaw can cause a condition called dumb rabies, where the animal's jaw hangs slack, and he is unable to close his mouth at all.

Treatment   The disease is invariably fatal. Any person bitten by a "mad" dog must be vaccinated. The original Pasteur treatment (for humans) has been abandoned for a less painful method, but there is still some danger of anaphylactic shock when these injections are given.

● *Cancer* is the common term for malignant tumors, which occur in animals just as frequently as they occur in people. There are many different types of cancer in dogs, but some sites are more common than others. Mammary tumors are very common in the bitch, and primary bone tumors in the giant breeds. There is a type of dog leukemia very similar to the human version. Tumors can be either primary, such as a kidney tumor that forms from kidney tissue, or secondary, such as a tumor in the lung that has migrated from the mammary gland.

Cause Not known.

Symptoms Morphologic change, a bump or lump. If it occurs in an internal organ, it will manifest itself with symptoms specific to that organ. For instance, a liver tumor will cause symptoms of liver disease, a kidney tumor symptoms of kidney disease.

Treatment Depends on the part of the body affected and the innate characteristics of the tumor. The doctor will check for lymph-node enlargement around the tumor and for lesions in the lungs, which indicate that the tumor has metastasized. If it has, there is no point in surgery. The cancer may then be treated with chemo- or radiation therapy by doctors who specialize in these techniques, often with considerable success.

EDUCATING YOUR DOG: OBEDIENCE TRAINING AND CORRECTING HIS FAULTS

There are four basic ways to get your dog trained: the classroom, the kennel, at home, and do-it-yourself.

The Classroom

Classes are held in a specific place at a specific time each week. About ten or fifteen owners bring their dogs, and the instructor shows them how to teach the dog each command. Classes have several advantages: they are relatively inexpensive; you see and hear exactly how each command is to be executed; the dog learns to follow orders in the presence of other dogs, which also teaches him to disregard distractions and nips in the bud any inclination to fight with other dogs. However, if you miss even one class, you and your dog fall behind. Also, most classes are aimed toward earning an obedience degree, which makes the training far more exacting and rigorous than is actually necessary. And although the dog may learn the basic commands, there is no way to deal in a classroom with specific behavioral problems that occur in the home.

The Kennel

Your dog is boarded for a couple of weeks and receives intensive

OBEDIENCE TRAINING   147

obedience training from an expert. When he is returned to you, you are taught how to execute the basic commands. This requires little work on your part. In fact you pay good money so that someone else will do the job for you. The degree of success depends on the quality of follow-up lessons that you receive after the dog is trained. In some cases, while the dog is almost certainly trained, you are not. You have lost one of the great opportunities to become involved with your pet, and you know little more about dog training than you did to begin with. If you don't execute the commands correctly, the dog will not listen to you, and there's a good chance of this because you weren't present to learn the commands in the first place.

On the other hand, some trainers provide a few follow-up sessions in the home. In this case, kennel training is extraordinarily successful, since the owner is taught what to do in the home environment. This method is often very effective with shy and spoiled dogs.

At Home

A trainer comes to your home and trains you and your dog simultaneously. The trainer teaches you how to work with the dog, and corrects your faults as well as the dog's. This is the most costly method, and it requires work on your part. You are expected to practice with the dog. You can't expect the trainer to come once a week and do magic.

Do-It-Yourself

This is the method proposed in this book. We give you instructions, and you train the dog yourself.

Even if you decide to employ a dog trainer, you should read this section. It will help you understand what the trainer is doing and why and what to do if and when problems occur. It will also help you understand your dog. There is no substitute for knowledge.

To begin with, any dog of any size, age or sex can be obedience-trained, unless he has an aggressive personality (see p. 47), in which case he should be left to a professional. Training can begin when the dog is as young as seven weeks old or as old as eleven years. The important thing, of course, is not age but personality, and you must study your dog's before you begin (see p. 46).

Actually, seven to twelve weeks is the best time to start, because this is when the dog's personality is being formed. Training then becomes a matter of not only teaching the dog how to behave himself but accustoming him to the human voice and touch. If the dog is shy, you can bring him out. If he is stubborn, he will quickly learn that stubbornness doesn't please.

For a training area, choose a quiet place in either your house or your backyard. The area should be free from distractions so that you and your dog can concentrate on each other. Whenever you teach him anything new, you should always return to this original quiet environment. This is true for each separate command. As soon as the dog understands the command perfectly, move to a busy environment. The dog is no good to you if he heels in your apartment and strains at the leash when you are walking outside. But the idea is to teach him first. Eventually he will be alert to the sound of your voice and will follow orders no matter how many horns are blaring or how many people stop you for conversation. The length of time you spend in the quiet area depends almost entirely on the dog's personality.

If you spend ten minutes a day with your dog every day for two weeks and then gradually increase the time until the dog is spending as much as twenty to thirty minutes a day practicing, he will learn the whole course in six to twelve weeks. If you spend five minutes a day with him, it will take longer. If you spend thirty minutes in one long session every other week, the dog will never learn, and you will become increasingly frustrated. The key is a regular schedule. If you haven't got much time, schedule shorter training sessions and resign yourself to taking longer to finish the course. There's nothing wrong with this; we all know people who went to law school at night and ultimately passed the bar exam.

Your three major training tools are those we have already mentioned—hands, voice and heart—but it is helpful to have at least two others: a corrective collar and a six-foot leather leash. A shake-can, a throw-chain and a water pistol will make your arsenal of training tools complete.

Hands Your hands are used to place the dog in the desired position—for example, the "sit" position. It is ridiculous to suppose that a dog will understand what "sit" means unless you show him, and you show him with your hands. With your hands at the end of the leash you have complete control over the dog. You lead him into desirable behavior, and when he errs, you correct him by jerking the leash. The dog does not really understand that your hands are applying the jolt, and therefore does not become hand-shy. The hands give signals that reinforce vocal commands. They are also, as we have said, used for patting and stroking, communicating to the dog that you are pleased.

Voice   The voice is used to give the basic commands of "sit," "heel," "stay," "down" and "come," and to speak to the dog by name. The name is spoken in combination with the commands of motion—"heel" and "come"—never with the stationary commands—"sit," "stay" or "down." The name must never be spoken harshly or in conjunction with correction but always enthusiastically or with affection. Thus the dog learns that his name is good, and whenever he hears his name spoken, he will expect good things to follow. The voice is also used for "okay," which is a release: either a release from one command followed by another, as in "Okay, Sidney, come," or a release from training—when you say "okay" and the dog is allowed to do whatever he wants. The voice is used for "no," which is the single word of correction. "No" is the only negative word that you should ever say to your dog.

The tone of the voice conveys as much (or more) information to the dog as the words themselves. For instance, if you say "come" with enthusiasm, the dog is as likely to respond to your enthusiasm as he is to the word. "Stay" is spoken evenly in a level tone or with a slight upward inflection. "Heel" is said authoritatively, never harshly. "Sit" is spoken with an upward lilt at the end and is drawn out to give the word a steadying effect. "Down" has a downward tone at the end so that the dog hears the idea of "down" in your voice. This may sound foolish, but dogs are sensitive to tone and inflection. Your tone of voice must always be calm, even and cheerful. The amount of excitement you communicate is determined by the dog's personality. You will want to communicate as little excitement as possible to a nervous dog, for example, while a great deal of enthusiasm may help to get a sedate dog moving.

The voice is also used for praise. Every time that the dog does what he is supposed to do, you must praise him. "Good boy, good Sidney." This is true whether or not you have helped him. For example, when you are teaching "sit," you push the dog into a "sit" position with your hand. As soon as he is in the proper position, you must praise him as though he thought of sitting all by himself. You will find that during most training sessions, you are a constant chatterbox. Even a little silliness gets better results than silence.

Heart   The love you have for your dog will teach him obedience faster than anything else you can offer. This may sound sentimental, but it is true. The dog feels it in your hands and hears it in your voice, and the more of it he hears and feels, the more he wants to please. If you get angry, remember it's not the dog's fault. You have lost control. Stop the training session immediately and ask yourself what you are doing wrong. Find the *reason* for the dog's failure. Don't punish him for it.

The Collar   What you want for training is what is sometimes called a choke collar. Because it should not be used to choke the dog, we prefer to call it a corrective collar. There are two types. The *nylon* corrective collar is used on puppies, fragile dogs, and dogs with docile dispositions or long, silky coats. It is useful because it communicates a correction without injuring a delicate neck or damaging a silky coat. The *metal* corrective collar is made of metal links welded together for additional strength. The links come in various sizes, but we recommend small-linked collars only. While the larger links may appear to provide additional strength, in fact they have a tendency to get tangled, which destroys the effectiveness of the corrective jerk. The metal collar is designed for larger breeds and for dogs with stubborn dispositions and strong, well-muscled necks. Applying a correction with a nylon collar to a dog of this nature is much the same as applying a table fork to the side of a charging bull.

The corrective collar comes in many lengths, each designed for a specific size neck. When you buy a collar, measure your dog's neck and get one that is three inches longer than the size of the dog's neck. Never buy a collar that is too small or too large. If the collar is oversized, the dog can put it in his mouth and choke. Therefore, if your dog is still a puppy, do not buy a collar that he will "grow into" but resign yourself to buying a new collar every time his neck becomes a little larger. Also, don't make the mistake of letting the collar get tight before you invest in a new one. We have seen dogs with great necks bulging over tight collars, which is not only harmful to the dog but makes him mean.

The Leash   There are many different kinds of leashes, and most of them are useless as training devices. The rhinestone leash, for example, is lovely to look at, but hurts the hands. The very short leather leash looks smart on Dobermans, but is utterly useless for training. The chain-link leash looks strong and effective, but in fact it is difficult to detect weaknesses in the chain, which can suddenly snap, leaving the dog completely out of control. The dog becomes excited by his unexpected freedom and makes a mad dash for home across busy streets and through heavy traffic.

The six-foot leather leash is the perfect training device. It is long enough, without being so long that the dog gets tangled in it. It is smooth to the hands and strong, and weak spots in it show up before the leash is in danger of breaking. Canvas and nylon leashes are acceptable substitutes but sometimes burn the hands during the application of a firm correction.

The Shake-Can   This is described on page 48. The shake-can is used in conjunction with the word "no" for correction. Its object is to startle, not to frighten or hurt, the dog. You can shake it behind your back, at your side or even above your head, but you must never shake it *at* the dog or toward him. With a sensitive or shy dog, it is often best not to use a shake-can at all.

The Throw-Chain   This is a variation of the shake-can, made by tying a couple of knots in a corrective collar—not the one that is around the dog's neck. It is used in conjunction with "no" and is thrown to the side or behind your back on the floor. The effect, again, is to startle the dog. It also reminds him of the chain collar around his neck, which reinforces the fact that you are in control. The throw-chain is probably best used with sensitive dogs who can't tolerate a shake-can.

The Water Pistol   This is fun to use, and the effects are sometimes miraculous. Any type of pistol will do, but it's worth noting that the simple 29¢ transparent variety is as useful as the $1.99 pistol molded out of tri-colored plastic. *Do not* borrow your son's cap gun. Small explosions are jangling even to human ears.

The water pistol is used only for special problems, such as going into the garbage, eating plants or jumping on the kitchen counter. When you catch the dog in the act of doing something wrong, you shoot straight and say "no." A direct stream of water aimed at the dog's mouth or chest will get the point across quickly and effectively. *Do not* aim for the eyes. *Do not* add lye, turpentine, fuel oil or even common dishwashing liquid to the water. The dog will learn no more from the resulting injury than he will learn from a squirt of H_2O.

Successful Training

Training is a four-part process that includes the repetition of commands, a certain tone of voice to evoke a certain kind of response, physical reinforcement and praise. The essence of successful training is the coordination of these four. The trick is to manage the whole process without letting on to your dog how clumsy you actually feel. With a bit of practice, you will get better at it.

The Corrective Jerk

The most important physical act you will perform in the whole process of training is the *corrective jerk*, which must be applied smoothly, efficiently and firmly without causing injury and yet with enough force to get the point across. Most people err toward the gentle side.

Hold the collar by one ring in your left hand. Lift the other end by the ring in your right hand. Thread the chain or nylon through the ring in your left hand until a loop is formed. There is a right and a wrong way to place this loop over the dog's head. If the collar forms a letter P, it is the correct way. If it forms a 9, it is incorrect.

Attach the leash to the collar. Slip the loop of the leash over your right thumb. With the leash hanging from your thumb, take the middle of the leash in your left hand, form a loop with it and drape it over your right thumb. You now have four thicknesses of leather across the palm of your right hand. Close your fingers over the leather so that they are pointing toward you. Hold your left hand with the fingers pointing down. Grasp the leash with your left hand, placing it next to your right hand. The fingers of your left hand will be pointing away from your body so that both hands hold the leash but in opposite directions. The leash is attached to the dog's collar, stretches diagonally across the front of your body to your hands, and has a slight amount of slack in it.

With the dog standing or sitting at your left side, you are now in a position to administer the corrective jerk. You and the dog are now facing in the same direction. You are holding the leash as we have described above, and your arms should be curved, your hands resting just below your waist with hands and arms relatively relaxed so that you do not communicate unnecessary tension to the dog. To apply the correction, you jerk quickly to the right and then return your hands to the original position. For a brief couple of seconds, the dog will feel an unpleasant jolt at his neck. The effect is to surprise him. He should feel no pain. It is important that you adjust the force of the jerk to the dog's size, weight and personality. A very small dog requires a gentle jerk; a large and stubborn dog, a hard jerk. The jerk

The correct way to hold the leash—with the collar forming the letter P—to give a corrective jerk. The chain will release after the jerk, and the collar will return to normal.

The wrong way to hold the leash—with the collar forming a 9. If you jerk the chain, it will not release.

Slip the loop of the leash over your right thumb.

Take the middle of the leash in your left hand, form a loop with it, and drape it over your right thumb.

You now have four thicknesses of leather across the palm of your right hand.

Close your fingers over the leather so that they are pointing toward you. Grasp the leash with your left hand, placing it next to the right hand. Both hands hold the leash, but in opposite directions.

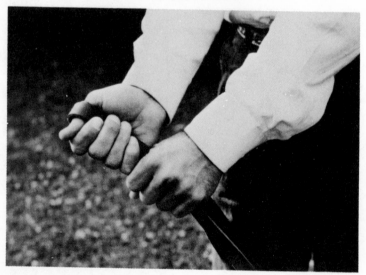

The leash is attached to the dog's collar, stretches diagonally across the front of your body to your hands, and has a slight amount of slack in it. You are now in a position to administer the corrective jerk.

To apply the correction, you jerk quickly to the right and then return the hands to the original position.

PHOTOS ON BOTH PAGES BY FRANCINE MEISLER

should not be forceful enough to knock the dog off his feet.

At the very moment that you apply the corrective jerk, you also say "no," the single word necessary to convey your disapproval. Ultimately the dog will stop whatever he is doing at the sound of the word, whether or not you apply the corrective jerk.

Always go to the dog to correct him. Never ask him to come to you. Praise always follows immediately on the heels of correction and must be meted out according to the dog's personality. If the dog is nervous, praise should be brief and quiet. A shy dog needs lavish, loving praise in a quiet tone of voice. For a stubborn, sedate or responsive dog, the praise may be steady, vociferous and enthusiastic.

Never practice the corrective jerk on the dog, because you will be correcting him even though he has done nothing wrong. He will not understand the purpose of the jerk and will become jerk-shy or unresponsive. In order to improve your technique, borrow a friend's wrist, and he can tell you how the jerk feels to him. Practice is more important than you may think, because you *must* learn to apply the jerk efficiently. If you are too soft when you correct the dog, you will have to do it again and again, and with each application, the jerk loses effectiveness. The idea is to get the message across with a *single* application.

Repetition

A dog learns commands the same way an eight-year-old child learns the multiplication tables—by repeating and repeating and repeating until they are fixed in his memory. It's your job to fix the correct and desirable behavior in the dog's memory, which is a great deal easier than you may think. Repeat each lesson over and over again until the dog knows exactly what is expected of him and which act is connected with each word.

It is easier for him to remember if you concentrate on one command at a time. If he sits a hundred times to the word "sit," there is little chance that he will confuse "sit" with "heel." Once he has "sit" firmly fixed in his brain, it is time to learn "heel." Some dogs, of course, learn more quickly than others, but any dog will learn eventually if he is allowed to concentrate on one thing at a time.

Leash Breaking

Teaching the dog to get used to the leash is not nearly as difficult or dangerous as teaching a horse to wear a bridle. Most people make the mistake of not putting the dog on leash until he's over three months old. By this time, he will fight it, simply because he's not used to it and it frightens him. To avoid this reaction, put a collar and leash on the dog as soon as you get him home. A short leash (three or four feet long) is not as likely to tangle around his legs as a six-foot training leash. Or you can substitute a length of heavy clothesline. The idea is to get the dog used to the weight. When you are home, let him drag the leash around the house or yard. When you take him out, snap the leash on and walk him. *Do not* let the dog wear the leash when you are not home or are so busy that you can't watch him. If the leash got caught on something, it could choke him.

The Commands

The basic commands are "sit," "sit/stay," "heel," "down," "down/stay" and "come." You can also teach the dog "go to your place," which is convenient if you live in an apartment or small house.

The first training sessions should not last more than five minutes, and you can hold several of these throughout the day. As the dog matures, you can give fewer and longer lessons, but never let the dog get overtired or bored. If you do, he will make mistakes. Always end a session with a word of praise and release the dog from training with the word "okay."

SIT

If you are opening the door to pick up the morning newspaper, you want the dog to sit. If you are coming to the traffic light at the corner, you want the dog to sit. "Sit" is the easiest command for the dog to learn, and it can be taught when he is eight weeks old.

1. Begin with the dog on your left side so that you and he are facing in the same direction. Hold the leash in your right hand with the loop hooked over your thumb. Take the middle of the leash with your left hand, make a loop and drape it over your right thumb so that you have four thicknesses of leather in your right palm. The leash goes across your body diagonally and attaches to the dog's collar.

2. Push down on the dog's rump with your left hand as you pull up with the leash in your right hand and say "sit," elongating the word.

The dog feels the physical pressure on his rump, hears the verbal command and feels the upward pull of the leash at his neck. Most dogs will get the idea after ten to fifteen tries and begin to respond without the pressure of your hand on the rump. Each time the dog sits, you praise him whether or not you are applying pressure.

SIT / STAY

This means that the dog sits and stays in position with a hand signal

Push down on the dog's rump with your left hand as you pull up with the leash in your right hand and say "sit."

The dog feels the physical pressure on his rump, hears the verbal command, and feels the upward pull of the leash at his neck.

and/or verbal command. Ultimately he will stay in position for one to three minutes. He may be taught the command right after you have taught him to sit.

After you have got the dog in the "sit" position, give the command "stay." At the same time, hold your left hand with flattened palm, fingers together and pointing down, directly in front of the dog's face and about five inches from his nose. In this brief instant, his vision is blocked and he sees nothing but the flat of your hand. Simultaneously with the verbal command and hand signal, pull up on the leash with your right hand and hold it taut. This forces the

Each time the dog sits, you praise him, whether or not you are applying pressure.

Hold your left hand with flattened palm, fingers together and pointing down, directly in front of the dog's face and about five inches from his nose.

dog to remain in the "sit/stay" position.

Now remove your left hand from in front of the dog's face and at the same time pivot in front of the dog, using your left foot as a pivot and lifting only your right foot from the ground. As you step in front of the dog, you are blocking him from moving. In addition, you have kept your left foot on the ground and have moved only the right, which is the foot farthest away from the dog's eyes. Repeat the whole procedure ten or fifteen times.

Now, while the dog is in the stay position, transfer the leash to your left hand and take up about three feet of slack in your right.

Remove your left hand from in front of the dog's face; at the same time, pivot in front of the dog, using your left foot as a pivot and lifting only your right foot from the ground.

You are going to test him by creating a distraction, and at the same time you will maintain control with the leash. Start moving to the left and to the right, constantly repeating "stay" and at the same time pulling up with the leash in your right hand so that it is difficult for the dog to move. The dog begins to associate "stay" with tension in the leash. Every time the dog gets up and tries to follow you, repeat "stay," and pull up on the leash. Every time the dog returns to the desired position, praise him. Continue until you are confident the dog will stay at a distance of about two to three feet from you.

Increase the distance to six feet, which is the length of the leash, and repeat the moving. When the dog is steady at a distance of six feet, start walking around him. This is when most dogs will try to follow. The dog is permitted to follow with his head only, not his body. Every time he moves his body, put him back in position, and every time he is in the correct position, praise him. Walk around the dog slowly, first a quarter-circle, then back; next a half-circle, then back; and finally a complete circle, even lifting your leg and walking over the dog, all the time repeating the command "stay" and reinforcing it with tension in the leash. Practice until the dog remains in position no matter what.

The final step is to practice with a slack leash. The dog has learned the meaning of the command "stay," and he should remain in position of his own accord. Place him in "stay," pivot in front of him, back away from him and start circling. If he follows you, correct him with a firm jerk and "no." When he returns to the desired position, praise him.

HEEL

A heeling dog walks next to you on your *left* side so that you can carry a rifle on your right side if you are out shooting duck. A dog may be taught to heel when he is three months old. Place him in the "sit" position at your left side. Both of you are now facing in the same direction. Hold the leash as directed for the corrective jerk (p. 152). Give the command "Silver, heel" and step off with your left foot. You use the dog's name because this helps to get his attention, and because the name is always spoken with commands of motion. Your tone of voice should be firm and authoritative but not harsh. You step off with your *left* foot because it is closer to the dog's eyes than your right and will give him the idea that he is supposed to move forward.

As you give the command and step off, apply a corrective jerk, thus communicating to the dog that he is supposed to walk. Walk forward in a straight line. The dog will start walking and pull in front of you. Let the leash feed out to the end, and when the dog comes to the end of the leash, he will automatically receive a corrective jerk and turn around. Say "Silver, heel," jerk to the right, turn around, pivoting quickly on your *right* foot, and walk in the opposite direction. The dog will come alongside you and then barge ahead again. Let the leash feed to the end, repeat the correction, and turn to walk in the opposite direction. Repeat this until the dog starts to respond to the correction.

Then instead of making U-turns or complete turns, start making *right* turns. Imagine a square in the center of the room and follow

the pattern. If you wander all over the place, both you and the dog will become confused, but if you walk in a square, you know exactly where you are going and where you want the dog to be. Walk in a straight line and turn right. Every time you turn, say "Silver, heel." After three such turns you will have completed the square.

Keep the square small in the beginning. This will give the dog little opportunity to get ahead of you and as long as he remains exactly at your side, you may continue to praise him. When you start feeling comfortable, increase the size of the square. Practice until the dog is heeling perfectly.

Now you can start making sharp turns in unexpected directions. The first few times, the dog will be confused. He may bump into you, so be careful not to step on his toes. Practice until the dog is

letter-perfect. As soon as you feel comfortable with him, move to a busy sidewalk and get him used to people and traffic, praising him constantly.

The key to teaching the "heel" command is verbal communication. As you walk with the dog, keep talking to him. This will focus his attention on you and the job at hand, and it will help him relax. Every time you turn, repeat the command "Silver, heel," and every time the dog responds, praise him.

It is important to hold the leash correctly. Many people keep the leash taut and continually pull the dog back. This is not heeling. It is holding the dog, and it will make him want to strain all the more. Be relaxed and calm and give the leash plenty of slack. If the dog runs in front of you, don't be afraid to give him a hard correction.

One very hard correction is worth a dozen weak corrections, which will only make the dog jerk-shy.

● ***Lagging Behind*** Do not correct the dog for lagging behind. Encourage him with your voice—"Silver, heel, atta boy, atta boy, Silver, heel, come on, boy," etc. Most laggers are a little sedate and will respond better to enthusiasm than criticism. If you quicken your pace and even run a little bit, the dog will get the idea that heeling is fun and will start to walk faster.

● ***Bearing Inward*** If the dog bears inward toward your legs, use

your *left* hand to guide him alongside of you. *Do not* hold the dog with your hand. Just place your arm straight down with flattened hand in between the dog's body and your legs. Constantly repeat the command "Silver, heel" until the dog gets the idea of where he's supposed to be.

● **Bearing Outward** There are two solutions to this problem. First, every time the dog bears outward, jerk to the right and repeat the command "Silver, heel." Second, practice in a hallway and keep the dog close to the wall so that he is unable to bear out. If you are working outdoors, you may practice next to a fence, which has the additional advantage of corners where you will have to turn.

● **Digging In**   A dog digs in when he is frightened. Don't correct him for it. Practice on a carpeted or grassy surface so he won't hurt his pads, pull him forward with the leash and encourage him with your voice. Keep your tone high-pitched, gentle and affectionate. Too much enthusiasm may frighten the dog even more, so you want to keep your voice soft. "Come on, Silver, come on, boy, atta boy," etc.

AUTOMATIC SIT

The object in heeling is to get the dog to walk when you walk and sit when you stand still. You want the dog to sit without being told to sit—hence the automatic sit. This is useful when you are walking down the sidewalk, meet a friend and stop for a conversation. It is particularly useful when you come to a corner and have to wait for a stoplight to turn green.

While you are walking with the dog and he is correctly at heel at your left side, slow down, pull up with the leash, and as you come to a stop, say "siiiiiiit . . . ," drawing the word out. The key to teaching this command is to come to a stop gradually so that the dog knows you are going to stop and is prepared for it. When you pull up on the leash, this reinforces the idea and eases the dog into position by holding his head back.

After practicing this ten or fifteen times, try coming to a stop without giving the command. If the dog does not automatically sit, give a firm correction and say "no." If the dog seems recalcitrant, repeat the whole process from the beginning until he's got it. When he does sit, praise him copiously.

DOWN

The importance of the "down" command is to give you instantaneous and complete control over the dog at any time and in any place. You say "down," and the dog will stop whatever he is doing and flop on the ground. "Down" is one of the more difficult commands to teach, so be patient.

INTRODUCTORY TECHNIQUE FOR SMALL OR NERVOUS DOGS

1.   Place the dog in "sit/stay" at your left side.

2.   Kneel beside the dog and hold the leash in your right hand only, as for "sit."

3.   Place the thumb of your *left* hand on the *right* side of the dog's

front paws, the index finger of your *left* hand in between the paws to keep them from grinding against each other, and the rest of your hand around the paws in a firm but gentle grasp. Holding the paws thus in your *left* hand, give the command "downnnn," inflecting your voice downwards and at the same time pulling the dog's paws out from underneath him and sliding him into the down position. Praise him. Practice ten to fifteen times.

4. Next you must practice "down" while standing in front of the dog because eventually he must respond when you are standing in front of him and some distance away. Place the dog in "sit/stay" at your left side and pivot in front of him, using your left foot as a pivot. Kneel, grasp his paws and slide him into position while you give the command "down."

Put your left thumb on the right side of the dog's front paws. your index finger in between the paws to keep them from grinding against each other. and the rest of your hand around the paws in a firm but gentle grasp.

Holding the paws in your left hand, give the command "downnn," inflecting your voice downward and at the same time pulling the dog's paws out from under him and sliding him into the "down" position.

You can also force a dog into the "down" position by applying pressure to the leash with your foot. (This is called the sliding-leash technique.)

The leash is extremely important when teaching "down," because you must maintain control without choking the dog, without pulling him up and out of position, and at the same time without giving him the opportunity to bolt or resist. You must hold the leash taut above your head, a difficult maneuver because you are kneeling and busy with your left hand. In the beginning stages, the corrective jerk is not employed, and the leash is used only to keep the dog in position. Do not be alarmed if the dog becomes playful and rolls over on his side or slides around on his belly. As long as he is down, he deserves and should receive your praise.

INTRODUCTORY TECHNIQUE FOR SEDATE DOGS AND VERY LARGE DOGS AND SECOND STEP FOR ALL DOGS TAUGHT "DOWN" BY FIRST METHOD*

1. Place the dog in the "sit/stay" position at your left side.

2. Hold the leash with your right hand as directed for teaching "sit." Allow no slack in the leash.

3. Bring your left hand over the dog's head and push down with flattened palm against the collar where it clips to the leash. At the same time give the verbal command "down." The dog hears the verbal command, feels the pressure against his collar pushing him down and sees the hand making a sliding, downward motion, which

*This incorporates the hand signal.

he will soon recognize as the hand signal for the command. The dog may fight you at first. Remain steady and calm and repeat the lesson over and over until he gets it. If the fight becomes intense, stop the lesson, review "sit," "stay" and "heel," praise the dog, and then try again.

4. Every time the dog goes into the "down" position, praise him whether or not you have forced him to do it.

5. Practice until the dog stops resisting.

6. Now you must do the same thing while you stand in front of the dog. Place the dog in "sit/stay" at your left side. Pivot around so that you are standing in front of him.

7. Take the leash in your *left* hand and kneel. You use your *right*

BOTH PHOTOS BY FRANCINE MEISLER

hand to push the dog down because this is the hand you will eventually use to give the signal.

8. With your flattened palm, push down on the collar just above the leash clip, and at the same time say "dowwwwwn," inflecting downward.

9. Practice this technique until the dog does it perfectly. He is now expected to take the lesson seriously and will not be allowed to roll over, wriggle around, lick your fingers, etc. The moment he starts any of these tactics, put him in "sit/stay" and start the lesson over.

10. When the dog no longer resists hand pressure, teach him the command while you are standing in front of him, as opposed to kneeling. Place the dog in "sit/stay" and pivot until you are standing about two feet in front of him, holding the slack leash in your left hand.

11. Raise your right arm straight up in the air with flattened palm and fingers extended. Give the command "down" very slowly at the same time that you swing your right arm downward until the flattened palm meets the leash. The very slight pressure of your palm against the leash will suggest to the dog that he should lie down.

12. Praise the dog and repeat the lesson ten or fifteen times.

13. Increase the distance between you and the dog to about three feet. Hold the leash in your *left* hand, as before. Raise your right arm above your head, and as you give the command, swing your arm downward, this time not touching the leash with your palm, but continuing the motion until your arm is resting at your side. This is the hand signal you will henceforth use for the "down" command.

14. If the dog moves out of position at any time or if he fails to respond, you must now apply the corrective jerk. This is not easy. You are holding the leash in your *left* instead of your *right* hand and are not accustomed to jerking the dog from this position. If you have any doubts about your jerking ability, practice on your best friend's arm until you've got it right. One or two good corrections at this point will banish all resistance, while thirty or forty ineffectual jerks may ruin the dog forever.

15. Gradually increase the distance between you and the dog. As long as you are in a contained area like your house or backyard, you can let go of the leash and conduct practice sessions from some distance. The dog should now respond to hand and voice alone without leash pressure. If he does not respond to "no," then continue practicing with the leash until he gets it.

FRANCINE MEISLER

16. Practice with vocal or hand signal, or both. Eventually the dog will learn to respond to either. The vocal signal is useful in those situations where the dog can't see your hand, and the hand signal is useful when the dog can't hear your voice.

DOWN / STAY

Lying down is one thing. Staying down is another. The purpose is to put the dog in the "down" position for three minutes to an hour. This allows you to take him on a picnic in the park, ride in the car with him, have dinner with him in the same room, and entertain lots of guests without having him constantly underfoot.

"Down/stay" is taught in the same manner as "sit/stay."

1. Place the dog in the "down" position. Hold the leash in your left hand, as for "down."

2. Using your right hand, which is the hand you have just used for the down signal, give the signal for "stay." Stand in front of the dog at a distance of about two feet so that you can actually block him from moving with both your hand and body. Raise the flattened palm of your right hand, with the fingers pointing up. Place it about five or six inches in front of the dog's face, and at the same time give the command "stayyyyyy . . ."

3. Back away from the dog and begin to circle around him, constantly repeating the command, constantly circling, and praising the dog as long as he remains in position.

4. If the dog starts to follow you with his body, tighten up on the leash and give a corrective jerk accompanied by the word "no."

5. Practice until the dog knows the command well.

6. Remove the leash from the dog's collar and lay it in front of him. Although the leash is no longer attached to the dog, he will see it, and it will remind him that you are still in control. At this point he should pay attention to your voice and hand. Practice by circling, walking around him, stepping over him, constantly giving the command "stay," and constantly praising him.

7. If the dog starts to follow you with his body, give the correction "no." If he responds to the correction, praise him. If he does not, return to practice sessions with the leash attached to the dog's collar and reinforce "no" with a corrective jerk. After each correction praise him. *Practice sessions without the leash are essential if you want the dog to stay in the down position for long periods of time.*

8. Practice in confined areas full of noise and distraction.

DOWN / STAY IN THE CAR
Training the dog to behave himself in the car requires two people, a driver and a trainer. The trainer is responsible for the dog while the car is in motion.

1. Leash the dog.

2. Put him on the back seat of the car in the down/stay position. The trainer sits beside him and holds the leash in his left hand.

3. Every time the dog gets up, the trainer gives a hard corrective jerk and says "no." After each correction, the dog is praised.

4. Practice until the dog stays in position for the duration of the car ride.

5. The trainer moves to the front seat but leaves the leash attached to the dog's collar. Every time the dog gets up, the trainer gives a hard correction and says "no." When the dog lies down, he is praised.

6. Practice until you are confident that the dog will remain in position while you are driving.

GO TO YOUR PLACE
This command is a variation of the "down/stay" command, and is useful if you live in small quarters and want to keep the dog out

A Siberian Husky "in her place"

from underfoot. "Go to your place" means that the dog has one or more specific spots in the house which are his, where he will be expected to go on command, lie down and stay. He should eventually stay in place an hour or more. Make the place comfortable for him and convenient for you. Give him a piece of carpet, a blanket or a covered cushion to lie on. His bed is a perfect spot, and you can make additional areas for him in other rooms if you so choose. *The most important thing is to remember that his place is not one of banishment,* but a place where he can rest, be comfortable, play quietly, and watch the members of his family.

1. Place the collar and leash on the dog. Hold the leash as for heel with both hands.

2. Say "Silver, place," and lead the dog to his place and put him in "down/stay." Your tone of voice should be firm and matter-of-fact. As soon as the dog lies down, praise him.

3. Practice with the dog on the leash fifteen or twenty times.

4. Take the leash off and try giving the command. If the dog goes to his place, praise him enthusiastically. If he does not, snap the leash back on and practice some more.

This command is taught by repetition only. Do not correct the dog if he fails to respond. Too much correction will make him feel that he is being banished, and he will become sulky and resentful. Constant praise, on the other hand, will tell him that his place is a happy one, and he will soon agree with you that that is where he wants to be.

COME

The purpose of this command is to teach the dog to come when you call him regardless of what he is doing. It is the most difficult command to teach and also the most important, because if your dog comes when you call him, you are going to save his life someday. You begin by teaching the command indoors, but eventually you will expect the dog to come in any environment.

Before you teach "come," you must put yourself in a positive frame of mind. Banish all negative thoughts and words from your head. You are a good person. You never get angry, impatient or frustrated. You are brimming over with love and affection. In short, you are the kind of person your dog will want to come to. The worst problem people have with this command is when they call the dog to them for punishment or correction. The dog is no fool. He is afraid to come because he doesn't know what is going to happen, but he suspects that it will be something bad. *This is why you must always go to the dog to correct him, never call him to you.* It is also imperative that you never use his name in a negative way, because you are going to call him by name and his name should have only pleasant associations. If you do these two things, half the battle is won.

1. Place the dog in "sit/stay."

2. Pivot in front of the dog and back away until you are at the end of the leash, and the dog is six feet away.

3. Take the leash in your left hand as for "down."

4. Say the command "Okay, Silver, come." If you have ended each training session with the release, "okay," the dog is already familiar with this word and knows that it means good things follow. As you give the command, jerk the leash with your left hand, and swing your right arm around in a wide arc toward your chest. This is the hand signal for "come," and is the opposite of the hand signal for "down."

5. When you jerk the leash, the dog will start coming toward you. As he comes, draw the leash in like a fishing line, all the time

ALL PHOTOS BY FRANCINE MEISLER

praising the dog: "Come on, boy, good boy, good boy ..." The friendlier and more affectionate you are, the more inclined the dog will be to come to you. Do not worry about his style at this point. The important thing is to get him coming. Be firm but use a light tone and a high-pitched voice.

6. Practice until the dog comes without hesitation every time you give the command.

Now you must teach the dog to stop, sit in front of you and wait for the next command. You don't want the dog running past you or leaping up and knocking you over. He has to go somewhere, and the safest and most convenient thing is to have him sit at your feet.

1. Take the leash in your left hand.

2. Give the hand signal and the command: "Okay, Silver, come."

3. As the dog comes toward you, pull up on the leash and say "sit." Maintain leash control at all times. You do not want the dog to sit to your right or left but square in front of you, and the key to positioning him is pulling straight up with the leash so he has no place else to go.

4. Repeat the lesson until he's got it.

5. Increase the distance between you and the dog by walking backward as the dog comes. Practice.

6. When you are practicing indoors or in fenced areas, drop the leash and back away from the dog, gradually increasing the distance between you.

IMPROVING YOUR TECHNIQUE
In all training, the key is practice. *Once your dog learns the basic commands he will never forget them, but it is helpful to give him a refresher course once or twice a week.*

SPECIAL LIMITATIONS
The first and most obvious is illness. Never try to train a dog while he is feeling under the weather. Training is hard work, and the dog must be in good physical condition to have enough energy for it. Also, illness may make him feel mean and a little snappish even if he is normally sweet and responsive.

Dogs with Long Bodies and Short Legs   The Dachshund in particular takes longer to train because of physical limitations, not because he is stubborn or lacks the will to please. His long body and very short legs make the "sit" position difficult for him and extremely difficult to maintain. Be patient with him and don't force him to "stay" in this position for long periods of time. Also, because of his short legs, he is not speedy in "coming." Large amounts of praise make him anxious to obey.

Dogs with Short Noses   The Pekingese, the Pug and the Bulldog all have breathing problems. If you overwork one of these dogs, he may collapse. Keep training sessions short, no more than five or ten minutes, but schedule more than one session each day. The Bulldog can also be a bit stubborn at times, so you'll have to learn the difference between a real asthma attack and a fake one.

Dogs with Floppy Ears   The danger here is that long, pendulous ears may get caught in the corrective collar, and a strong jerk will injure the ear, causing bleeding or internal bruising which leads to hematoma. In addition, since floppy ears are extremely sensitive, the dog feels pain when his leathers (ear flaps) get caught, even if no damage is actually inflicted.

Breeds susceptible to ear trauma are the entire sporting group without exception; among the hounds, the Afghan, Basset, Beagle, Black and Tan Coonhound, Bloodhound, Dachshund, Foxhound, Harrier, Otter Hound, Rhodesian Ridgeback and Saluki; among working dogs—although to a lesser extent because the leathers tend to be shorter—the Bernese Mountain Dog, Briard, Bullmastiff, Komondor, Mastiff, Newfoundland, Puli and St. Bernard; among the terriers, the Bedlington and Dandie Dinmont; and among nonsporting dogs, the Bichon Frise, the Dalmatian, the Lhasa Apso, the Poodle and the Tibetan Terrier. The English Toy Spaniel, the Pekingese and the Shih Tzu are also susceptible, but less so because they are so small. A hard corrective jerk is totally uncalled for, and therefore the risk of catching the ears is minimized.

Dogs with Delicate Necks   In this case, the problem is obvious. A hard corrective jerk may injure the dog. You must learn the art of jerking the dog hard enough to get the point across but not hard enough to hurt him. Puppies and toy dogs are the most obvious candidates for neck injury, but some of the larger dogs are delicate as well. Among these are the Whippet and the Shetland Sheepdog.

Dogs with Long, Silky Hair   If you wish to preserve the long, silky coat around the neck, you have one of two choices. If the dog is small or very compliant, you may train him with a nylon corrective collar. If he is large and stubborn, you can try using the metal corrective collar and removing it immediately after training sessions. Dogs in this category are the Afghan, Rough Collie, Great Pyrenees, Komondor, Kuvasz, Old English Sheepdog, Puli, Samoyed, Shetland Sheepdog, Skye Terrier, Soft-Coated Wheaten Terrier, Chow, Keeshond, Lhasa Apso, Poodle (depending on his haircut) and Tibetan Terrier. Examine the neck carefully after each training session. At the first signs of damage to the coat, you must substitute a nylon collar.

Personality Pointers

Most of this chapter has been directed toward the responsive dog who is basically an orderly, clean creature, willing to please, intelligent and quick to learn. Breeds that typically fall into this category are the Golden and Labrador Retrievers, Basset Hound, Bloodhound, Bernese Mountain Dog, Bouvier des Flandres, some Boxers, Briard, Doberman Pinscher, German Shepherd, Great Dane, Great Pyrenees, Newfoundland, Corgi, Maltese, Pekingese, Pug and Poodle.

Among these breeds, the Doberman and the German Shepherd are particularly sensitive to abuse. They must never be threatened, beaten or punished—NEVER. Negative treatment is quick to develop mistrust in these beautiful, highly intelligent animals, and besides, they learn so easily that such treatment is not required. If you lavish kindness and affection on these dogs and treat them with respect, they can learn how to do anything that a dog can do.

THE NERVOUS DOG

The nervous dog is often the result of bad breeding. He is a pacer, constantly moving and panting. He may have a tendency to wet when he greets you at the door. He is by far the most difficult to teach, because every sound and movement serves to distract him from the job at hand. He is not stupid, yet he seems to gather every fiber of cunning against you. He may also be excessively affectionate, with moist nose and nervous wet chops constantly aimed for your lap.

He needs firm correction and quiet, brief praise, never extravagant praise which will only increase his nervousness and give him additional strength to resist. The trick is to keep his attention. This may be done with constant, quiet and soothing chatter during training sessions. He should be exercised before every session, which will help to burn off his excess energy. And the more training he gets, the calmer he will become. Susceptible breeds are the German Shorthaired Pointer, Irish Setter, Vizsla, Weimaraner, Black and Tan Coonhound, Borzoi, Greyhound, Norwegian Elkhound, some Boxers, Puli and Fox Terrier.

Sit   Before you place him in the sit position, stroke his backside so he will get used to the feel of your hand and will not be startled when you apply pressure. When you push down with your left hand, hold the leash very taut with your right so that it is difficult for him to move out of position. Keeping your left leg right up against his body will help him maintain the proper position. As soon as the dog sits, praise him in a calm, quiet voice and then release him almost immediately from the position so that praise sticks in his mind. Do not overpraise and do not expect immediate success.

Sit / Stay   In the beginning, when you walk around the dog, do not make a complete circle but always remain in his view so that he can watch you. His head will follow every motion, and this is okay. The problem is to keep his body from following you as well. To do this, maintain a firm tension in the leash but do not hold it so taut that the dog feels uncomfortable. You want only to keep him in his place.

Heel If you vary your pace, the dog will pay closer attention to what you are doing. He requires a lot of correction, but to avoid making him jerk-shy, let him go to the end of the leash and correct himself as often as possible. Praise him frequently but quietly. If he tries to jump on you, give him a firm correction. Teach him this command in a quiet area for an extended period of time.

Automatic Sit The nervous dog has difficulty with this command. When he comes to the street corner, he is easily distracted by cars, horns and milling people. He may sit, then immediately get up and try to cross the street. Correction must be extra firm to prevent him from making the mistake again.

Down There is nothing the nervous dog wants to do less than lie down. Even when he is asleep, he seems to be in constant motion—twitching, dreaming, sometimes wetting. Once you get him to lie down, he will want to jump up again and start pacing, or he will try to slide along the ground on his belly, wagging his tail, panting and licking his chops. Don't give up. Limit training sessions to five minutes and release the dog with "okay" and a note of praise. Be prepared to spend twice as long teaching this command as you will spend on any other.

Down / Stay Never expect a nervous dog to stay down for an extensive period of time. He is incapable of such dignified behavior. However, practice will lengthen the time and calm him down. Keep training sessions short and *never* unsnap the dog from his leash in public places. "Go to your place" is essential for the nervous dog if you hope to prevent unpleasant accidents from happening around the house. Also giving him a place and expecting him to stay there is one of the most effective ways of calming him down, particularly if you have company. Do not encourage guests to be overly affectionate or they will spend all evening with the dog's twitching, panting head in their laps.

Come The nervous dog likes this command because it means he can get up and walk toward you. He may not, however, like the idea of walking in a straight line. If you force him to do this, he may resist the leash, bite at it or mouth it. When he comes to you, he would rather jump up and lick your face than sit quietly before you. Hold the leash taut at all times and guide him firmly into position. Do not overcorrect him, but keep up firm guidance, constant chatter and quiet praise. Take plenty of time in a distraction-free environment, make lessions short and don't ever trust him to come to you outdoors. He may—and he may not.

THE SHY DOG

The dog with a shy personality is never an unpleasant character unless he is mishandled and his shyness turns to aggression. In fact, this dog is particularly dear to our hearts because obedience training brings out the best in him. Once he is trained, he will obey willingly, even though somewhere inside his head a nagging little voice tells him that he is afraid. Training will not cure the dog of his shyness, but it will teach him how to be brave. He must never be abused with either your hands or your voice, for abuse will make him aggressive out of fear. Praise should be quiet, sincere, loving, affectionate and constant, for this will increase his confidence. The corrective jerk must be employed as little as possible. Shake-cans, throw-chains and water pistols must not be used.

Breeds susceptible to shyness are the Afghan, Borzoi, Greyhound, Saluki, Whippet, Shetland Sheepdog and mixed breeds who have been battered on the street.

Sit   Allow him to get used to the feel of your hand on his rump before you apply pressure. The leash should not be slack, but if it is held too tightly at his throat you will frighten him, his eyes will bulge and he will start to pant. Kneeling next to the dog while you teach the command may make him feel less shy. Do not correct him at first, but repeat the lesson over and over until he gets it.

Sit / Stay   He probably won't budge because he is afraid to move. Constantly reassure him with a quiet, soothing voice and praise him throughout the lesson. This command is the most important command that you will teach the shy dog. The reason is that he will naturally excel at it, for which he will receive effusive praise and thus gain confidence.

Heel   The shy dog will have little trouble learning to heel indoors. Praise him and don't jerk hard. Let him go ahead of you in the beginning and encourage any desire to explore on his part, which may help bring him out of his shyness. When you take him outdoors, work at first only on grassy surfaces. If he is frightened, he may dig in with his feet, and if he does this on concrete, he will injure his pads. If he refuses to budge, get down on your knees and encourage him to move forward. Once he agrees to move, you may begin the "heel" exercise.

Automatic Sit   No problem here. A reluctance to move is accompanied by a willingness to sit.

Down   This command should be taught, if possible, without the use of the corrective jerk. Be extremely gentle and affectionate, keep training sessions short and give several a day until the dog gets it. Be prepared to spend additional time on this command.

Down / Stay   This is easy to teach if the dog has been taught the "sit/stay" correctly. In the latter case, he has received plenty of praise, so he knows that he excels in the "stay" department. He will easily transfer this knowledge to "down/stay." Teaching him to "go to his place" has many advantages. He will feel safe and secure in his place, particularly when you have strangers in the house. Getting underfoot is not good for the shy dog at all; it confuses and frightens him. Warn guests not to approach him suddenly or handle him roughly.

Come   You are really going to have to put yourself out on this one. Be extra loving and affectionate. Get down on your knees and coax the dog to come to you. Run backward so that he can see your face while you are running and at the same time call him to you. Practice indoors for an extensive period of time, and when you go outdoors, practice at first on grass. Only after he overcomes his fear should you teach him to sit in front of you. Be gentle with the leash. Do not employ the corrective jerk.

THE STUBBORN DOG
This dog is difficult to deal with because he likes to think that he is the boss. It is your job to get this idea out of his head as soon as possible. Corrections must be firm, even hard at times. As soon as the dog responds, you must praise him loudly and enthusiastically. A stubborn dog will often use all his intelligence in the fight against you, but he suffers from the disadvantage that you are more intelligent than he. Don't ever let him forget it. Exercise him thoroughly before all training sessions. Hunting dogs, hounds, terriers and even some of the working dogs tend to fall in this category; these dogs have tenacity bred into them in order to give them additional endurance and strength. Among the stubborn breeds are the German Short-haired, English, Gordon and Irish Setters, some of the Spaniels, the Weimaraner, the Afghan, Basenji, Beagle, Norwegian Elkhound, Rhodesian Ridgeback, Alaskan Malamute, Collie, Old English Sheepdog, Rottweiler, Samoyed, Schnauzer, Siberian Husky, terriers, the

Bulldog, Chow, Dalmatian and Keeshond.

Sit Push down hard with your hand, hold the dog in position and jerk up hard with the leash. He may whine and cry but don't believe him. He is neither hurt nor frightened but testing you to get his way. When he does achieve the correct position, effusive praise will convince him that behaving himself is worthwhile.

Sit / Stay The stubborn dog is going to fight you every inch of the way. He's going to sit and get up, sit and get up, sit and get up. You must constantly repeat the introductory steps, and later when he has these down, you must practice the circling technique over and over. Corrections must be extra firm followed by steady praise. Maintain a taut leash at all times. Keep this dog in a quiet training area as long as possible, and then spend an equal amount of time in noisy and distracting environments. Confront the dog with specific situations where you want him to stay—opening the door, feeding him his dinner, getting out of the car. Do not move on to another command until he knows this one so thoroughly that you barely have to speak the word for him to obey. In the process of teaching the first two commands of "sit" and "stay," you are establishing control over the stubborn dog and making the following training sessions much easier.

Heel The stubborn dog may come to the end of the leash, jump, paw at the leash, even bark and growl. You must remember that he is not feeling aggressive so much as annoyed. He requires firm correction. If he refuses to move at all, call him to you, praise and encourage him. If he is a full-grown dog, you can encourage him with the corrective jerk. Give the command "Silver, heel" and jerk him forward. Once he has learned the command in a quiet, distraction-free environment, he will not have much trouble on a busy sidewalk.

Automatic Sit Initially he may need a couple of hard corrections, but once he knows "heel" and "sit," he will have little difficulty putting the two commands together.

Down With this command, the stubborn dog has the opportunity to resist to the most annoying degree. You must pull his paws out from under him so quickly that he never has a chance to disagree. Then praise him enthusiastically. Be firm but not harsh with corrective measures. One little trick he plays even after he knows the command is to lie down partially—that is, with his legs flat against the ground and his belly somehow suspended. This takes a great deal of effort on his part but is a lot more fun than doing exactly as you say. *Do not praise him* until his entire body is resting and relaxed against the ground.

Down / Stay   Once down, he may or may not be inclined to stay that way. Be firm with corrections.

Come   The stubborn dog will fight the leash, may even back away from you instead of advancing in the desired manner. When you issue the command, give a quick, hard jerk with the leash to reinforce the idea that he is supposed to move forward. Insist on good form from the very beginning. Make him come and make him sit before you. Praise him when he deserves it.

THE SEDATE DOG
The sedate dog is affectionate but not terribly willing. Don't be fooled by his demeanor. While he often appears to be a big, slobbering fool, he is in fact not stupid. Sometimes training can be abbreviated by teaching him the commands of motion first to get him moving, which is what he likes least to do. Corrections should be firm, never harsh or aggressive; and praise must at all times be lavish, enthusiastic, even silly. If you can get him to wag his tail, even briefly, this is a step in the right direction. The very large breeds tend to fall into this category, with the lumbering St. Bernard serving as the perfect example. Others are the Irish Wolfhound, Mastiff and an occasional Bullmastiff. The trick is to be gentle and insistent and to draw the dog out. Never exercise one of these breeds before training.

Sit   The problem here is to keep the sedate dog from lying down. If he does this, don't correct him for the error but lift him up with your hands and place him in the correct position. With a full-grown St. Bernard, this is not easy. In this case, wrap your arms around the dog's midsection and hoist—excellent exercise for you if you can keep from fainting. When the dog is in the proper position, praise him with all the breath you have left.

Sit / Stay   Staying is what the sedate dog is all about. In fact, you may think he has learned the command before this is in fact the case. Check by putting him in position, jerking very gently on the leash and giving the command. If he refuses to budge, then you know he's got it.

Heel   The sedate dog requires much patience and prattle during "heeling" lessons. Talk to him constantly: "Come on, atta boy, good boy," etc. If he starts to lag behind, quicken your pace. Be enthusiastic and cheerful; even run if necessary to give him incentive. He couldn't care less whether he works in a quiet area or a busy, noisy environment.

Automatic Sit   No problem here. He requires only mild correction and lots of praise.

Down   This is by far his favorite command. It is, however, essential to insist on the proper form and practice conscientiously to make sure he is lying down because *you* want him to, not because *he* wants to. Don't let him roll over and play; hold him in position with the leash.

Down / Stay   No problem. He will remain in this position literally for hours. "Go to your place" is convenient for the very large, sedate dog, especially if you live in small quarters. If he learns this command, you may sometimes forget that you even have a dog.

Come   The sedate dog will always come to you very slowly. Be enthusiastic with praise. Here is where affection really pays off because it is the only thing that will get this dog off the ground and moving toward you. The problem, again, is to get him to sit in front of you instead of lying down. You do this by chattering and praising him in a very excited tone of voice. Keep him in line with the leash, although a lot of tension in the leash is not necessary.

The great advantage of training your dog at home is that you can eliminate his bad habits in the process. It is pointless, for instance, to train a dog not to chew in the kennel environment, where there is nothing for him to chew—or not to leap on the furniture where there is no furniture. At home, there are many temptations, some of which are naturally enticing and others that the owner has in fact invented himself.

THE BEGGAR

This is the little fellow that we like least of all because his bad table manners are such an obvious reflection of owner indulgence. Some beggars learn the tricks of the trade naturally, but the great majority are *taught* to beg, and worst of all, the owner thinks it is cute.

The problem is solved by placing the collar and leash on the dog before you sit down to eat. When the dog comes begging, you grab the leash, give a firm corrective jerk and say "no." As the dog begins to get the idea that begging is wrong, you may reinforce this view by placing him in "down/stay" at mealtimes or by sending him to his place.

The Thief

Every dog is a thief by nature. He smells the pot roast on the kitchen counter and can't imagine who else it could be for. We knew a carefree chap who stole and consumed a roast beef, string and all. Unless you are prepared to keep a twenty-four-hour watch in the kitchen or to never allow the dog in, you must put an end to thievery.

Put a leash on the dog and set a tasty morsel on the counter. Sit and wait. When he goes for the food, grab the dog by the leash, apply a corrective jerk and say "no." When the dog becomes less brazen and steals only in your absence, you will have to hide in wait for him to catch him in the act. Alternatives to leash and collar corrections are a neat rattle of the shake-can or squirt of the water pistol.

The Chewer

If chewing is not properly handled while the dog is young, it will become a lifelong habit, and the older dog who chews can literally eat you out of house and home. The upholstery, baseboards and even the drapes are likely candidates for destruction. Older dogs chew out of boredom, usually when nobody is home to stop them. Breeds prone to chewing are the hunting and retrieving dogs, who are energetic and sometimes tense, and are bred to carry things in their mouths; nervous and high-strung dogs; and the German Shorthaired Pointer, Golden and Labrador Retrievers, Gordon and Irish Setters, Vizslas, Weimaraners, Afghans, Norwegian Elkhounds, Collies, Samoyeds, Siberian Huskies and Fox Terriers.

Most people think that the only solution is to confine the chewer behind a puppy gate in an area where he cannot damage anything—for example, the bathroom. But there are always the towels and the toilet paper. What you really want is to turn a chewer into a nonchewer—and this is how it is done.

The best way is to catch the dog in the act, give a firm corrective jerk and say "no." This could take several hours of your time, but it may be worth the effort. Another technique is to coat his favorite chewing objects with a bitter spray, which you can purchase from a pet store for just this purpose. You can also use a paste of alum and water, but it must be used sparingly, since large doses can irritate the gastrointestinal lining.

THE DEFOLIATOR

It is difficult to imagine a dog owner who does not love gardening, but most of us have found it difficult to keep both dog and plants alive and healthy in the same environment. What a dog can do to a plant is outrageous, but what a plant can do to a dog is even worse. Many common house and garden plants are poisonous if the dog ingests them and can cause anything from simple diarrhea to convulsions and death (see p. 231).

The dog has two methods of defoliation: eating the leaves, stems and flowers; and digging, which can ruin the lawn or lay a whole garden bare to the roots. For the plant eater, there are several methods of attack. There are a number of commercial products that may be added to the soil, tied around the stems or sprayed on the leaves. Sometimes these are effective deterrents, and sometimes they are not. Mothballs placed in the soil sometimes work. The training method is to catch the dog in the act and give a corrective jerk, a firm "no," a rattle of a shake-can or squirt of a water pistol. Another idea is to buy a cheap plant, coat the leaves with a solution of alum and water and put the plant in some very obvious place as a decoy. After the dog chomps on this one, he'll never go near a plant again.

For the digger, there are a couple of other methods. If the dog digs a lot of holes, leave one hole open and fill it with water. Some dogs don't like water and won't go near it. Another solution is put chicken wire or a rock in the hole and cover it with earth. When the dog digs, he will jab his paws, and this may solve the problem. Best of all is to catch the dog in the act and correct him for it.

THE BARKER

To the neighbors it sounds like a circus next door. Typical offenders include some of the sporting breeds, terriers and toys. Among the worst are the Weimaraner, Fox Terrier, Scottish Terrier, Chihuahua and Toy Poodle. A very nervous, high-strung dog may bark every time he hears an interesting noise in the hallway. If he does this while you are home, let him wear his collar and leash around the house and give him a firm corrective jerk and a "no" every time he opens his mouth.

Unfortunately more dogs yap while they are alone. They do it because they are lonely and bored. The dog who has been allowed to sleep in bed with his master will often develop this offensive habit. He is not used to being left alone and will begin his crescendo of howls, pathetic cries and yelps the moment the owner closes the front door.

Correction is difficult and requires ingenuity on your part. If the dog seems to object to confinement, perhaps he will bark less if he is allowed the run of the house. But if he reacts to every strange sound, you may have to confine him to the quietest part of the house until your return. Playing the radio will sometimes soothe him and blot out street sounds. Another possibility is to prepare a tape recording of your own voice as it might sound during a training session, with the interjection of a sharp "no" every two or three minutes. Or you might go far enough away so that the dog starts to bark and then sneak back, burst through the door and rattle a shake-can. A persistent barker requires many, many corrections. Do not expect to break the habit with one or two tries.

THE GARBAGE GETTER

Eating garbage, as we have said before, is a dangerous as well as distasteful habit. All dogs are susceptible to it, but those most likely to succumb are the hunters and hounds because of their overactive noses. The Beagle is the example par excellence; he will swallow anything that remotely resembles food, and many things that do not.

What to do about it? First of all, garbage in the house and garbage in the yard next door present two different problems. You may be able to keep your own cans under lock and key, but it is very difficult to convince an angry, glowering neighbor that he should do the same. More than likely after cleaning up several overturned bins, he will be satisfied with no less than murder—and nothing is more gruesome than a dog who dies from warfarin, ground glass or some other compound that "accidentally" finds its way into last night's potato peels.

The only answer is to train the dog not to go into any garbage anywhere. Put the dog's leash on and take the lid off the garbage can, leave the room and wait. Sooner or later you will hear the telltale crunch of jaws. Back in the kitchen you go, grab the leash and give the dog a firm correction with the word "no." Repeat this exercise until you can leave the room for several hours without the dog doing wrong. Then practice the exercise with the backyard garbage can.

COPROPHAGY

Coprophagy is when the dog eats his own feces. Any dog who indulges in this nasty habit needs a veterinary examination to determine whether he is malnourished or has worms. If that is not the case, there are other reasons. From the dog's point of view, his feces smell a lot like last night's supper, and if he deposits them on paper or in his run, he may return to them later and mistake them for a second feeding. Hunting dogs in particular get into this habit because they are bred to carry things in their mouths. For the most part, however, coprophagy occurs when the dog is bored. Considering the fact that dogs are by nature extremely curious about feces and spend a great deal of time sniffing and interpreting them, it is one of nature's small miracles that the great majority of dogs have no inclination to consume them at all.

For those who do, there are only two possible solutions. The first is to separate the dog from his feces as soon as they have been deposited. If the dog lives in a kennel, you must keep his run clean at all times. If the dog is paper-trained, you may have to housebreak him. Also, since coprophagy is a symptom of boredom, you should schedule more exercise and attention for the dog. The second solution is to make the feces less appealing by coating them with hot pepper, or by putting MSG or meat tenderizer in his food, which makes the stool taste bad. Corrective techniques with leash and collar are not wanted here. They only serve to reinforce the dog's sense of loneliness and rejection.

THE FEAR-WETTER
The fear-wetter is usually high-strung, nervous and a little shy. He was born with this personality, but rough handling has increased these qualities. The sound of a human voice is often enough to make him lose control of his bladder. It's important to realize that he doesn't *want* to do this. He just can't seem to help himself. Naturally, the more often he is guilty of the offense, the more annoyed you become, which only increases his fear.

Fear-wetting is not a housebreaking problem. Although it may help to cut down his water intake, other housebreaking techniques are not effective in solving this problem. The only sound method is to reeducate the dog, put him through an obedience course, eliminate all punishment from his daily fare and keep corrections to a minimum. *The wetting itself should never be corrected.* The trick is to teach him what a good boy he is, supply him with large amounts of praise, love and affection, put his fears to rest and bring him out of his shyness.

THE BULLY
This fellow is at the other end of the spectrum. He is not quite aggressive but thinks along those lines and must be cured of it quickly and efficiently before he develops a serious problem. This is the dog who growls and bites at his leash during training sessions.

You may think this is cute while the dog is still a puppy, but you have to consider the consequences of letting him grow up that way.

Growling, howling, barking or leash-attack during training is known as back talk. There is only one solution. Treat this fault as though the dog disobeyed your orders altogether. Apply a firm correction with the leash and say "no." Repeat this every time the dog shows any inclination toward aggressive behavior. Praise him afterwards.

THE FIGHTER

This is the dog who fights with other males. Among the most common offenders are the Weimaraner, Rhodesian Ridgeback, all the terriers and some of the more spoiled toys. Interestingly, the very large dogs are not particularly aggressive toward one another, but if one of them is attacked by a feisty little Chihuahua, it is fair to assume that the latter will get his head bitten off. For some reason these tiny dogs have no concept of size.

There is very little you can do with a dog fighter except prevent him from fighting. When you are walking down the street with him, maintain good leash control at all times. If the dog should happen to get free, and if a fight should occur, get out of the way. A dog who is busily engaged in chewing up another dog can't distinguish between a hairy leg and a naked finger. You can stop the fight by stepping behind the dog, grabbing him by the tail or by the hind leg, and hoisting him off-balance. Never get your face or hands caught in the middle of the fray. Other alternatives are to spray the dogs with a hose or to startle them by banging two pots together.

The best solution is to socialize your dog with other dogs very early in life. Most dogs who have been allowed to enjoy good relations with their own kind never become fighters, nor do they become particularly abject or submissive. They are simply comfortable around other dogs and their hackles never rise. Terriers are exceptional in this regard. Terriers often take themselves too seriously and will sometimes mutilate and even murder to establish dominance.

THE ACROBAT

The acrobat is the dog who leaps on the furniture—or on your favorite uncle when he walks in the door. Just about any dog will become an acrobat if it pays off. Puppies very often are offenders when they are only a few weeks old, and of course there is nothing more gratifying to the new master than a little ball of fur who shows his affection by leaping up to lick your face. Encourage these displays, however, and before you know it, you'll have an eighty-pound adolescent knocking you over the second you walk in the door.

By the same token, if you let this little chap sleep in your bed, what's to stop him from nesting on the couch or in your favorite armchair? You may not think this is so bad, but a nesting dog is more than just a creature who takes a nap. He is also a creature who scratches and scrabbles with his toenails to make a comfortable spot for himself. As you can well imagine, he quickly tears the finest upholstery to shreds.

The moral of this story is to be firm and consistent when the dog is young. Don't allow him to jump up and lick your face. And don't allow him to jump on the furniture. At the first signs of such behavior, get out the shake-can and give it a rattle or two. *If you never allow a puppy to jump, he will never do it.*

Once the dog has learned this behavior, other, more forceful methods must be employed. When the dog jumps on the furniture, you may have to *throw* a shake-can in his direction to get the point across, or have to have him wear his collar and leash around the house for a quick correction. The same holds for the dog who jumps on you when you come in the door. Place the collar and leash on the dog. Have a friend or another member of the family come knocking. Hold the leash firmly. When the door opens, the dog will try to jump. Deliver a firm corrective jerk and say "no." Then praise the dog. Repeat this many times, each time following with the command "sit" and hearty praise when the dog obeys orders.

The Sneak

The sneak is the clever character who has somehow figured out how to behave while you are home and misbehave while you are gone. This dog is a smart cookie, almost too smart to live with. As long as you are in the house, he will sleep in his place or lie at your feet, the very model of canine perfection. The moment the door snaps shut behind you, he's up on the bed, the couch or your Moroccan armchair.

The approach here is to outsneak the sneak. You could record your voice on tape, as we suggested earlier; or blow up balloons and plant them under a bedspread, blanket or sheet so that they will burst when the dog leaps up on the bed; or put mousetraps under newspaper and tape the paper down so that when the traps snap shut, the noise will frighten him. These procedures must be repeated perhaps a dozen times before the dog learns his lesson, but if you are persistent, you can rest assured that he'll learn.

THE RUNAWAY

This dog is overly enthusiastic about going outside and will try to do so whenever you open the door. He may do this regardless of the fact that he is obedience-trained and knows the command "sit/stay." Naturally you don't want to teach him that it is wrong to go outside. You want merely to impress upon him the fact that it is wrong to go outside unless you want him to.

Leash the dog and have a friend or another member of the family ring the doorbell. Stand about two feet away from the door. Place the dog in the "sit/stay" position and keep a firm grip on the leash. Then open the door, and when the dog tries to bolt, give a hard corrective jerk and say "no." Leave the door open. Place the dog in the "sit/stay" position and praise him. Wait for him to make another run and repeat the correction. Do this until he no longer tries to run away. Then repeat the whole exercise from the beginning. After several days of practice, he will no longer be a runaway. You must remember thereafter to put him in "sit/stay" every time the doorbell rings. Ultimately he will learn to take the position automatically.

THE CAR CHASER

In most cases, it is far better to confine your dog than to let him run free. If he never has the opportunity to chase cars, of course he will never do it. However, there are exceptions to this rule. Among these are the hunting dogs, who obviously cannot be confined while you are out hunting. If your dog is a car chaser, the very moment he comes close to a road he is in a lot of trouble.

Again the corrective method is to use the collar and leash. Have a friend drive around the block in front of your house several times. Every time the dog takes off after the car, let him run to the end of the leash, give a hard corrective jerk and say "no." The jerk should be very sudden and forceful enough to actually lift the dog off the ground. Be merciless. You are saving your dog's life. After you have practiced with the leash, you may replace it with a twenty-foot length of clothesline to give the dog what appears to be additional mobility. If he bolts for the car, let him go to the end of the rope and then jerk him off his feet. After all corrections, be sure to praise him. You may also correct the dog by tossing a shake-can from the car window.

THE LOVER

The lover is the dog who mounts—not just females in heat, but your leg, the neighbor's leg, Aunt Sally's leg and small children. Male dogs are most often accused of this behavior, but we have actually seen spayed females do it. This is a persistent and obnoxious practice, and the solution is once again collar and leash. Let the dog wear them around the house, and every time he mounts anything, even a table leg, give him a hard correction and a "no." It is usually not difficult to correct this problem.

GROOMING AND EXERCISE

Grooming is important for a number of reasons. It helps keep both the dog and your house free of dirt and parasites. If you have ever lived for as much as fifteen minutes in a flea-ridden house, you will know how important this is. Also, of course, the well-groomed dog is a beautiful dog. A longhaired dog, such as a Collie, who has just been shampooed, dried and brushed out is a spectacular creature to behold, and in spite of the fact that he can't see himself in the mirror, he knows it.

It is not a bad idea to take your dog to a groomer at least once to have him done professionally, even if you own a shorthaired dog that requires little attention. This will give you the opportunity to see how the dog *ought* to look and, more importantly, to ask questions about his grooming. If you own a dog with a difficult hairdo, you may choose to have him groomed by a professional on a regular basis. Those who haven't the time, the desire or the manual dexterity to learn to do the job themselves should not feel ashamed of having it done by someone else. You can keep the price down by having the dog groomed every four to six weeks and brushing him thoroughly in between. Be sure, however, that the groomer uses healthy and humane methods. Tranquilizers should not be necessary.

Basic grooming for any dog means both daily and monthly care. You should develop a regular, routine procedure that the dog recognizes as such. Dogs depend on a schedule; they need it and love it, and above all, it smooths their tempers. Ideally, the dog

All dogs benefit from professional care. Here a part Pomeranian, part Dachshund is being groomed by the Shaggy Dog groomers.

should be trained to lie down as often as possible during the procedure. This will relax him to the degree that he may even fall asleep. Of course for leg and belly work, he must be taught to stand. If you go to Westminster or any of the big dog shows and visit the grooming area in back, you will see dogs standing like statues under the brush and comb. Grooming is part of their routine, and they have learned to enjoy it.

The best age to start grooming the dog is as soon as he is weaned from his mother. Up until this point, she has groomed him herself by licking and smoothing his coat with her tongue. The puppy is

This Irish Water Spaniel stands like a statue on his grooming table backstage at the Westminster Dog Show.

used to physical attention and will not be surprised by it. If you want to have the dog groomed professionally, now is the time to introduce him to the grooming shop. If he goes to a professional at this early age and is treated properly, he will never have any problem with it.

Puppy grooming is easy and rewarding because for the most part you don't have to worry about bathing and clipping. The important thing is not to scare the puppy. You can start by brushing him, even if he doesn't have much coat. Use a soft-bristled brush so you don't injure his skin, and talk to him in a quiet tone of voice. If he gets dirty, you will have to bathe him, but you must be very careful to dry him completely afterwards and to keep him out of drafts. Puppies are particularly subject to upper respiratory infection.

Even with a small puppy, you should set up an area that means business. You should not start by placing the dog in your lap. Choose a table the top of which is about four or five inches higher than your knees. If the dog is small, the table can be a little higher than this, but for a large dog, you will need plenty of room between the table level and the top line of the dog. Expensive grooming tables are not necessary but are convenient if you intend to travel with the dog, since they are lightweight and adjustable and fold and pack easily.

Put a rubber mat on top of the table—a shower mat will do. This is important; it gives the dog traction and makes him feel secure. If he slips and slides around on a slick surface, he will become increasingly nervous and difficult to manage. From the beginning you should use a *loop* to hold the dog's head in place. Otherwise, if he visits a professional groomer, he may be frightened by it. Professional tables have loops attached, but you can devise one by hanging a show lead from a hook in the ceiling and adjusting the length until it holds the dog's head securely, without choking him. *When you use a loop, you must never turn your back on the dog, even for a second.* The reason is obvious: if the dog loses his footing or becomes frightened and tries to jump off the table, he can choke to death or break his neck.

Daily Procedure

Brush the dog thoroughly. This is important for the longhaired dog because it helps prevent tangles and mats from developing, and for the shorthaired dog because it stimulates the production of oil in his skin, keeps his coat glossy and helps to confine dog hair to one area of the house. While you are brushing the dog, you can also give him his daily health examination.

In this day of soft dog foods, teeth have become increasingly problematic. Toothbrushing is considered an optional procedure, but if you get your dog used to it while he is still young, he will not cause much trouble when you brush his teeth later. A toothbrush, of course, will not remove tartar, but it may help prevent tartar from forming. Baking soda and water makes a fine toothpaste, or you can buy special dog toothpastes from your veterinarian. You don't need to brush the teeth every day, but several times a month would certainly be beneficial.

Creases Loose-skinned dogs like Bulldogs have a face full of creases, which tend to retain dampness and provide the perfect breeding ground for bacteria and infection. These creases should be checked daily. Hold them open with your fingers and apply cornstarch to the wrinkles on a regular basis.

Tear Stains Some dogs, like Poodles, tear excessively. The tears are acid and stain the fur around the eyes. White-coated dogs are particularly susceptible. Because the stain is so close to the eye, it is not safe to bleach it out, but you can rinse the area with clear water and put a little petroleum jelly under the eye. Tears will roll over the petroleum jelly and fall to the ground instead of staining the coat.

Monthly Procedure

If you have kept up on the daily procedure, the monthly procedure will not be troublesome, and if you take the dog to a grooming shop, it will not be terribly expensive.

Brushing the Dog Out Even shorthaired dogs should be brushed out before bathing, and it is absolutely essential for the longhaired dog. Otherwise mats and tangles solidify and get bigger. Brushing means more than just a surface brushing, which will make the dog look fluffy but will leave the mats underneath. Millions of dollars are spent each year on products that claim to remove mats. Actually nothing but hard work with a comb and brush will do the job.

If the dog is not severely matted, you can break up the mats with your fingers, and some of these can then be worked out with a comb and brush. Others must be cut out. Mats form near the skin. There is a little area between the skin and the mat, and you have to get a clipper blade in here to cut the mat away. A very close mat requires a very close blade, which actually shaves the area. In some cases, it is necessary to do this in order to remove the matted hair. A badly matted dog may have to be stripped down all over.

Certain areas on the dog are more subject to matting than others. These include the hair on the feet and behind the ears. Matting in the ear and neck area is aggravated by the dog's collar, so longhaired breeds should not be allowed to wear collars except on outings and during exercise and obedience sessions. As soon as the dog is brought inside, his collar should be removed and the neck area brushed out.

STEPHEN PROCU[?]

ABOVE: To clip a dog's nails, grasp his paw gently.

ABOVE RIGHT: Slip the nail into the slot of the clipper.

RIGHT: Be careful not to cut into the quick.

Clipping the Nails This should be initiated when the dog is a puppy. If you wait until he is full grown before you expose him to nail clippers, you may have to have a veterinarian do it, which is an unnecessary expense.

Clipping keeps the pads tight and the toes from splaying. Filing and smoothing the rough edges afterwards prevents the dog from catching and tearing his nails. If nails are left to grow, they may actually curl back into the pad, which is extremely painful to the dog and will temporarily cripple him.

Be careful not to clip the nails too close or you will cut the quick, which hurts the dog and also bleeds profusely. It is better to clip too little than too much. Furthermore, as the nail grows, the quick grows longer, making it extremely difficult to cut the nails short enough if they have not been attended to on a regular basis. In this case, the only solution is to have the veterinarian do the job and promise yourself that you won't let it happen in the future.

Do not use human toenail clippers on your dog. Get a special pair from a pet store. These resemble a pair of pliers but have a small slot through which the nail fits at the cutting end. As you squeeze the handles together, a little blade shoots out and nips off the nail. The advantage to these clippers is that you can control the amount of nail removed by putting only that much into the slot.

Preliminary Haircut Most clipping and scissoring should be done after the bath, but a longhaired dog should be clipped on the belly and around his feet before he is bathed. If his coat has been allowed to grow too long, he should receive a pre-bath rough clipping all over. There's no point in wasting time bathing and drying hair that's going to be removed anyway.

Bathing Most dogs can use a bath on an average of about once a month. A dog's skin is much more delicate than human skin, primarily because it is not so exposed, and too frequent bathing will remove the oils that keep it healthy.

On the other hand, most dogs are fragrant animals. Those with excessively oily coats, such as water dogs, can get to smell pretty doggy. There is also the occasional roll in the mud, not to speak of even less savory substances, which make a dog rather "high" at times. Bathing is good for the dog on two levels. It helps remove irritants, dirt and bacteria, and it makes the dog more pleasant for human beings to live with.

Choose a shampoo that is appropriate for your dog's coat—if possible, a tearless shampoo that will not sting his eyes. In a pinch, you can use baby shampoo, although we don't recommend it on a regular basis. There are tearless shampoos manufactured specifically for dogs, and in the long run these are better suited to the dog's coat. If the dog has fleas or ticks, or if he runs outside and you want to prevent him from getting them, you can bathe him in a flea-and-tick shampoo.

During the bath, it's a good idea to plug the dog's ears with cotton or to hold a finger in his ear while you are washing that area. If you are not using a tearless shampoo, close his eyes and run some petroleum jelly across the lids, or put a few drops of mineral oil in his eyes. Rinse the eyes out with clear water or an eyewash afterwards.

Many dogs do not like being immersed in a tub of water. A rubber shower mat in the bottom of the tub to give the dog traction will help; so will filling it with only a few inches of water. If the dog is frightened by this, use a spray instead, or take the dog in the shower with you. Many dogs who hate the idea of immersion actually enjoy a gentle shower, and this is a perfectly effective method of getting the dog clean. It is also much easier to manage a very large dog in the shower than it is to keep him steady in a tub. Shampoo the dog twice, working from back to front and bottom to top so that he will have soap in his face for the least amount of time. Rinse after both shampoos, and rinse thoroughly after the last one. If you don't remove every bit of shampoo from the dog's fur, it may work its way down to his skin and cause flaking and irritation.

Dry Bath   Longhaired dogs, especially those with a lot of white in their fur, may look dirty more often than once a month. An alternative to more frequent bathing is the dry bath. There are dry shampoos on the market, but cornstarch is the cheapest and most effective. Work the cornstarch into the coat and then brush it out. This will remove a considerable amount of dirt. But be sure to brush the coat well and remove as much of the powder as possible. If the dog licks himself and gets a lot of cornstarch in his system, it could upset his stomach.

Alcohol Bath   Breeds with double coats, like the Husky, are bathed less frequently. It is possible to bathe such a dog, but because the undercoat is almost impervious to water, the dog requires meticulous rinsing. Otherwise shampoo works its way into the undercoat and causes flaking and itching. Instead of using shampoo, you can rinse the dog in a solution of rubbing alcohol and water, which has a cleansing effect and is not likely to cause irritation.

Drying the Dog   Shorthaired dogs can be rubbed with a towel and then put in a warm, draft-free room until they are perfectly dry, or you can hasten the process with a hair dryer. Longhaired dogs may be *patted* with a towel, but rubbing will cause tangles and mats to start forming. Finish drying the dog with a hot-air dryer, holding the dryer in one area at a time and brushing at that spot. *Always* keep the dog indoors until he is thoroughly dry. If he goes outside, his wet coat will pick up dirt and debris and he may catch cold.

Scissoring, Shaping and Clipping   This is the final step and by far the most dangerous one. We do not believe that clipping procedures can be learned from books. If you are interested in doing your own clipping and scissoring, we advise you to take a course in it. Clippers and scissors are as sharp as surgical instruments, capable of cutting off the tongue, a testicle or an ear. With razor-sharp clippers, it is possible to open the skin. Also, because clipper blades heat up, you must check and cool them frequently in a cooling lubricant; otherwise they can inflict severe burns.

Weather and living conditions have a great deal to do with the quality of your dog's coat. The outdoor dog develops a more lustrous coat because he needs it to protect him from the weather. Longhaired dogs in particular benefit from spending long periods of time outdoors in the winter.

The indoor or apartment dog sheds continually because he lives in an atmosphere of warm, dry heat and unnatural lighting. His coat tends to thin out and his skin may become dry. A humidifier may help rectify the latter situation, but nothing except cold weather will keep a longhaired dog's coat as beautiful as it was meant to be. On the other hand, the dog who spends most of his time indoors is less likely to pick up ticks and fleas.

Exercise

All the grooming in the world will not make a dog beautiful if his diet or exercise are poor, and the latter is more apt to be deficient than the former these days. Most of us seem to think that if we throw the dog outdoors every once in a while he will get all the exercise he needs. This is not altogether true, and it is not even possible if you live in the city or in suburbs where leash laws are strictly enforced.

The first word to be said about exercise is "safety." Nothing that endangers your dog's life can be considered healthy exercise, except for certain kinds of working dogs whose professions entail some risk—the professional guard dog, police dog, war dog, sheep guard and cattle dog and to some degree the hunting dog and the sled dog. In general, most dogs live in safe environments, and it's the owner's job to provide them with safe exercise. This means you don't hitch a dog to the back of your car while you ride and he runs. It means you don't let him chase you on your bicycle. It means you don't let him off his leash on streets with heavy traffic. And in terms of what modern science knows about the body and how it operates, safety means something else as well.

No dog should be kept indoors most of the time and then taken out on weekends to run his brains out. If the dog is not exercised fully *every day*, his exercise must be controlled when he does get it. This is particularly important for the larger dogs and dogs subject to hip dysplasia.

The rules for exercise are as follows:

1. If possible, exercise your dog regularly. If this is not possible, control his exercise so that he suffers no ill effects.

2. Never exercise your dog immediately after a large meal. This is especially important for large dogs subject to gastric torsion.

The Puppy The puppy gets a considerable amount of exercise just in growing. In addition, he plays with his litter mates and adopts all sorts of positions and stances that stretch and develop his muscles. Once you bring the puppy home, however, he no longer has litter mates to play with, so the job is up to you. If you have children, they can help. Puppies love to chase balls and sticks; this is excellent exercise as long as you make certain that the ball is too large to lodge in the puppy's throat, and that the stick will not splinter. You may also purchase inexpensive hard-rubber pull toys that the dog will take in his mouth at one end while you pull at the other. The strain of pulling is excellent exercise for the legs and shoulders. Going upstairs is good exercise—it stretches out the leg and back muscles—but going downstairs should be avoided; if this is done to excess, it will damage the puppy's shoulders. One good exercise is to run upstairs with the puppy, and then, because it is good exercise for you, carry him down.

Save your longest outdoor exercise period for the evening. Take the puppy outside and play with him until he seems to be getting tired. This will help him sleep during the night. Outdoor exercise is extremely valuable for the young puppy, but you must *always remember* not to run him to death. Be sensitive to signs of fatigue,

lying down, panting, etc., for overwork will put too much stress on his soft bones and tender muscles. By the time he reaches six months, he will be able to exercise on a more businesslike basis, and it will be good for him to do so.

The Inside Dog   The dog who lives most of his life indoors presents the most difficult problem. He may *need* to run, even *like* to run, but because he is confined, he cannot. As a result, his physique, coat and temperament all suffer. The best plan is to think of some form of exercise that you and the dog can enjoy together. This is not always possible. You can't take a dog on the tennis court, for a run at the Y, or to a public swimming pool—more's the pity. However, many confined owners have started jogging, and have found that this is one form of exercise they and their dogs can do together. Before jogging, both you and the dog should get complete physical examinations to determine whether or not it is safe for you to run. You should also take the time to build yourselves up gradually. Start by running short distances and gradually increase them until you are running a mile or more. *Always* keep the dog on leash. He may not be able to run as fast, but a slow, steady pace is safer than a wild, free sprint.

A long walk is also beneficial for both you and your dog, and in many cases, especially among the giant breeds, a walk provides adequate exercise. Of course the walk must be more than just giving the dog the opportunity to relieve himself. You must be prepared to spend a good twenty minutes to half an hour once or twice a day. Walking in combination with some indoor or outdoor play is even more invigorating, and you may continue the same games you instituted when the dog was a puppy—retrieving, and pulling rubber toys with the mouth.

Many cities provide special dog runs where you can take the dog and release him for long periods of time. Since there are other dogs present and since most runs enforce scoop laws, you must remain present to supervise, but the dog run is still an excellent alternative for the owner who objects to jogging.

The Outdoors Dog   Many people erroneously believe that a dog who lives outdoors gets exercise automatically. In some cases this is true. Put a hunting dog in a fenced yard or a twenty-foot run and he will probably race around. Some dogs, however, like some people, are inveterate lazies. We knew a dog named Skipper who was left to roam the neighborhood completely free of leash and chose to spend most of his time curled up on his front porch. When he *did*

An empty parking lot is a great place for city exercise. Make sure that the lot is enclosed unless your dog is off-leash trained like this German Shepherd.

BOTH PICTURES BY TIMOTHY REMY

move, he moved slowly and methodically; no one ever saw him run. Often the owner is inclined to leave such a dog to his own devices. The dog is happy; he doesn't bark and he doesn't disturb the neighbors. He sleeps well at night—at any time, for that matter. But it may not be good for him to lie around. In this case, the owner should provide the initiative, using the same techniques as those required for the dog who lives cooped up in an apartment.

The Pregnant Bitch   For the normal bitch, nothing could be more important to a swift and easy delivery than good muscle tone. Therefore, even after she becomes pregnant, you must make sure that she receives regular exercise. As her pregnancy advances, you must see that she does not overtax herself and that her exercise is controlled and supervised. Extensive stretching and pulling at the wrong muscles at the wrong time could result in a premature delivery. Do not let her exercise immediately after eating; this could cause considerable discomfort, although since she will be eating three or four small meals a day, it is not likely to cause serious damage.

The Fat Dog   Controlled exercise combined with a controlled diet is the only efficient way of turning the fat dog into a sleek beauty. If the dog has been allowed to go to fat, you probably have not been exercising him correctly in the first place, so you will have to watch him carefully in the beginning, limiting his activities at first and gradually building him up. Since overweight people tend to have overweight dogs, jogging may be an excellent program for both of you. Fat dogs tend to be lazy dogs, so it may take a good deal of convincing on your part to get this dog to run. On the other hand, he may have to convince you.

The Neutered Dog   Again, combine exercise with a good diet, and the dog will not go to fat.

The Skinny Dog   Exercise burns calories, of course, but since it improves muscle tone, it also helps maintain a respectable weight. If the dog is excessively thin, he probably has something wrong with him medically and ought to be thoroughly checked out. Once you are satisfied that the dog is not ill, start him on a controlled exercise program. Many dogs with excessive nervous energy tend to burn up fat just pacing around the house. Exercise will help relax the dog and is therefore a more productive way of using excess energy.

The Sick Dog   Did you ever feel like running around the block when you had the flu? Leave the poor fellow alone. Once he recuperates, go easy for a few days until he has regained his strength.

HOW TO DEAL WITH EMERGENCIES

The object of this chapter is to teach you how to keep your dog from dying before his time. We are not going to teach you fancy bandaging techniques or how to suture a wound. The dog owner has to deal with this sort of emergency only once or twice in a dog's lifetime and does not have the knowledge, technical skill, experience, equipment or medication to treat a severe injury adequately. The veterinarian, on the other hand, has all of these things at his disposal. In most emergencies, your only hope is to get your dog to the veterinarian as swiftly and safely as possible. This is true for everything from snake bites to internal injuries. But in many cases, a little quick action on the owner's part may save the dog's life. The problem is to be able to distinguish what will save the dog from what will hasten his demise—and this is precisely where old wives' tales and "neighborly advice" may interfere with sound judgment.

Safety First

Most emergencies could be prevented if the owner took the attitude that his dog was no more sensible than a child. Some dogs, it's true, have an amazing gift for avoiding problems—some have intelligence and foresight, and some are trained remarkably well. But the average dog is constantly confronted by perilous and confusing situations that we expect him by some miracle to figure out, although this requires the mental ability to make comparisons, distinctions and judgments. It is not reasonable to expect a dog to know the difference between an electrical cord and piece of rope, a balcony and a front porch, or a dish of bleach and a bowl of soup. Our rule is this: Take the same safety precautions for your dog that you would take for a small child.

This means that you must inspect your home, yard and garage carefully and eliminate possible hazards. Puppies, and some older dogs as well, have a vital curiosity and a strong desire to chew. Both qualities can mean trouble. In most cases, obedience training will teach the dog how to control his more desperate urges, and you will find that as the dog learns how to behave himself better, you will be able to relax the rules. In the meantime, this chapter will make you aware of some of the accidents that can happen, how to prevent them, and how to deal with an emergency should it arise.

The Automobile

The automobile is probably the leading canine killer in this country and is certainly the leading cause of injury. An orthopedic surgeon at the University of Pennsylvania Small Animal Hospital estimates that 90 percent of all fractures seen at that hospital are caused when dogs are hit by cars. While we tend to think that such accidents occur only in rural or suburban areas where dogs are allowed to run free, they also occur frequently in the city.

Having your dog walk by your side on the city streets without the restraint of a leash is not exercise. It's an ego trip, particularly if the dog is not off-leash trained. It takes a professional trainer sixteen to twenty once-a-week sessions to train a dog to "come" off-leash. Even so, he would never allow that dog to walk along the sidewalk of a busy, heavily trafficked street without a leash. Too many things can happen.

Dogs can also get into trouble inside the car. Your dog should not be allowed to hang over the front seat and disturb the driver, who can have a bad accident if his arm is jostled or his attention distracted. A dog hanging halfway out the window can get a serious eye injury or fall out of the window or snap at passers-by. Dogs allowed such freedom are a particular nuisance to bike riders and toll-booth operators.

THE RULES

1. If you live in the suburbs or country, never allow your dog to run free, even if this means building a seven-foot fence around him.

2. If you live in the city, never allow your dog off-leash except in parks where dogs are allowed and in designated dog runs.

3. Train your dog to lie quietly on the back seat of the car while you are driving, and keep the windows open only enough to let air in and out of the car—not enough to allow the dog to stick his head outside.

If your dog is struck by an automobile, go to your RX cabinet (see p. 60) and get the following items:
1. Gauze
2. Blanket
3. Board

You will also need a pair of scissors to cut the gauze and a friend to help you carry the dog if the dog weighs twenty-five pounds or more. Make no attempt to lift the dog and cradle him in your arms; this may impede his breathing.

Step 1: Apply a muzzle. No matter how docile the dog is under ordinary conditions, he may be half crazed with pain. Cut a long strip of gauze. Make a single-tie loop, slip it over the dog's muzzle in between his nose and the hinge of his jaw and tighten it down. Bring both ends of the gauze underneath the dog's chin and tie again in a knot. Bring both ends of the gauze behind the dog's ears and tie in a knot at the back of his head. If the dog is *short-nosed*, take both ends of the gauze, draw them firmly over the crown of his head between his ears and tie to the original loops around the muzzle. This will prevent the gauze from slipping off the dog's face. Clip the gauze ends short.

Step 2: Slip the dog gently onto the board, which you will use as a stretcher.

Shock   If the dog is severely injured, he will probably go into shock. Shock is not emotional. It is a physiological response to severe injury, blood loss, trauma or severe illness. When a dog goes into shock, his circulatory system slows down so that it is no longer able to supply the tissues of his body and brain with enough oxygen to keep him alive. If you lift the dog's lips, you will see that his gums

An emergency muzzle should be applied before handling an injured dog. In the following pictures, Dr. McLellan demonstrates the technique.

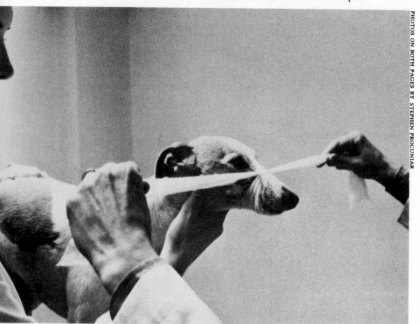

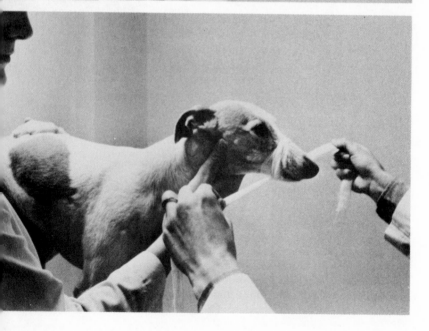

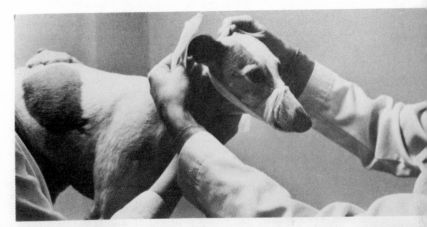

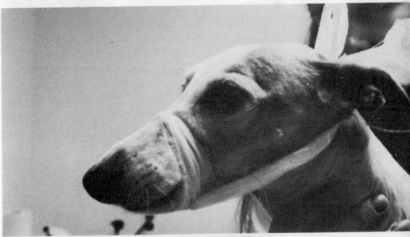

An emergency muzzle
for a short-nosed dog.

are pale, and if you press your finger into the gum, it will turn white. Normally, the gums will regain color within a second or so, but if the animal is in shock, the indentation regains color slowly.

Step 3: If the dog goes into shock, cover him with a blanket and move him immediately to a warm, sheltered place. Make sure that the board is resting at a slight angle so the dog's head is lower than his hindquarters. This will help the blood get to his brain and may prevent brain damage.

Step 4: If the dog has trouble breathing, turn him on his sternum so that he is lying on his stomach with his legs out to the side. If he stops breathing altogether, go to step 5.

Step 5: Remove the muzzle and apply *artificial respiration*. Open the dog's mouth, and using your thumb and first two fingers, pull out the dog's tongue so that you can see deep into his throat. Clean out blood and mucus to make an air passage. Close the dog's mouth and hold it closed. Take a deep breath. Cover the dog's nose with your mouth, making sure that your lips are pressed tightly against the dog's muzzle so that no air escapes. Breathe air gently into the nose until the dog's chest expands. Release until the chest relaxes. Take another breath and repeat about ten to twelve times a minute.

Step 6: Once the dog is breathing, take him immediately to the veterinarian.

PHOTOS ON BOTH PAGES BY STEPHEN PROCUNIAR

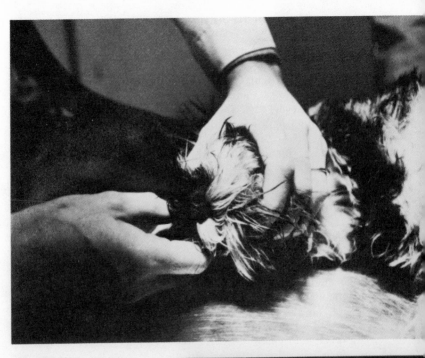

Bikes, Both with and without Motors

Bikes pose a particular danger, because they often drive the most well-mannered pup into a state of frenzy. Dogs who are allowed to chase bikes, even when the owner is at the handlebars, frequently get injured when they misjudge distances and somehow get tangled up in the wheels. Bike chasing is therefore not good exercise but the lazy owner's method of avoiding a walk in the park.

THE RULES

1. Don't allow your dog to chase you while you are riding a bike.
2. Don't let your dog loose in areas where there are a lot of bikes or motorcycles.

If your dog is struck by a bike, proceed as though he had been struck by an automobile. Take him immediately to a veterinarian, who can accurately determine the extent of injury.

Dog Fights

Dog fights occur when the dog is out of the owner's control. Dogs get seriously bitten and people may also get injured when they try to intervene.

THE RULES

1. Don't let your dog run free.
2. If you make the mistake of doing so and your dog gets in a fight, don't try to separate the animals by dividing them near the head, face or neck. If the dog has a long tail, grab him by the tail; or grab him by the back foot and hoist him off-balance.

If your dog gets bitten by another dog, clip the hair away from the wound and cleanse it with hydrogen peroxide. Watch the area for swelling. The danger with a puncture wound is that the surface skin may heal, leaving a pocket of infection underneath. For this reason, it's important to take the dog immediately to the veterinarian for further treatment.

Heat Prostration

Because dogs don't sweat like humans, the only way they can eliminate body heat is by panting. While he is panting, the dog salivates and produces extra moisture, and it is the evaporation of this moisture on the tongue and in the mouth that cools the blood and ultimately cools the dog. If the dog can't pant enough to cool himself, his temperature will soar and he'll go into heat prostration.

The following symptoms indicate heat prostration: glazed eyes, struggling for breath, foaming at the mouth, vomiting, pacing and other frantic behavior, and a soaring temperature; in the final stages, pale or blue gums and convulsions, followed by coma and death.

Heat prostration is most likely to occur in the following circumstances:

In a Closed Automobile   Particularly in summer, when the temperature of a closed, parked automobile under the hot sun can rise to 150°F. in a matter of minutes.

At a Show

On the Street or Terrace   The short-nosed breeds are especially prone to heat prostration—the Lhasas, Pekingeses, Bulldogs, Boston Terriers, Pugs—because they can't pant effectively. Some of these animals will actually go into heat prostration just walking down the street on a hot day. Heat prostration may also result if the dog is left out on a terrace under the blazing sun.

At the Beach   If the dog runs wild and overheats himself, he may try to drink a lot of "beach" water to cool himself off. But instead of hydrating the dog, the water dehydrates him because he is absorbing salt along with the water.

THE RULES

1.   Don't leave your dog in a closed car in summer. If you absolutely must leave him, park in the shade and check frequently to make sure that he is all right or that the shade has not moved away from the car.

2.   Don't overexercise the short-nosed breeds when it is hot outside, and as soon as the dog shows signs of stress, get him inside to air conditioning.

3.   Don't lock a dog out on the terrace during the summer.

4. When you go to the beach, take a supply of cool, fresh water and don't let your dog drink salt water along the shore.

If your dog should suffer from heat prostration, go to your RX cabinet (see p. 60) and get the following items:

1. Rectal thermometer
2. Petroleum jelly
3. Board

You will also need plenty of cold water and perhaps ice.

Step 1: Get the dog out of the heat and if possible into a cool, air-conditioned room.

Step 2: Douse him with cold water to get his temperature down as quickly as possible.

Step 3: Check his temperature frequently to find out whether it is going down.

Step 4: Continue cooling procedures until his temperature has returned to normal.

Step 5: Take the dog immediately to the veterinarian—even if his temperature drops, but especially if it does not. If the dog's condition is severe, pack him in ice while you transport him. *Do not transport him in the back part of a station wagon or hatchback if the engine is located in the rear of the car,* because the engine makes that part of the car hot. Place him on the back seat on his sternum with his feet extended to the sides to facilitate breathing. If the dog is relatively motionless, you may open the windows fully for good air flow. If the dog is frantic, open the windows only wide enough to permit air flow but not wide enough for the dog to put his head outside.

Sunburn

Sunburn occurs at the beach, particularly when the dog is pink-skinned or has very pale pigmentation.

The Rule Don't allow pale-skinned dogs to spend long hours in the sun unless you acclimate them gradually, as you would a red-headed child.

If your dog should suffer from sunburn, move him to a cool, shady area. Soothing powders, such as equal parts of zinc oxide and talcum or boric-acid powder, may be applied. If blistering or itching are pronounced, veterinary treatment will be necessary.

Salt Water

Except in the case of heatstroke, salt water does not really bring about an emergency situation, but it can cause serious problems if the owner is not alert. Certain ear and skin problems develop when the dog is allowed to swim in salty or brackish water. This is no reason to keep your dog out of the water, but it's a good reason to rinse him off afterwards and to be on the lookout for hot spots, which are particularly common during the summer months. A hot spot occurs for a number of reasons. It may start as an itchy spot that the dog feels after he has been swimming in salt water or water with a lot of bacteria in it. The dog starts scratching and the irritated area enlarges until there are huge sores on the skin which cause the dog considerable discomfort.

THE RULES

1. Rinse the dog with fresh water after he has been swimming in salt or polluted water.

2. Examine his skin carefully for inflammation or irritation.

3. Examine his ears for debris or inflammation.

If your dog suffers from hot spots, you may ease his discomfort with aspirin.

High-Rise Disease

"There's a disease we have in major cities," says Dr. Susan McLellan, "called high-rise disease. It's when the dog goes out the window."

Puppies are particularly curious and apt to get into trouble, but even older dogs may get excited if they are left alone. The dog will jump up in an effort to see out or even to get out, and if there's no screen to stop him, out he goes.

Terraces offer a similar kind of danger. Some owners put chicken wire around the bottom of the terrace, but even this is not foolproof. Dogs have been known to leap fences six feet high. The terrace provides the additional dangers of exorbitant heat in summer and cold in winter. Most dogs cannot stand these extremes of temperature and should never be locked out on the terrace to fend for themselves.

THE RULES

1. If you must leave the windows open for air, buy screens or steel gates for them that the dog can't gnaw through.

2. Allow your dog out on the terrace only if you are prepared to supervise him at all times.

Electric Shock

Electric cords are particularly dangerous to puppies, who mistake them for strings and are tempted to chew on them. The effect seems to be equally severe whether the dog is large or small. It can cause shock, severe burns in the mouth, electrocution and death.

The Rule If you leave your dog alone, make sure that there are no electric cords available for chewing. Unplug all lamp cords and wrap them around the lamp bases—at least until the dog has matured beyond the chewing stages of puppyhood.

If your dog has received an electric shock, disconnect the source of electricity and insulate yourself before you touch the dog. Wear rubber gloves and pry him away from the cord with a rolling pin or wooden kitchen spoon.

Step 1: If he has stopped breathing, give him artificial respiration (see p. 218).

Step 2: Take him to the veterinarian immediately.

Burns

Dogs know about fire, but hot pots and pans look innocent. A serious accident can occur if the dog knocks a hot pot over, or if a pot of boiling water or hot soup gets spilled on him.

THE RULES

1. Take the same precautions that you would take for a child. Keep pot handles turned toward the center of the stove. If your dog likes to follow you around while you are cooking, banish him from the

kitchen whenever you are doing a lot of fetching and carrying—
unless you are prepared to move slowly and thus avoid an accidental
tackling maneuver.

2. Teach the dog not to leap up on the counter and stove.

If your dog gets burned, do not touch the dog until you have washed
your hands. The skin itself is one of the body's major protective
devices against infection. Thus when the skin is burned, a layer or
even several layers of insulation against bacteria are effectively
destroyed.

You can treat small burns yourself. Apply butter, petroleum jelly
or a commercial product considered safe for children. Or brew some
strong tea, dip a clean cloth in it and apply it to the burn. If large
areas of skin are affected, there is danger of serious infection and
water loss resulting in dehydration. Spread a clean cloth with
petroleum jelly so that it won't stick to the burn and cover the wound
with it while you transport the dog to the veterinarian.

Pins and Needles

Pins and needles, especially with strings or threads attached, are
some of the more common items that a veterinarian will find in a
dog's belly. The dog starts by chewing on the thread and ends up
swallowing the needle. Other common dangers include soft rubber
toys with squeakies, small rubber balls, hard-plastic children's toys,
baby rattles, baby-bottle nipples with the smell of milk on them,
buttery corncobs from the garbage, roast strings, bones and bone
chips. Such items can cause intestinal blockage, or even rupture.

THE RULES

1. Don't leave these objects around the house.

2. Teach the dog not to go into the garbage (see p. 191).

If your dog swallows a foreign object:

1. If the object is soft, such as a baby-bottle nipple, or round, such
as a hard-rubber ball, you may induce vomiting unless you believe
that the object has already entered the intestinal tract.

2. If the object is sharp or has threads or strings attached, get the
dog to the veterinarian as soon as possible.

Sticks and Stones

Sticks and stones won't break his bones, but we can't promise that they won't hurt him. They are the outdoor equivalents to pins and needles—yummy to chew and hard not to swallow. They cause intestinal blockage and sometimes rupture. They are particularly tempting to the household dog who is only rarely allowed outdoors and gets a little carried away when he arrives in the country for the first time in the season.

The Rule   If your dog is not used to grazing, supervise him rather closely for the first few times he enjoys the great outdoors.

If your dog chews and swallows sticks and stones, take him to the veterinarian immediately. Do not induce vomiting.

Chemicals and Poisons

"My dog eat laundry detergent? Never!"

Well, don't be so sure, because plenty of dogs have done it. We haven't yet figured out the taste appeal, but laundry detergents are very toxic, especially the biodegradable detergents, which are caustic and burn the esophagus. Dogs also find the sweet taste of antifreeze appealing. Fuel oils are poisonous. When they are delivered to city buildings, puddles of oil are often left on the sidewalk. The dog walks through them and licks his feet to clean them. Dogs left alone in old buildings can get lead poisoning when they chew on walls made of old plaster and painted with lead-based paint. In winter when the streets and walks are salted to melt the snow, the dog will lick the salt off his feet; if he absorbs enough of it, he'll get a serious gastrointestinal upset. Paint and turpentine can get on the dog's coat while your house or apartment is being painted. Both will cause serious irritation and burning of the skin: worst of all, when the dog licks his fur, he ingests these poisons. Rodenticides, insecticides, snail bait, weedkillers and nitrate fertilizers are extremely dangerous to animals, sometimes appealing in taste and often present in the dog's environment. Many popular house and garden plants are also poisonous.

THE RULES

1. Keep all household chemicals and poisons out of the dog's

reach. This may include cosmetics, pens, paints, and glazes, especially if your dog belongs to one of the omnivorous breeds, likes to chew, or displays an excessive curiosity.

2. If your dog shows an interest in plants, hang them from the ceiling where he cannot reach them, keep them in a room where he is not allowed to go, or train him not to eat them (see p. 190). You may also get various anti-animal compounds and devices at plant and hardware stores.

3. If you must use fertilizers and weedkillers, use types that are nontoxic to animals. Otherwise, keep your dog indoors until the effects of the poison have worn away.

4. If you use insect poisons and sprays indoors, keep the dog out of the room until the room has been aired and the poison has dried.

5. Rodenticides should be applied out of the reach of domestic animals—or not at all. The same goes for snail bait.

6. If the dog walks in oil or salt, wash his pads thoroughly with fresh, clean water.

7. If your dog chews at the walls or windowsills, check his diet with the veterinarian. A change in diet may rectify his bad eating habits. If he continues to chew, try painting his favorite spots with a solution of alum and water.

If your dogs ingests a poison, the following first-aid treatments may save his life. Remember, every poison must be treated according to the effect it has on the body. If the substance is caustic, do not induce vomiting.

● If you know what the dog has eaten, read the label to find out the proper antidote; or call your local poison control center for advice.

● If there is no label or the label is missing, put a sample of the poisonous substance in a small container and take it with you to the veterinarian for chemical analysis.

PRESCRIPTION DRUGS	
The following prescription drugs ingested by dogs resulted in calls to a poison control center:	
Darvon Thyroid medication Donnatal Benadryl Digitalis	Administer emetic. Call the veterinarian. In the case of barbiturates, administer emetic only if the dog is fully conscious. Otherwise the dog may choke to death on his own vomit.

PRESCRIPTION DRUGS	
The dog's own eardrops Various barbiturates	*Do not exercise the dog. Call immediately for veterinary assistance.*

OVER-THE-COUNTER DRUGS	
The following over-the-counter drugs ingested by dogs resulted in calls to a poison control center:	
Caffeine tablets Cough drops (sweet taste) Laxative Vitamins	If the dog ingests any of these items in large quantity, administer emetic. *Call immediately for veterinary assistance.*

INSECTICIDES	
The following insecticides ingested by dogs resulted in calls to a poison control center:	
Hornet spray Insect spray (sprayed on meat) Roach traps (taste sweet) Flypaper Flea collar	Most insecticides are convulsants. If the dog gets spray on his skin, wash with water and detergent. If he ingests the poison, induce vomiting. *Call immediately for veterinary assistance.*

RODENTICIDES AND PESTICIDES	
Warfarin laid down in cereal base	There is nothing you can do. *Call immediately for veterinary assistance.*
Thallium	There is nothing you can do. *Call immediately for veterinary assistance.*
Snail bait	Induce vomiting immediately. If symptoms are already present (uneasiness, muscle tremors, convulsions), *do not induce vomiting. Call immediately for veterinary assistance.*

REMODELING PRODUCTS	
The following products ingested by dogs resulted in calls to a poison control center:	
Paintbrush cleaner Paint thinner	These are petroleum distillates, and corrosive. On the skin, flood with water and wash with mild detergent. If ingested, *do not induce vomiting. Call immediately for veterinary assistance.*
Turpentine	On the skin, flood with water and wash with mild detergent. If ingested, *do not induce vomiting. Call immediately for veterinary assistance.*
Putty	If ingested, *call immediately for veterinary assistance.*
Plaster	*Do not induce vomiting. Call immediately for veterinary assistance.*
Rustoleum Oil-base paint	On the skin, clean with rag dampened with turpentine, then flood with water and wash with mild detergent. If ingested, *call immediately for veterinary assistance.*
Lead paint (chewed)	*Call immediately for veterinary assistance.*
Latex (water-based paint)	On the skin, flood with water. If ingested, *call immediately for veterinary assistance.*
Dried paint	On the coat, clip away the hair, and soothe skin with mineral oil.

CLEANING AGENTS	
Borax Cleanser Toilet bowl cleansers	*Do not give emetics.* These substances are corrosive and will cause further damage if the dog vomits them up. Administer water and dilute vinegar solution. Administer demulcent. *Call immediately for veterinary assistance.*
Pine-oil cleaner	*Call immediately for veterinary assistance.*

CLEANING AGENTS	
Laundry detergents	*Do not give emetics.* Administer water, and administer demulcent. *Call immediately for veterinary assistance.*

AUTOMOTIVE PRODUCTS	
Battery acid	*Do not give emetics.* This is a corrosive substance. Administer baking soda in water. *Call immediately for veterinary assistance.*
Antifreeze	Administer emetic. *Rush to the veterinarian.*
Sidewalk salt	Give plenty of water. For vomiting and diarrhea, give Pepto-Bismol. If vomiting and diarrhea persist, call for veterinary assistance.
Fuel oil	*Do not induce vomiting.* This is a petroleum distillate, and corrosive. *Call immediately for veterinary assistance.*

MISCELLANEOUS ITEMS	
Resulting in calls to a poison control center:	
Shampoo	Induce vomiting. Call for veterinary assistance.
Nail polish	*Do not induce vomiting. Call immediately for veterinary assistance.*
One ballpoint pen and ink	Induce vomiting. *Call immediately for veterinary assistance.*
One book of matches	Will not harm the dog.
Kitchen matches	Induce vomiting. *Call immediately for veterinary assistance.*
One tasty bowl of ceramic glaze	*Do not induce vomiting. Call immediately for veterinary assistance.*

POISONOUS PLANTS

Here is a list of some of the more common poisonous plants growing in the house and garden.

Seeds	Leaves	
Apple	Avocado	Administer emetic, followed by demulcent. *Call immediately for veterinary assistance.*
Apricot	Buttercup	
Crabapple	Cherry	
Peach	Nightshade	
Bird of paradise	Hydrangea	This list is not complete. If your dog eats a plant not on this list, no matter how innocent that plant may seem, seek veterinary advice immediately. The one exception is grass.
Black locust	Iris	
Castor bean	Jerusalem cherry	
Cherry	Jimson weed	
Delphinium	Philodendron	
Flax	Poinsettia	
Morning glory	Potato	
Narcissus	Rhododendron	
Nutmeg	Tomato	
Sweet pea		
	Nuts	
Bulbs	Acorn	
Daffodil	Horse chestnut	
Hyacinth		
Jonquil	*Flowers*	
Tulip	Lily of the valley	
Berries		
Nightshade		
Holly		
English ivy		
Mistletoe		
Virginia creeper		

FERTILIZERS AND WEEDKILLERS

Fertilizers	These, especially nitrate compounds, are toxic if ingested. If symptoms are not yet apparent, administer emetic. If the dog shows symptoms (cyanosis, difficult breathing, congested lungs), administer mineral oil orally and seek veterinary assistance.
Weedkillers	Most weedkillers are toxic only if ingested in large amounts. However, dinitro- compounds can be absorbed through the skin. If plants sprayed with herbicides are ingested, induce vomiting. Seek veterinary assistance.

Flesh Wounds

For a laceration or puncture wound that is bleeding profusely, press a clean cloth next to the wound and apply pressure with your fingers to staunch the flow of blood. *Do not use a tourniquet* for the following reasons:

1. Most people don't know how to put a tourniquet on an animal so that it will do any good.

2. There is risk of losing the limb when you apply a tourniquet.

3. A tourniquet is only useful on a limb or tail, and then only if an artery has been cut. This situation is extremely rare. An animal can have half the skin torn off his legs without artery damage. *If* an artery is cut, pressure around the upper part of the extremity will usually slow down the bleeding, and is much safer than a tourniquet.

Self-mutilation   The dog's mouth actually has some antiseptic action, and he will try to clean his own wounds by licking at them. Unless his teeth are bad or he has infected gums, this may have a positive effect. However, if he begins to worry and bite at a wound, he may incidentally cause additional trauma.

Sometimes a dog will start biting and licking at a spot for no apparent reason. Once he starts to worry the spot, he causes a lot of irritation and the skin begins to thicken—which starts up a vicious cycle, with more licking and more irritation.

If the dog is biting or licking at the stitches in a wound, the veterinarian may be able to help you devise a protective collar that will prevent him from causing himself further injury. If he caused the wound himself, the veterinarian may suggest anti-inflammatory medications to lessen the itching sensation, and if this doesn't work, radiation therapy or injections of painkilling drugs

The Muscles and Bones

If your dog is limping badly, the muscles may be damaged, but the leg is probably not broken. If he has broken his leg, he will place no weight on it at all. The best thing to do in either case is to get the dog to the veterinarian as soon as possible. Do not try to splint the leg yourself for the following reasons:

1. It is usually too painful for the animal.

2. It is easy to bandage a splint too tightly, which will cause swelling in the extremity. In our experience, attempts on the part of the owner usually end in disaster.

Gastrointestinal Emergencies

Vomiting After the dog vomits, he will want to drink a lot of water, but you must take all food and water away. Giving him additional water after he has vomited will only cause him to vomit again. Wait until vomiting stops, then give him a few swallows of water or an ice cube to lick. These measures will prevent dehydration. Administer a stomach sedative.

Diarrhea Profuse diarrhea *without vomiting* is another matter. Give the dog as much water as he wants because he is losing a lot of water in his stool. Administer a stomach sedative.

If vomiting or diarrhea continue, call the veterinarian.

Bloat More properly known as "gastric dilatation-torsion complex," bloat constitutes a major emergency and requires prompt veterinary attention. It most commonly occurs in the giant breeds but can occur in the hunting breeds as well, particularly after a heavy feeding followed by strenuous exercise.

The symptoms of bloat are uneasiness, discomfort, nausea, gagging, repeated efforts to swallow, tenseness around the stomach and abdomen, obvious distension of the abdomen, reluctance to lie down, difficulty breathing and circulatory collapse followed by shock. The dog's reluctance to lie down is often taken by the owner to mean that he is improving, but actually it is a sign of impending death.

If you wait until the dog goes into shock, the chances of his survival are slim indeed. There is no first-aid treatment. Thus as soon as the dog exhibits the first symptoms, it is imperative to get him prompt veterinary attention. The veterinarian will try to relieve the gas in the dog's stomach by inserting a stomach tube. If the stomach is twisted, however, the veterinarian will be unable to insert the tube and will have to operate. Grave risks accompany this type of emergency surgery. After surgery the dog will be placed in intensive care. If the dog survives, the danger is not yet over. When bloat has occurred once, it is likely to recur. The owner must restrict the dog's exercise and feed him several small meals a day, as opposed to a single big meal. The dog may return to a normal regimen only after his stomach has regained muscle tone.

CALLEA PHOTO

A German Shorthaired Pointer proudly shows off her puppies.

12

SEX, REPRODUCTION AND BIRTH CONTROL*

If you own a beautiful bitch and decide you would like to breed her, there are four questions you should ask yourself first:

1. What are you going to do with the puppies? Unless you are a breeder or connected with a breeder, there is always the difficulty of finding customers who are willing to provide safe and reliable homes. In many cases, you will have to resort to advertising, which is costly.

2. Should your bitch really be bred? Many people are blind to their dog's faults. Some faults may certainly be overlooked if the dog has a superior temperament and a sound constitution, but some faults should never be bred. These include traits like cleft palate, cryptorchidism in males or hip dysplasia. There are varying degrees of faultiness, but you must be objective enough to distinguish those faults that are harmful and should not be passed on from those that are minor.

3. Are you prepared for the work involved in seeing a bitch through her pregnancy and delivery, in helping her wean the pups and in caring for them when they're big enough to run around making little puddles and mounds all over everything? You must be prepared to feed these puppies on a relentless schedule four or five times a day

---

* This chapter was prepared with the help of our medical consultant, Dr. Susan McLellan. All controversial questions were also referred to the University of Pennsylvania's Small Animal Hospital.

This West Highland White Terrier puppy comes from a long line of champions. Below is her grandfather's pedigree.

CERTIFIED PEDIGREE

Name of Dog: CH KAR RIC'S EXTRA EDITION   Sex: MALE   Reg No.: R767101

Breed: WEST HIGHLAND WHITE TERRIER   Color: WHITE

Date Whelped: AUGUST 29, 1969   Breeder: DORIS H EISENBERG

Sire 1: CH RAINSBOROWE REDVERS (UNITED KINGDOM) R319300 5-65

  3: BANKER OF BRANSTON 493AQ 71582/56

    7: BARRISTER OF BRANSTON 2041AG

    8: BINTY OF BRANSTON 1657AG

  4: RAINSBOROWE MICHALA 9087/60

    9: FAMECHECK MUSKETEER 562AS

    10: RAINSBOROWE TREASURE

Dam 2: CH KAR RIC'S TALK OF THE TOWN R557992 8-68

  5: CH LOCHGLEN GUARDSMAN R407566 9-65

    11: CH LOCHGLEN DRUID R323336 8-64

    12: LOCHGLEN ENCHANTRESS R337438 8-64

  6: CH KAR RIC'S GAMBLE R337666 11-64

    13: CH ELFINBROOK SIMON R240664 12-59

    14: CH KAR RIC'S FOOLISH FANCY R302415 11-62

The Seal of The American Kennel Club affixed hereto certifies that this pedigree has been compiled from official Stud Book records.

Date Issued: 2-5-79   RLC

and to clean up after them at least as often. You must be prepared to hand-raise the puppies if something goes wrong—if they are orphaned or rejected by their mother.

4. Can you afford it? The medical expense involved in raising a litter includes prebreeding, prenatal and postnatal examinations of the bitch by a veterinarian, cost of vaginal smears and laboratory tests, examination of the pups, worming and vaccinations. You will also have to buy vitamin and mineral supplements and all the other medications prescribed by the veterinarian, as well as extra dog food and protein supplements for both the puppies and the bitch. All of this adds up to a considerable sum. It is worth noting that the money you get for the puppies rarely compensates for the cost of having them in the first place.

If you can answer all these questions to your own satisfaction, then go ahead and breed your dog. It is indeed a wonderful experience to raise a litter.

The Reproductive Cycle

The male dog has no cycle. He will be attracted by the scent of a bitch in heat every day of his life as long as he is fertile. Young and castrated males are often the first to notice that a bitch is in heat. As the stud becomes older and wiser, he will take no notice of her except during her acceptance period, which is only four or five days. Often, on the last day of the acceptance period, he will become disinterested, for he knows by her scent that she is no longer fertile.

The female has one or two and sometimes even three cycles a year. The Basenji, a breed that has been domesticated for a relatively short period of time, has only one season like her wild counterpart, the wolf. Most bitches, however, go into heat twice a year, approximately every six months, although this varies greatly. Typically, the heat periods occur in the spring and the fall, but this timing is not consistent, especially with the advent of the apartment dog, who is protected from seasonal changes. The heat cycle is regulated by hormones and may be artificially induced, although there are attendant risks. Dr. Leon Whitney discovered that bitches tend to go into heat both when the days get shorter and when they get longer, so the largest number of heat periods occur in February and August. A bitch in heat can also influence the heat period of another bitch. According to Dr. David Senior of the University of Pennsylvania's

Small Animal Hospital, "Kennel managers notice that bitches housed together will cycle in unison. This could be equivalent to the 'boarding house' effect seen in people." With all of these factors to contend with, the heat cycle of any particular bitch is difficult to predict with any reliability.

The bitch spends three to five months in anestrus. This is the period when she is not cycling at all. The cycle begins with proestrus, which is marked by a swelling of the vulva and a watery, bloody discharge that lasts from five to twelve days. The length of proestrus varies substantially from dog to dog, and during this period she is not fertile, will not conceive and usually will not accept the advances of a male. Proestrus is followed by estrus, which is when the bitch actually ovulates. The watery, bloody discharge begins to be replaced by an amber or brownish mucoid discharge that lasts for a variable period of time, usually seven to nine days, and is the first indication that the dog is ready to be bred. Ovulation occurs one to five days after the discharge changes, and the female will now "stand" for the male. As a general rule, the dog should be bred on the tenth to twelfth day after the first signs of bleeding, or the first and fourth day after the first acceptance of the male dog. If the dog is not bred, the discharge will become a milky-white color, diminish and gradually disappear. The vulva will shrink, and the bitch will return to normal.

Things You Should Know about a Bitch in Season

First of all, as we have already said, the heat cycle is subject to a number of influences and can't always be reliably predicted. Also, the pattern for each bitch is somewhat different, and therefore the exact day on which the bitch should be bred may be difficult to determine.

For years breeders swore that the change in discharge was a reliable sign of ovulation, but this turned out not to be invariably so. Some breeders swear that the first day the bitch will accept a male is a reliable indication, but again this turns out not always to be accurate. The only really reliable method of determining when the bitch is ready is a vaginal smear taken by the veterinarian, and even this test is not 100 percent foolproof. Certainly, if you have any questions, you ought to have a smear taken.

Some bitches have "silent heats," which means that they manage to go through all the internal changes without a single outward sign. The discharge may be minimal or apparently nonexistent. If you examine the bitch, you may notice a slight change in her vulva, although even this can be difficult to detect. But in spite of the lack of outward signs, the bitch is just as fertile as one who bleeds copiously. Many misalliances occur with these animals because the owner is unaware of the condition and allows his bitch too much freedom. At the other end of the spectrum is the bitch who bleeds profusely throughout her period and ovulates even though the color of her discharge never changes. In both of these cases, it is difficult to tell exactly when the bitch is ready to breed.

When we speak of "profuse" or "copious" bleeding, we don't mean that the bitch loses a lot of blood. The discharge is watery, and the amount of blood loss is not great, even in the case of a very large animal. Also, most bitches keep themselves remarkably clean during this period, so you don't have to worry about a mess.

This is a period when you should make a special effort to keep the bitch comfortable. She should receive additional outings, since in many cases she will have to relieve herself more frequently. Occasionally there is evidence of psychological change during the heat cycle. The bitch may become a little depressed, irritable and snappish, even though she ordinarily has a very sweet and tolerant personality. These changes are nothing to worry about as long as the dog is healthy and normal.

If you do not wish to breed your dog, you must keep her under control at all times. If you live in the country and your dog is used to a certain amount of freedom, you'll have to contain her during her heat cycle even if you live behind a fence. Otherwise she will attract every Romeo in the neighborhood, which will be a great inconvenience to both you and your neighbors, and dogs have been known to invent very clever methods of getting under, around and over fences. Many states have laws against allowing a bitch in season to run free, and if your dog gets caught at it, you may have to pay a fine.

If you decide not to spay your bitch and also not to breed her for the length of her reproductive life, you should know that her fertile years will not end in menopause. In other words, you will have to take the same precautions whether the bitch is two years old or ten years old, because at ten she can and will get pregnant.

A pregnant ten-year-old is in a rather precarious situation. It is often difficult for her to give birth. She may conceive only one or two puppies who grow to an abnormally large size, increasing delivery problems still more. Even if she manages to give birth normally, she may have trouble nursing her puppies, or the strain of pregnancy and lactation may be too great for her. The puppies may not do very well either. For the welfare of all concerned, it is advisable to put an end to a bitch's reproductive life by the time she reaches eight (in the giant breeds, perhaps younger).

At the other end of the scale is the very young bitch who goes into heat for the first time when she is six to eight months old. Some breeders feel that a dog will not go into heat until she is physically mature enough to handle pregnancy and lactation, and that it is therefore safe to breed a bitch coming into heat for the first time. We disagree with this. Most bitches experience their first heat cycle before they are a year old, when the great majority have not yet reached adulthood in terms of size and weight. Years ago, fanciers believed that breeding a dog at this time would stunt her growth. This is questionable, but pregnancy and lactation take a great toll on the young animal. As a general rule we advise not breeding before the second heat, and in some cases—for example, in the giant breeds—it may be worth waiting until the third.

Some breeders of Bulldogs and other dogs with large heads and narrow pelvises believe that it is best to breed these dogs at the first heat. The pelvis is thought to be more elastic at this time, which supposedly will minimize birth difficulties. But there is no scientific basis for this opinion.

If you are breeding your bitch for the first time, try to mate her with a stud who is competent and experienced. He will probably make no attempt to mount her until she is ready to accept him, and while she might shy away from a clumsy amateur, she will be much more inclined to accept the advances of an expert.

Establish the mating date well in advance, although, as we have indicated, this is not always easy to do. If the owner of the chosen stud does not know you, he may ask for pictures and the right to approve the bitch in person before any mating takes place. He will certainly ask for her pedigree.

At the first signs of bleeding, contact the stud owner again and tell him when your bitch will be ready. He will probably help you with travel arrangements so that her departure, arrival and return will occur at your mutual convenience. He will also ask that you have her examined by a veterinarian and declared free of infectious diseases. He will probably also ask for a blood test to establish that she is negative for canine brucellosis (see p. 258). You should ask for an equivalent clean bill of health for the stud and proof of his fertility. Both stud and bitch should be in excellent health, free of internal and external parasites and in prime condition.

Before you send off your bitch, get a contract from the stud's owner with all the conditions in writing. In exchange for the stud's service, his owner will probably ask for a fee or for the puppy of his choice from the litter. In the latter case, make sure that the contract specifies alternative arrangements should the bitch deliver only one pup. Have it in writing that the stud will not be mated with any other bitch on the same day or on the day preceding the day he is mated to yours, and that you are entitled to a second service at no additional fee if your bitch should happen to come home not pregnant. Other conditions vary and are worth discussing with your local kennel club.

The Mechanics of Mating

If you can arrange to be present at the actual mating of your bitch, then by all means do. There are several advantages. If this is your first time at the mating game, you will acquire valuable experience from the stud's owner or handler, who has presumably supervised matings before. Your presence will help keep the bitch calm, and you will be on hand to make sure that she is bred to the right stud. This is particularly important if you are having her mated to a popular male who has a long list of admirers waiting in the wings. Your presence will eliminate the possibility of a last-minute substitution.

Ideally the bitch should arrive at the stud's the day before she is mated, so she will have time to settle down. She should be mated on the second day after she indicates that she will accept the male. You can test this by placing your hand on her back at the root of her tail. If she stands rigid, and swings her tail to the side, this usually indicates that she is ready. Or you can present her to the male and see how she responds to him.

The male, whose claws should be trimmed short to prevent injury to the bitch, will mount, and male and female will be locked together in the tie. After the male has entered, he will lift his leg over the bitch's back and swing around so that the two animals are facing in opposite directions. If he has difficulty assuming this position naturally, the handler will help him because it is by far the most comfortable position for the dogs to be in. The tie will last anywhere from a few seconds to forty-five minutes, although on the average it is accomplished in twenty to thirty minutes. It should never be interrupted. The erect penis is locked into the bitch by muscular constriction at the opening of the vagina, and if the male is pulled out, he may be seriously injured.

There are many theories about the nature and purpose of the long tie, but there seems to be no biological necessity for it. A successful mating can be accomplished with a very short tie, or none at all if the handler is able to hold the erect penis at the lips of the vagina so that ejaculation occurs in the proper place. Naturalist David Mech has suggested that the tie actually has a social function in the wild. Because wolves only mate once a year, this provides the only opportunity for close physical intimacy between male and female and is therefore lengthened to make the "love" relationship or social tie stronger. The mating process is a matter of some importance for the entire pack, which forms a circle around the pair. Some of the more aggressive males engage in ritualized attacks of the male partner, while others defend him. All of this occurs, of course, while the male and female are standing back to back and interminably locked together.

It is sometimes desirable to mate two animals with a discrepancy in physical size. In such cases, the handler devises a platform of some sort to elevate the smaller animal. Some dogs, usually those who are kept outdoors, resent human interference, but they should be trained to accept the assistance of a handler. The general consensus is that if you throw two dogs in a pen and hope for the best, the chances of a successful mating are minimized. On the other hand, too much interference can also have a harmful effect. It's usually best to allow the animals to do what comes naturally and intervene only when there is trouble.

Some experts advise muzzling a nervous or skittish bitch to prevent her from attacking the male. Our opinion is that a bitch with such a temperament should not be bred at all and will not raise good-tempered pups.

Before the dogs are mated, they should be allowed to exercise and relieve themselves. The latter is particularly important for the female, who will not be allowed to relieve herself for several hours after the mating. Some experts believe that both dogs should be fed a large meal before they copulate; others hold that the stomachs of both should be relatively empty. It is up to the individual dogs and the handlers involved. Some young males become so excited that they vomit during copulation, but this bothers the human beings on hand more than the dogs.

Some males faint while they are copulating. This may indicate either that the stud is a little older than he ought to be or that he has been overused in the past months and needs a rest.

After mating, the female should be led away from the mating room or pen to rest for at least several hours before traveling home.

Some breeders feel that there should be a second mating, usually around forty-eight hours after the first. Although this is not necessary if the first mating occurs at the proper time, it helps ensure pregnancy if you have doubts about the exact day of ovulation.

Some people believe that if a misalliance occurs and the bitch delivers a litter of mongrels, her capacity for breeding purebreds is forever ruined. This is a myth. No litter has any effect whatsoever on puppies born later after a proper mating. Each separate litter is determined by the genetic input of both individual parents involved, not by past history. However, a misalliance can occur after a proper mating has been accomplished. As long as the bitch will accept a male, she may be fertile and may possibly conceive puppies from another father. For this reason, many stud owners insist on keeping the bitch for the duration of her acceptance period, even after a mating has been accomplished. The puppies born from this mating will reflect on the stud, and if inferior puppies are born, the stud's reputation will be damaged. In this case, you may be expected to pay a boarding fee.

Artificial Insemination

While this may seem like an attractive alternative to you if you don't want to send your bitch away, it is really only a useful procedure when bitch and stud absolutely refuse to mate. In this case you must obtain a form from the AKC and follow Kennel Club restrictions. First of all, you will save nothing on travel because both bitch and stud must be present for the artificial mating. Also the same veterinarian must perform the extraction and insemination. These rules help eliminate the chances of a faulty mating and make sure that the puppies will be registerable.

Pregnancy

The dog's period of gestation varies from fifty-five to seventy days, with the average around sixty-three days. It is hard to determine the exact day of delivery, since the total gestation period is measured from the day of conception, which is not necessarily the day of mating.

Toward the end of gestation, the bitch will develop swollen breasts. If she is uncomfortable, have your veterinarian examine her. You will, of course, be giving her extra food (see p. 80), and you must also make sure that she does not lie around and get lazy. An easy delivery is determined partly by her muscle tone. Don't let her overexercise at any one given period of time, but make sure she gets small doses of exercise at various periods during the day. She will also need to relieve herself more frequently than usual, so if she lives inside, you will have to walk her more often.

False Pregnancy

This is not considered abnormal in dogs. It may occur whether or not the dog has been mated and is particularly disappointing when the owner has been expecting a litter of puppies. He sits out the gestation period with his bitch and suddenly realizes that nothing is happening, that a conception never actually occurred. False pregnancy is not psychological in dogs as it is thought to be in humans but is the result of physical events in the body. When the ovum is exuded from the ovary, a small body of tissue called the corpus luteum, which secretes the hormones of pregnancy, is formed in its place. The corpus luteum is more persistent in dogs than in many other animals and continues to secrete hormones for a month to two months at a time. This causes the false pregnancy, which usually occurs a month or two after the regular cycle. In most cases, the changes are minor—a slight enlargement of the mammary glands which disappears after a week or so.

In some cases, however, the bitch will develop milk, build a nest for the puppies and mother old shoes or little stuffed toys. In extreme cases, she will suffer a false pregnancy after every heat cycle and her mammary glands will become quite enlarged and painful. Lactational changes in the mammary glands may cause little cysts to form from clumps of mammary tissue that have become occluded, scarred and possibly infected, and sometimes the encysted glands have to be surgically removed because the veterinarian is unable to tell by a simple examination whether these lumps are cysts or malignant tumors. A false pregnancy should last no longer than a week or two. If it continues, the veterinarian should examine the dog to find out if anything else is wrong.

Although false pregnancy is not considered abnormal, in severe cases the veterinarian may recommend spaying, which will put an end to the condition. Severe, prolonged and frequent false pregnancies are physically and psychologically exhausting for both dog and owner.

Whelping

Three weeks after breeding, the bitch should be examined by the veterinarian to determine if she is really pregnant. A week or so before the puppies are born, the bitch will begin to nose around the house looking for a whelping place. If you want to avoid the possibility that she will choose the floor of your closet and whelp on your best pair of sneakers, you should provide a place for her and get her used to it.

If your bitch is rather small, a cardboard box from the grocery store is quite adequate. Cut away one side, leaving only a low ledge so the puppies won't get out but the bitch can climb in and out easily. For a larger bitch, you will probably want to supply a wooden whelping box, which is easy to make. The box should be at least one and one-half times as long as the bitch and twice as wide so that she can lie down lengthwise to nurse the puppies and extend her feet to the side. The box should not be so big that the puppies can wander off and get lost, nor so small that the bitch is uncomfortable. If the bitch is very large and clumsy, build a rail around the inside of the box so that any puppies who manage to stray away from the center will not be inadvertently smothered under the bitch's body. Again, three sides of the box should be tall and the fourth merely a ledge.

Cover the bottom of the box with old sheets or a blanket with a tight weave so that the puppies cannot get caught in it. Torn newspapers are convenient because they are cheap, easy to dispose of and usually in ample supply. Whatever you put in the bottom of the box will have to be changed frequently. If you use blankets as the whelping bed, cover them with newspapers to soak up the blood and debris during the birth process.

About a week before the delivery, the bitch should be reexamined by the veterinarian. At this time he may want to take an X-ray. This will not harm the bitch or fetuses at this late stage of pregnancy. Twelve to twenty-four hours before delivery, the bitch will become restless and try to build a nest, shredding and tearing at the newspapers that you have provided for her. She will usually lose her appetite. At this time her temperature will drop to 98°–100°F. As soon as her temperature drops, call the veterinarian to warn him of the impending delivery so that he can prepare to be on hand for emergency calls or an emergency visit.

Have the following equipment on hand:

A stack of newspapers
Nylon thread

A sharp pair of scissors

A stack of clean linen, including baby receiving blankets, towels and washcloths

Several cans of simulated bitch's milk

Two or three small animal nursers or baby bottles with preemie nipples for larger breeds

Cotton balls

Mineral oil

As the hour of delivery nears, the bitch will become increasingly restless, tearing and scratching at the paper in her whelping box, pacing back and forth. If you are very attentive, you might see a whitish mucoid discharge coming from her vagina, which indicates that the cervix is dilating. Next you will notice that the bitch is straining as though to expel something, which is in fact exactly what she is trying to do. She may become anxious and preoccupied, and you can help her through this period by stroking her gently and talking to her in quiet, soothing tones.

Before the puppy appears, you will see a bubblelike sac at the vulva. The mother may reach around and rupture this sac with her teeth. Shortly thereafter, the puppy's head or feet will appear as the mother contracts and forces the puppy out. If the puppy appears feet-first, this is not considered abnormal, but it may cause a problem if the puppy's head is not forced through the birth canal. You can help by grasping the feet with a clean washcloth or towel and gently pulling with the contractions. Pull upwards and out. As you start to feel the puppy coming through the pelvic canal, lift down. Usually the puppy will flop right out; you can then remove the membranes from his mouth and make sure that he starts to breathe.

Don't be afraid to intervene if necessary. If the puppy appears in a breech position, the chances are you will be able to deliver it much faster than the mother could. Sometimes the puppy will be completely through the pelvic canal and just sitting in the vaginal tract. Because the impaction of the puppy against the pelvic canal is gone, contractions may stop, even though the puppy is only partially delivered. If contractions cease or if the delivery seems to be taking a long time, you *must not wait for contractions*; you must continue your efforts to extract the puppy, who is no longer receiving oxygen from the umbilical cord. All traction must be exerted *gently*, for the sake of both the dam and her pup. But time is of the essence. You have only a few minutes to accomplish the delivery and still have a chance of delivering a puppy who is both alive and healthy. Throughout this process, *you must never insert your fingers into the vagina. If you do so, you may contaminate the uterus by introducing foreign bacteria.*

Normally, the mother will remove the sac from each puppy and clean the puppy vigorously with her tongue. Some breeders object to the fact that the bitch eats the placenta and either try to remove it or limit the number that she consumes. But since we don't yet fully understand the purpose of this act, we feel this is one area where it's best to leave well enough alone and do not recommend removing the placentas.

In some cases, the mother will not remove the sac from the puppy. If this happens, you must do it. Tie the umbilical cord with nylon thread about a half-inch away from the puppy's abdomen and cut below the thread with a sharp pair of scissors. Considering all the bacteria present in the whelping environment, there is no need to sterilize either the scissors or the umbilical cord. *The most important thing is to get the membranes away from the puppy's face and head and to swab out the puppy's mouth* If the puppy looks weak and isn't making breathing motions, put it in a clean towel and rub vigorously along its sides. Most owners go too easy, so remember that you have nothing to lose by rubbing hard.

Throughout the delivery process, you should be constantly reassuring the mother. In between puppies, offer her a few swallows of water. Do not give her great quantities and do not encourage her to eat a meal. Most bitches will refuse to eat until they are finished whelping. It's hard to tell exactly when this is unless you have had an X-ray taken and know how many pups to expect. The bitch can go many hours between births, and after each, contractions may not begin again for some time. You will have to wait and watch the bitch. If she goes into labor again, you know another puppy is on the way.

When the bitch has finally delivered the last puppy, remove all soiled newspapers from her whelping bed and replace them with fresh. Try to do this without disturbing the bitch and her puppies, for by this time she should be curled up around them and the puppies should be happily nursing. Call the veterinarian to tell him the news and ask him when you should bring the dogs in for examination. He will want to examine the bitch to make sure that she has expelled all the placentas, and he will want to check the puppies for any abnormalities.

Twenty-four to forty-eight hours after birth, the bitch's appetite will return to normal, and there is nothing wrong with putting her back on the same diet she ate before whelping.

·   ·   ·

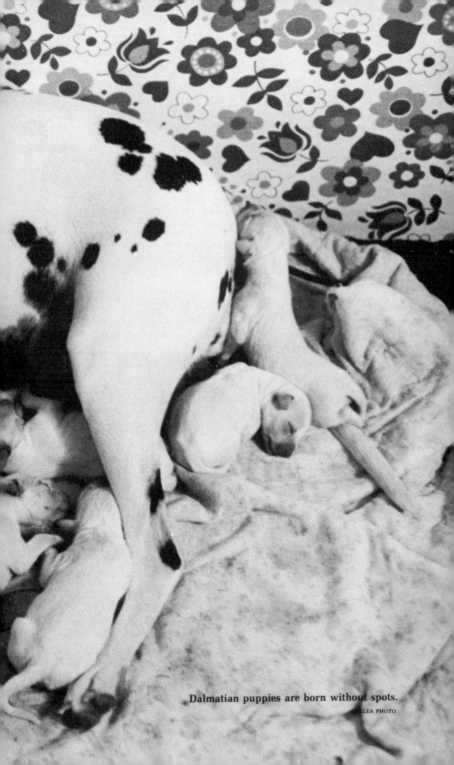

Dalmatian puppies are born without spots.

Signs of Trouble

1.   A pregnancy exceeding seventy days has gone on too long, and a veterinarian should be consulted.

2.   Most bitches will not make much noise during labor. If the bitch screams and acts like she is in a lot of pain, this may mean that she is impacted and the puppies can't be born normally. Consult the veterinarian.

3.   If the bitch strains longer than an hour and a half without producing a puppy, consult the veterinarian.

4.   If the bitch is straining and straining and you see a bubble at the vaginal opening, but no pup is produced, call the veterinarian. This usually means that the puppy is in the birth canal but for some reason can't be delivered normally.

5.   If the bitch is in labor for an hour or less before delivering the first puppy and you see a greenish discharge, consult the veterinarian. This is a sign that the placenta has become detached from the puppy, who is then essentially without an oxygen supply. If a puppy has already been born, the greenish discharge may be the placenta following and is not necessarily cause for concern.

6.   After the bitch has delivered one or two pups, contractions may stop for a period of three hours or more. This may mean simply that there are no more puppies, or it may mean that something has gone wrong. The veterinarian should examine the bitch to determine whether or not there are additional puppies still in utero.

7.   There is always a certain amount of bloody discharge during the birth process, but if you observe an extreme amount of hemorrhaging and the dog's gums and tongue are pale, call the veterinarian.

8.   If a puppy is partially delivered and you are unable to deliver the puppy the rest of the way, call the veterinarian.

9.   A day or so after delivery, you may notice a malodorous discharge. This indicates that one or more of the puppies is dead and has not been delivered. Consult the veterinarian.

10.   If the puppies cry excessively or start to nurse and then fall off the nipples, this may mean that the bitch is not producing enough milk. Have the mother examined to determine whether she does have milk. There are things that can be done to stimulate milk production.

11.   If her nipples are extremely hard, if they look discolored or bluish, or if the fluid looks like anything other than milk, you have cause for concern. These are symptoms of *mastitis* (see p. 253).

12. If the mother seems excessively restless, you should be concerned. This can vary a lot because a nervous dog is often quite upset. Any extreme behavior, however, should be reported to the veterinarian. For example, the bitch may constantly be licking the puppies or trying to carry them from place to place.

The Puppies

The puppies should start nursing within two hours after they are born. Often they will nurse immediately and should certainly be encouraged to do so. You can help the situation by talking to the mother in between births and keeping her as relaxed as possible so that she has the opportunity to get used to the puppies. The antibodies that give the puppies their early immunity are in the first milk or colostrum, and can be absorbed by the puppies only in the first one or two days. If the first milk appears to be orange-colored or serum-like, do not be alarmed. This is the normal color and consistency of colostrum.

First and Second Weeks   The puppies will be completely sustained by the mother.

Third Week   The puppies start to open their eyes and move around. At this time, you can begin supplemental feedings, especially if the litter is very large. Start by giving the puppies canned milk with a little broth and some strained baby meats mixed in. Dip your finger in this mixture and let the puppies suck it off. As they get a little older, they can be encouraged to lap the food from a pan.

Fourth Week   Start to wean the puppies by separating them from the dam during the day. Feed them four meals during the day and let them nurse at night. One meal should consist of a combination of dairy products: canned milk, cottage cheese, yogurt and cooked eggs. Three meals should consist of baby beef, veal or lamb mixed with baby cereal. The strained meats can be either plain or mixed with vegetables. The mixture should be moist and runny.

Fifth and Sixth Weeks   As soon as the puppies are eating well, start them on puppy feed mashed up well with the mixture you used during the preceding week. Again, the mixture should be very liquid; if necessary add extra canned milk or broth. As the puppies get older, increase the amount of feed and decrease the amount of liquid until weaning, which occurs at around the end of the sixth week.

Beginning of the Seventh Week   Take the puppies away from the dam completely. They should be eating well by now and can slowly be introduced to a regular puppy diet consisting of one part canned food mixed with three parts moistened-down feed. Lean meat, cooked eggs and canned milk may be added as supplements (see p. 77).

Some bitches encourage weaning, others do not, but most go back to nursing if given the opportunity. At four to five weeks the puppies start cutting their baby teeth, so it's imperative to start the weaning process whether the mother wills it or not.

Once the puppies are weaned, the mother's mammary glands may be swollen and sore because she will continue to lactate until the sucking stimulation she received from the puppies has been absent for a while. Usually the glands dry up on their own. You can apply cold packs for fifteen minutes three times a day, or massage gently with camphorated oil three times a day if they seem to bother her. If they are excessively sore, consult your veterinarian.

NOTE: All dietary changes should be accomplished slowly over a period of several days to prevent digestive upsets. Should the puppies develop diarrhea, consult your veterinarian immediately.

Seven to Eight Weeks   It's time for the puppies to leave home.

Natal and Postnatal Problems

Eighty to 90 percent of all pregnancies, births and nursings go well, which is a high percentage of success considering the genetic game of "Mastermind" that man has played in taming of the canine species. It's one of the great miracles of nature that the bitch has any maternal instinct left at all. Yet she does. As a general rule, we believe it is best to defer to these instincts. Many bitches have such strong maternal instincts that they resent interference, and we believe they should be respected as far as possible. Do what's necessary. Provide the basic elements of comfort, security and affection, and all will go well. But on the other hand, you have more to lose than the natural world, which is basically indifferent to the survival of the she-wolf and her cubs. And there are moments when you should step in.

Abnormal Delivery

In some cases the bitch is unable to whelp normally. This occurs most commonly with breeds prone to birth difficulties, such as the Bulldog. In addition to the fact that large-headed pups have to descend through a narrow pelvis, the conformation of the Bulldog's jaw sometimes makes it difficult for the bitch to sever the umbilical cords without injuring the pups. This last problem can be solved by removing the pups from their sacs yourself.

Abnormal presentation of the pups can also cause delivery problems. For example, the puppy appearing in "neck presentation" may call a halt to the whole process. An obstruction in the birth canal may prevent delivery; delivery may also be prevented if the bitch becomes overtired from straining for long periods of time.

In some cases, the veterinarian may be able to extract one puppy with forceps, and normal delivery of the succeeding pups will follow. In other cases, he may choose to perform a Caesarean section and remove the puppies through an abdominal incision. Some veterinarians routinely plan on Caesareans for Bulldogs and other breeds with similar problems.

Mastitis

This is a bacterial infection of the mammary gland. The glands become bluish and hard, and the milk may be discolored or blood-streaked. Sometimes the milk shows no signs of infection, even though it is present. If the mother displays the obvious symptoms, or the pups have difficulty nursing, have the bitch examined by the veterinarian. If the condition is allowed to progress, it will become generalized; the mother will become increasingly ill and the puppies may sicken and die. It can be treated with hot packs and antibiotics. In mild cases where only one or two glands are infected, these teats may be bandaged and the puppies allowed to nurse on the bitch's healthy teats.

Eclampsia

This may occur before delivery but is far more likely to occur after the bitch has delivered and is already nursing. Frequently it occurs as much as two to three weeks after the puppies are born. The exact cause is unknown. Since some bitches are predisposed to the condition, it may be a genetic inability to metabolize calcium. During lactation, a lot of calcium goes into the milk for the puppies, and the bitch becomes depleted. Vitamin and mineral supplements fed to the bitch during pregnancy and lactation may prevent it, but oversupplementation may *cause* it to occur. Therefore, all such supplements must be carefully regulated by the veterinarian.

The symptoms are frightening. The bitch first becomes restless and uncomfortable. Her jaw muscles become rigid, which gives the appearance of rabies. As eclampsia progresses, she develops a fever, her muscles stiffen, and she goes into convulsions. She requires immediate emergency treatment by the veterinarian. The puppies must not be allowed to nurse for at least a day, possibly longer. When nursing is resumed, the puppies should receive supplemental feedings of simulated bitch's milk. A bitch who has had eclampsia probably should not be bred again.

Metritis

This is an acute infection of the uterus caused by the retention of a placenta or dead fetus. Symptoms are fever, listlessness, depressed appetite, excessive thirst, vomiting and diarrhea. The bitch may show no interest in her puppies. She may not be able to produce enough milk, and in any event her milk will be toxic. She requires immediate veterinary attention and must be separated from her pups.

Fading Puppy Syndrome

"Fading puppy syndrome" is a catchall for a wide range of diseases. Some are infectious, such as herpes, which starts as a low-grade vaginitis in the bitch and is transmitted to the puppies during birth. The course of the disease is swift and almost always fatal, with the puppies dying two to three days after delivery. Bacterial infections progress more slowly. The puppy cries, eats poorly and has diarrhea, which may develop into bloody diarrhea or hemorrhagic gastroenteritis. If the puppies are ailing in any way, call the veterinarian at once.

The Orphaned Pup

Occasionally the bitch dies or becomes ill during or soon after the puppies are born, or she simply rejects them. Usually, if the bitch gives birth naturally in her home environment with her people around to soothe and protect her, she will do all that is expected of her. This is why most veterinarians will not deliver a bitch in their offices unless it is absolutely necessary to save the life and welfare of mother and/or pups.

In the unnatural surroundings of the doctor's office, the bitch may become frightened and confused. This occurs most often when she has been delivered via Caesarean section and not gone through the birth process. The natural progression of her instinctive behavior has been interrupted. She is groggy from anesthesia. She doesn't seem to recognize these strange little creatures crawling all over her.

The first step is to console her. Take the puppies away for a brief period of time. Then introduce them gradually, one at a time, allowing the mother to clean and inspect each puppy separately if she will do so. All the while, talk to her in quiet, soothing tones. If she still refuses to nurse, you must attach the puppies to her teats, hold her down and talk to her while the puppies suckle. It is essential that they nurse early in order to get the colostrum. Often, after the first day of strangeness, the hormones in the bitch's body stimulate her maternal instinct, and she'll be more than willing to take over.

However, if she cannot nurse or continues to reject the puppies, you will have to care for them yourself. This is why we recommend having several cans of simulated bitch's milk on hand. It can be purchased from a veterinarian or a pet store. If you are caught without a supply, you can temporarily substitute a homemade formula. The Gaines Institute recommends ½ cup cow's milk, ½ cup cream and an egg yolk. Your veterinarian may have other ideas.

The major advantage to the commercial formula is that it is remarkably similar to the milk that the puppies would receive from the bitch herself, meeting all caloric requirements while supplying nutrients in the correct proportion.

How Much to Feed

Amounts vary, depending on the size, age and breed of the puppy and individual differences. As a rule of thumb, underfeed for the first two to three days, then increase amounts until after each feeding each puppy's abdomen is nicely round without being bloated. The following chart gives average quantities of formula to be fed every day. Check with your veterinarian to make sure that recommended amounts are right for your puppies.

When the puppies are three weeks old, you can start the weaning process. Continue to feed the formula and at the same time start the puppies on solid food as described on page 77.

NEWBORN PUPPY FEEDING CHART

WEIGHT OF PUPPY	AMOUNT PER DAY	NUMBER OF FEEDINGS
2 ounces	4 teaspoons	8
4 ounces	8 teaspoons	8
6 ounces	4 tablespoons	8
8 ounces	6 tablespoons	6
12 ounces	10 tablespoons	5
1 pound	¾ cup	5
2 pounds	1 cup	4

NOTE: As the puppies grow older, amounts should be increased. For example, a two-pound newborn eats less than a two-pound two-week-old puppy.

How to Feed

Very small puppies can be fed with an eyedropper, but this is probably the least effective method. It is too easy to get too much in the puppy's mouth at once, which will cause him to sputter and choke. If milk gets in his lungs, he may develop pneumonia. *If you use an eyedropper, feed very slowly, squeezing only a drop or so at a time into the puppy's mouth.*

For years veterinarians recommended doll-size baby bottles for small puppies, but these days it's hard to find doll bottles with adequate nipples. Probably the best solution is to get two or three of Borden's *small-animal nursers*, which may be purchased from pet stores or through your veterinarian. The small-animal nurser is designed especially for puppies, with nipples tough enough to withstand their teeth and holes small enough to ensure that the puppy doesn't suck too much milk at once.

Place the puppy on his stomach in your lap. Wrap your left arm with a soft towel or baby receiving blanket, and curve it around so that the puppy may knead your arm with his front feet. Open the puppy's mouth with your right hand, and inject the bottle with your left, holding it high enough so that the nipple is completely filled with milk and the puppy won't suck air. When he is finished, burp him on your shoulder like a baby. Take a small piece of cotton dabbed in mineral oil and rub his abdomen and backside. Ordinarily the mother's tongue will do this to provide the stimulus for elimination.

Another feeding method is the stomach tube. You measure off a tube the length of the puppy from his mouth to his stomach, mark the correct length and then insert it through his mouth down the back of his throat to his stomach. This is much quicker than the nursing method, and if you have a large litter of puppies, it may save you a lot of time and work. Also there is less chance the puppy will get milk in his lungs and develop pneumonia. The disadvantages are that it's a little scary and not very aesthetic and that it requires some skill. If you decide to use this technique, have your veterinarian show you how to do it properly.

Signs of Trouble

The best way to tell if your puppies are receiving the proper nourishment is by the color and consistency of their stools and urine. The stool should be brown or yellow-brown, never green, whitish or clear in color. It should be of a pastelike consistency, neither watery nor lumpy. The urine should be clear or pale yellow. Dark urine is a sign of trouble.

Keeping Puppies Warm

The greatest danger to the newborn puppy is that he will get chilled. Normally the mother keeps her puppies warm with her own body heat, but when there is no mother, heat must be provided. Keep the puppies in a box with a heating pad covered with receiving blankets or a towel in the bottom. There are also special heating pads made especially for this purpose; these are impenetrable by puppy teeth and eliminate the problem of electric shock. Make sure the cord is completely buried; better yet, make a hole in the box and slip the cord through so that you can plug it in on the other side of the box. Puppies are also very sensitive to heat, and they burn easily. For this reason, it's best to cover only half the bottom of the box with the pad. If the puppies get too warm, they can scoot over to the other side of the box and cool off.

An alternative to the heating pad is a gooseneck lamp with a 150-watt bulb. Twist the neck of the lamp so that it heats only about half the box at a time. The only difficulty with this method is that it is hard to control the amount of heat, and you'll have to check fairly often to make sure that the temperature is maintained correctly. The temperature for newborns should be maintained at about 90° F., and should be reduced gradually about 10° each week until the puppies are four weeks old and can withstand temperatures of about 70°.

Inoculations

If the puppies have been unable to nurse normally, consult the veterinarian about early serum injections which will help them fight off infection. When you sell each puppy, make sure that you explain to the new owner that the puppy is *not* thoroughly immunized, and that a veterinarian should be consulted immediately.

Disorders of the Reproductive System

● *Canine brucellosis* is the scourge of the modern breeder. It is a bacterial disease caused by *Brucella canis*. One of the great problems is that the animal can have it or carry it and appear to be normal. Usual symptoms are abortion in the female and testicular swelling in the male. The animal can eventually become sterile from the disease, due to chronic infection. Genital contact is a frequent source of infection, or contact with the excretions of an aborting animal.

There is no vaccine against brucellosis, and there is no reliable cure. After the major infection is over, the animal may carry the organism and look perfectly healthy, but in fact he is capable of infecting a great many other dogs and even people. The only way to control the disease is by isolating the animal or having him put down. The owner must realize the public health aspect of the disease. There are a few documented human cases, usually in people who work in kennels where they are exposed to the disease in high concentration. It is a serious disease in humans, with fever, general malaise and other complications.

Brucellosis is becoming more and more prevalent, especially in large breeding kennels. Good breeders will carefully screen any new animals coming into their kennels to prevent an infected dog from contaminating the whole lot. Animals can be tested for brucella. *All* owners of breeding stock should demand brucella tests before allowing a mating to take place.

The Male

● *Cryptorchidism* is a condition in which one or both testicles are retained in the abdomen. Before birth, the testicles normally migrate from the abdomen down through the groin area and out into the scrotum. Sometimes one or both testicles fail to migrate and are retained in the abdomen or the groin area. This in itself causes the dog no real discomfort, but a retained testicle is more inclined to become tumorous. Also, when the testicle is not in its proper place, the blood vessels, especially those to the abdomen, may become twisted, blocking off the blood supply and killing the testicle. For these reasons, the veterinarian usually recommends that retained testicles be removed.

A bilateral cryptorchid (two retained testicles) is sterile and therefore cannot be bred, but a unilateral cryptorchid with one testicle properly in the scrotum is not necessarily sterile. Because cryptorchidism is considered a genetic disease, such an animal should not be bred.

● *Infections* of the testicle, epididymis or prepuce may occur, but they are not common. Any abnormal swelling of the testicles or discharge from the penis requires veterinary attention.

Many male dogs normally have a small amount of yellow/green discharge from the prepuce. This is quite normal if not extreme in quantity. If the male shows signs of irritation (licks constantly, etc.), he should be checked.

● *Prostate disease* See page 141.

● *Traumatic injuries* may occur because the male genitals, unlike the female's, are in a prominent location. Any blow to the abdomen or genital area should be treated by the veterinarian.

THE FEMALE

● *Vaginitis* is an infected vaginal tract, which is treated much the same as the corresponding human infection—with antibiotics, suppositories and douching, and sometimes in the older female, with estrogen hormones. *Vaginal hyperplasia* is a problem common to female Boxers; the vaginal tissues, which normally swell during the heat cycle, become overly swollen. Another problem is the vaginal tumor, which seems to be hormone-related. Symptoms of vaginal problems are a sticky, yellowish or greenish discharge, a raw or bumpy vulva, or protrusion from the vaginal area. Most vaginal problems are not life-threatening but should be examined and treated by the veterinarian.

● *Pyometra* is one of the most common diseases in the older, unspayed bitch. The name describes the disease perfectly—*pyo-*, meaning "pus," and *metra*, meaning "uterus." It's a disease in which the uterus actually fills with pus. Hormonal changes in the older female can increase the likelihood of infection. The lining of the uterus thickens and becomes a perfect medium for bacteria. A vaginal infection can then ascend through the cervix and establish itself in the uterus.

The condition is serious. If the uterus swells extensively, it may rupture and cause peritonitis, which is fatal. More often, however, the uterus just sits there while toxins from the infection are absorbed into the bloodstream and circulate throughout the animal's body. The dog can develop a secondary kidney infection, culminating in kidney failure.

In the normal German Shepherd, the uterus is about the size of a thin pencil, but in pyometra it can sometimes grow to four or five inches in diameter. In some cases, the bitch will develop a potbellied appearance because of the increase in abdominal mass. In other cases, she will appear normal and the owner must depend on other signs. Symptoms are abnormal vaginal discharge, especially not in conjunction with the heat cycle; a change in the animal's behavior; listlessness; vomiting; diarrhea; and increased drinking and urination (because of the effects on the kidney).

Often the condition is not recognized until the animal is extremely ill. Surgery is imperative, but is not always successful.

• *Ovarian tumors* sometimes occur in the older bitch, and unfortunately the majority of these tumors are cancerous. Symptoms are abnormal heat cycles, severe bleeding during the heat cycle, an overly long heat cycle or a swollen vulva after the heat cycle is over. Surgery is the only successful treatment, but often by the time surgery is performed, the tumor has already metastasized.

• *Mammary tumors* present a serious problem, not only because they can spread but also because they sometimes involve a whole chain of mammary glands.

Birth Control

Birth control is by far the most controversial subject in this book, partly because human beings have a lot of feelings about the dog's sexual life which are not really justified, and partly because veterinarians (who are also human) disagree on this subject more than any other. The idea that dogs have sexual instincts and feelings is true; that they constantly think about sex is not true; that the female should be allowed to have at least one heat and/or one litter is a matter of controversy. Spaying brings up other questions. Does it cause more problems than it solves? What about birth-control medications? Are they safe? Are they effective? These are questions we hope to answer here.

If you are the owner of a valuable brood bitch, birth control is a continual source of agitation. You know exactly where, when and how you want to breed her. The problem is how to convey this information to her. Nine chances out of ten, she'd prefer any old neighborhood Romeo to the stud of your choice. Your only hope is to know when the dog is in heat and keep her behind lock and key until the cycle is over. If the bitch does happen to get out—and some are good at it—you have the option of an abortion. Ask your veterinarian about birth-control medications. He probably won't recommend them. Although these medications are generally considered safe, you don't want to take any chances with pills and potions that might affect a valuable dog's future breeding career.

If you never intend to breed your dog, you have exactly two options: you can have the dog spayed or castrated and put an end to the problem once and for all, or you can choose to live with the problem forever. We are not entirely objective on the subject, but below are the pluses and minuses of both choices.

The Spay Operation (Ovario-Hysterectomy)

Unless you have your dog spayed at one of the humane organizations, which is a very acceptable alternative if you can't afford to go elsewhere, you may be shocked at how much spaying costs. You can shop around for a good price, but we don't recommend it. The best thing to do is to go to a veterinarian that you know, trust and like. It is often a bad sign if a doctor charges a low fee for a spay in an area where you know that other doctors charge more. In this case, a good price may mean a bad job, performed under less-than-acceptable conditions by a doctor who practices inferior technique.

Spaying is a major operation, equivalant to a human hysterectomy. Ask the veterinarian if he uses gas anesthesia. In a young, healthy dog, other methods are acceptable, but certainly in an older dog, gas anesthesia is essential. It is also more expensive. But because it is safer, we prefer that it be used on the younger dog as well.

When to Spay   Timing is crucial. When a dog is spayed too early in life, she will not develop normal female conformation. A popularly accepted time is between six and nine months. This is convenient for the owner because it is usually before the first heat. It is also convenient surgically because the reproductive tract is well developed, yet most dogs haven't developed too much abdominal fat, which makes surgery more difficult.

Some breeders swear that a bitch should be allowed to have at least one litter before she is spayed. Others disagree. Most vets feel there is no proof that this is in any way advantageous. It may also leave you with the problem of an unwanted litter to dispose of.

To Spay or Not to Spay   That is the question. "Spaying," says Dr. David Senior, "has been recommended for permanent contraception by veterinarians mostly because no other suitable alternatives were available. A drug called Cheque has been developed by Upjohn which may be a suitable alternative." (More about Cheque later.) In the meantime, there are additional arguments for spaying:

1.   According to both Dr. McLellan and Dr. Senior, spaying performed prior to the first estrus is almost 100 percent effective in preventing mammary carcinoma.

2.   Spaying at any age will prevent uterine infection. If the uterus is not there, it cannot become infected, which is one of the most common problems in older, unspayed females.

3.   Spaying will prevent false pregnancies.

4.   Spaying will prevent the formation of ovarian tumors, which are hard to detect and may spread to other parts of the body. If the ovaries are not there, they cannot develop tumors.

For these reasons, we believe that the spayed female tends to live a longer and happier life than a bitch who is not spayed.

Objections to spaying are as follows:

1.   There is a slight risk of anesthetic death and surgical complications during the operation.

2.   There is the chance that the dog will become fat and lazy, although some vets believe that obesity has nothing to do with spaying. One reason people believe the operation makes the dog fat is that it is usually performed when the dog is about eight months old, just about the time her metabolism begins to slow down normally. She just doesn't need the calories she used to need when she was in the growing stages, yet the owner continues to feed her the same amount of food.

Cheque

Cheque is used to prevent heat in the mature female dog who has gone through at least one heat period. It may be started any time after the last cycle, but must be started *at least thirty days before the first sign of the next cycle. It must be administered daily*, either directly by mouth or in the dog's food. It may be used safely up to two years; whether it can be used for longer periods of time depends on future test results. When you stop administering the drug, the heat cycle will return on the average within about seventy days. Cheque may be administered with no ill effects in conjunction with a wide range of other drugs, including heartworm medication, worming medication, vaccinations and anesthetics.

In about 45 percent of the tested animals a few adverse side effects were noted, particularly among immature bitches. These included masculinization resulting in enlargement of the clitoris and mounting behavior; in some cases, a slight vaginal discharge, and in some cases, an objectionable body odor. Cheque cannot be administered to an immature bitch who has not experienced at least one heat period or to any bitch with a prior history of certain ailments—for example, kidney or liver disease. It is not recommended for the show dog or for dogs intended for breeding purposes.

Castration

This is the other 100 percent effective method of birth control. It should not be done before the dog has reached puberty or he may not develop male characteristics, but if it is performed when he is about eight months old, there is little risk of complication from the surgery. Castration tends to modify behavior, particularly if the dog is young and not set in his ways. Recent studies indicate that castration inhibits the male urge to roam; thus the operation is often recommended for the suburban dog who tends to wander off and get into fights.

People who own a male and a female dog often decide to castrate the male because it is a simpler and less costly operation than a spay. Dr. McLellan says, "If you have to choose, spay the female. If the female comes into heat, she may *still* drive the male crazy, even though he can't impregnate her. Some castrated males are still capable of mounting and trying to mate."

There is no real objection to castration, except that the male *does* tend to gain weight. Again, this may be controlled by increasing his exercise and decreasing his food. On the other hand, there are not the same disease prevention factors as there are in the case of the spay. For these reasons, we generally do not recommend castration.

13

THE TRAVELING DOG AND THE DOG AS BOARDER

Many knowledgeable dog owners believe that one can travel with a dog safely and successfully only in a car. This is not really true. Most dogs enjoy car travel, while other forms of travel cause stress. Also, the rules for car travel don't change much from year to year; the rules and regulations for other forms of travel are constantly being revised, and it is difficult to keep abreast of all the changes. You can no longer take your dog with you on Amtrak trains, for example. On the other hand, airlines have improved greatly. But however you decide to go, here is what you should take with you:

Mortality Insurance If you own a high-priced show dog, a valuable breeding animal or a dog who has had the benefit of thousands of dollars' worth of training, you should speak to your personal insurance agent about obtaining mortality coverage. There are a number of companies in the United States that provide this type of insurance, which covers the dog in the case of accidental death, whether he travels by car, train, plane or boat—or stays at home and gets in an accident.

Documents At home or abroad, your two most valuable documents are a current health certificate and a rabies vaccination certificate. Don't leave without them. The former includes the owner's name and address; the breed, sex, age and color of the dog; his tag number; the type and date of his rabies vaccination; the date of his distemper vaccination; and the dates of any other vaccinations that have been administered. It certifies that the dog is free from communicable disease and from contact with same. The place, date and signature of the veterinarian appear at the bottom. The rabies certificate contains much of the same information plus a sworn statement that the dog has been inoculated. In many places you will need this; the health certificate alone won't do.

Travel Equipment
Can opener
Leash and collar
Bedding, extra blankets, toys
Poopscoop and plastic bags
First-aid equipment (see Chapter 3)
Grooming equipment (minimally, a comb and brush)
Food
Medicines (including heartworm preventive medication)
Food and water dishes
Supply of fresh water from home (to prevent a reaction to a strange water supply)
Spoon for canned food
Health certificate
Certificate of rabies vaccination

Traveling by Car

Accommodations   Most state parks and many private campgrounds permit campers to bring their dogs. The usual requirement is that you keep the dog on a six-foot leash at all times. When you make reservations for campsites, find out if dogs are acceptable and inquire about regulations.

"Touring with Towser" is a complete directory of hotels and motels in the United States and Canada where dogs are allowed to stay. You may purchase a copy of this booklet for a small fee from the Gaines Dog Research Center, 250 North Street, White Plains, N.Y. 10625.

Traveling by Rail

CANADIAN NATIONAL RAILROAD

Dogs are allowed to travel in the baggage car only. Consult the conductor in advance, and he will let you know when you may feed and water the dog. Dogs may travel *either* in a kennel or on a leash if muzzled. Cost is based on (1) the way the dog is shipped (leash and muzzle costs more than kennel); (2) the weight of the dog plus his kennel; and (3) so much per travel mile.

Traveling by Ship

Travel by sea is rapidly becoming a thing of the past. There are only a few shipping lines that still book passengers, and among these, even fewer that accept dogs.

CUNARD LINES

The *Queen Elizabeth II* is the only Cunard ship that has accommodations for dogs. Dogs are not permitted in the cabins but may be housed in a special kennel area, where kennel maids will care for and walk them. You are permitted to visit your dog and walk him yourself if you choose. Cunard provides portable kennels, but they must be reserved in advance and are included in the cost of the dog's ticket.

The *Queen Elizabeth II* goes to England and France. In England, the dog is subject to a six-month quarantine. There are no exceptions. The dog will be met by a quarantine official and escorted to the appropriate kennel. If you and your dog are going to France, you may bypass the quarantine, but the dog is subject to French regulations.

Cost: One dog, $160; each additional dog, $230

MOORE-MCCORMACK LINES

Dogs are not allowed in the cabins, but all passenger ships provide portable kennels. The dog will be fed scraps from the kitchen, but we recommend that you supply an adequate quantity of the dog's normal diet. You are allowed to walk the dog on deck. A health certificate and rabies inoculation are required.

Cost: One way to South America, $75

One way to Africa, $100

MARCH SHIPPING PASSENGER SERVICES

The *Lermontov* and *Pushkin* are the two ships that travel to Europe, and they both book dogs. We warn, however, that these are not luxury liners. Ships stop in England, Germany and France, and dogs are subject to the regulations of the country where they go ashore. A health certificate and rabies inoculation are required. The ships have built-in kennels, and you must provide your own shipping crate. The price includes food, and you are allowed to walk the dog on deck.

Cost: $74

Traveling by Air

Until quite recently, traveling by air with your dog could be a risky business. Horror stories were common—dogs frozen, overheated, battered; dogs who died from a lack of oxygen in the baggage compartment. Many serious breeders wouldn't even consider the prospect of putting their dogs on a plane. With the Animal Welfare Act of 1976—further updated and improved in 1977—the horrors of air travel for canines have just about come to an end. The U.S. Department of Agriculture in conjunction with the Civil Aeronautics Board has established very strict rules for the protection and humane treatment of dogs and other animals during air transport. Minimum air temperatures have been established at between 45° and 85° F. Crating, scheduling, health regulations and age minimums are now enforced. Naturally enough, these rules affect *you*. In order to fly your dog anywhere in the United States, you must conform to the following standards:

● The dog must be at least eight weeks old and weaned for at least five days. Younger puppies are not accepted because they are subject to dehydration.

● Females with suckling young will not be accepted.

● The dog must be caged in a shipping container that meets strict standards for size, ventilation, strength, sanitation and handling (to be discussed in detail later in this chapter).

● The dog may not be left at the terminal more than four hours in advance of flight departure—under unusual circumstances six hours is permitted, if the proper advance arrangements have been made. Other exceptions are made at those airports with animalports or where you may leave your dog in the care of humane-society employees for a cost of about $10 a day.

● If the dog is less than sixteen weeks old and will be in transit for more than twelve hours, you must provide food and water along with written feeding instructions. If he is older than sixteen weeks and will be in transit for more than twenty-four hours, you must arrange to have him watered every twelve hours and supply food along with written instructions. If you plan a long trip, check with your airlines well in advance. Some will not attend to dogs during flight.

● Policies about health certificates are not uniform, but in the great majority of cases, a health certificate *will* be required by either the airline or state animal-health officials upon arrival. To be on the safe side, have your veterinarian examine your dog and supply you with a health certificate within ten days of the trip.

The following additional facts should also be taken into consideration:

● Short-nosed dogs are affected more than other breeds by the thin air in the cargo compartment. With these dogs it's best to keep trips short if you must fly at all.

● Air transport of females in heat is allowed but not recommended. For breeding purposes, of course, it is often necessary.

Kennels

If your dog is not properly caged, the airlines may refuse to accept him on the carrier. The cage may be constructed of fiberglass, metal, rigid plastic, wickerwork or wood. Wooden crates must have a strong plywood framework with joints that the dog cannot claw or bite his way through. The cage must be large enough for the animal to stand up, turn around and lie down with normal posture and body movements. Appropriate dimensions are determined in the following manner as established by the International Air Transport Association:

Length of the kennel	Length of the dog from his nose to the root of his tail, *plus* his height from ground to elbow joint.
Width of the kennel	Width across his shoulders times two.
Height of the kennel	Height of the dog in standing position, including ears if they are upright.

Exceptions are made for coursing hounds with a high spinal arch. These include Whippets, Greyhounds, Borzois and Italian Greyhounds, who are all subject to spinal injury if allowed to turn around in a confined area. These breeds must be shipped in containers small enough to prevent the dog from turning around.

The cage must be strong enough to withstand shipping and free from internal protrusions that might cause injury. It must have a solid, leak-proof bottom covered with absorbent material unless there is a wire false bottom separating the dog from the floor. In the latter case, the mesh should be tiny enough to prevent the dog from catching and ripping his toenails.

At least the upper and lower third of *two opposite walls* or *8 percent of each wall* must be ventilated. There must be rims or knobs on the outside of the cage to prevent the ventilation from being blocked.

The cage must be fitted with proper handles so that the shipper can lift it in an upright position. It should be marked "Live Animal" with arrows indicating which end goes up. If the dog must be fed and watered during the trip, access should be provided to allow for this without releasing the dog from the cage.

Virtually every domestic air carrier sells kennels that meet these rigid standards, and your best bet is to buy one. Kennels cannot be rented for sanitary reasons, but once you buy one, it should probably last. The only hitch is that you *must* purchase the kennel from the airline on which the dog is traveling at the time.

Kennels may be purchased in six sizes, from carry-on to extra large. Prices range on the average from $5 to $40.

World Wide Pet Transport

If you are baffled by air travel or don't have the time to make arrangements yourself, World Wide Pet Transport will do the job for you. This company has facilities in every major city in this country to ship your animal to airports in the United States and abroad. In most cases, they pick up the animal at your home and deliver it to the home at point of destination. They book the dog's flight, provide veterinary services, make sure that the dog has the proper documents and board the dog overnight if that is necessary. They also build outsize or jumbo kennels according to airline specifications and regulation requirements. You may purchase oversize kennels from this company, *or any other part of their services*, without purchasing the entire package of services.

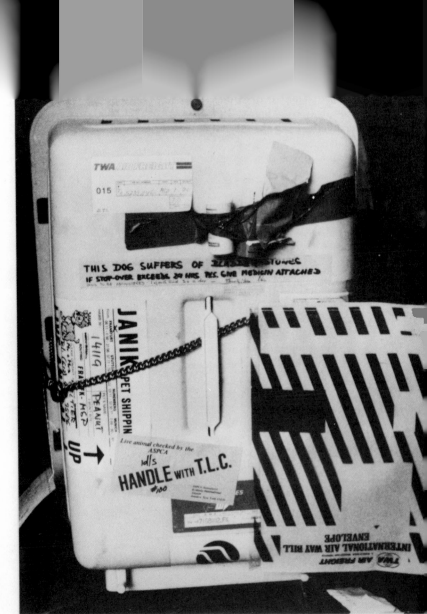

THIS DOG SUFFERS OF BLADDER STONES
IF STOP-OVER EXCEEDS 24 HRS. PLS. GIVE MEDICIN ATTACHED

JANIK PET SHIPPIN

UP →

Live animal checked by the ASPCA
HANDLE WITH T.L.C.

Richard Orzo, manager of the ASPCA Animalport at Kennedy International Airport, suggests that you attach explicit medical instructions to your animal's shipping kennel. In this case, the jar containing the medication opened in transit and the pills were lost, but instructions on the kennel made it possible for the Animalport veterinarian to represcribe without a long and difficult examination.

All orders and reservations must be made through the home office:

World Wide Pet Transport
96-01 Metropolitan Avenue
Forest Hills, New York 11375
Telephone: 212-544-8518
Call or write for an estimate of price.

The Animalport

The Animalport operated by the ASPCA at Kennedy International Airport was the first airport shelter in this country established for animal air travelers. Today, similar facilities have been opened at airports in Atlanta, San Francisco, Boston, Washington, D.C., and Hawaii. The Animalport sells crates, supplies information about airline regulations, and cares for animals during stopovers lasting anywhere from hours to days. Dogs are fed, watered and exercised. The dog's cage is cleaned, and he is examined for signs of illness. Veterinary attention is provided if necessary. Because the Animalports are operated by humane shelters, they are able to keep the cost of these services comparatively low.

Tips for Air Travel

As a general rule, dogs do not enjoy air travel. They have delicate noses, in some cases delicate breathing apparatuses, and in all cases delicate ears, which make air travel at best uncomfortable. The considerate owner will fly his dog as infrequently as possible and take him in the cabin with him whenever possible (which means whenever the airlines allow it).

If you have to ship the dog:

● Make sure he has attached to his kennel: health documents; food; feeding and watering instructions if necessary; your name, address and phone number; the name, address and phone number of the person who will pick him up, marked in bold letters: CONSIGNEE.

● Discuss tranquilizers in advance with your veterinarian. In no case give the dog human tranquilizers.

● Never muzzle the dog. If the dog is properly kenneled, a muzzle is unnecessary and will hinder his breathing.

● Avoid shipping your dog during peak traveling periods—rush

STEPHEN PROCUNIAR

Two puppies receive loving care at the Animalport.

hours and vacation and holiday times.

● Always reserve a kennel in advance. If possible, pick it up several days before the flight so the dog can play in it and get used to it. Put his blanket and a few familiar toys in it.

● Do not feed the dog for six to twelve hours before flight time, and give him only small amounts of water at a time.

● After the trip, release him from the kennel as soon as possible and allow him to relieve himself in an appropriate place. Give him food and water in small quantities only for the first two hours after arrival.

● During the summer, fly your dog only during the evening or early morning hours. Some airlines will not accept dogs if the temperature climbs too high.

● Always choose as direct a route as possible. If you change planes mid-route, you may be expected to pick up your dog in the baggage area and reboard him on the second airplane. If you change to a different airline, you will be expected to pay a second fee.

Insurance

The most important question to ask when you are making advance reservations is whether the airline will insure your dog—if so, for how much, and if the dog is worth more than the prescribed amount, whether additional insurance may be obtained. Often if you are flying with the dog in the cabin or air cargo section as excess baggage, the airline does not consider insurance necessary and provides none or a limited amount. In this case, you might want to take out your own insurance for him.

Another option is to ship the dog *air freight* or *air cargo* and buy insurance through the freight office. If you are making the trip with your dog, this is to your disadvantage, since it will cost you considerably more. You are giving up the $18 pet fee offered in conjunction with your ticket and must pay freight charges—usually based on dimensional weight of the kennel—and the insurance fees as well.

Insurance for pets on international flights is notably hard to come by. Some carriers require you to sign a paper releasing the airline of any responsibility.

Flying with Your Dog

Cost: $18

Dogs allowed in cabin; one pet per container and one container per cabin. The kennel must be small enough to fit under the seat (less than 8 inches high):	Allegheny American Braniff Eastern North Central Northwest	Pan American TWA United Continental Western
No dogs allowed in cabins:	Delta National Ozark Piedmont	Southern Golden West Air California

Additional restrictions*:

1. No dogs may fly in the cabin to quarantined areas.

2. If you take a dog, you are allowed no additional carry-on baggage.

3. No child under twelve years old is allowed to carry on a pet.

4. No pets allowed on commuter flights.

5. Reservations will *not* be confirmed until airline personnel inspect the pet and container.

Exceptions:

1. All airlines allow properly harnessed guide dogs in the cabin unless the dog is flying to a quarantine area. In the latter case, check with the airline for details.

2. Some airlines allow two puppies in one container if they are less than ten weeks old.

Dogs as Excess Baggage   If the airline will not accept dogs in the cabin or the dog is too large to fit under the seat, he flies in the cargo section as excess baggage, and you may have to observe additional restrictions. Again, check the airline.

Once you've got your dog where he's going, you have to be sure he meets state regulations. These vary from state to state, and since they are often difficult to come by, you'll find them listed at the end of this chapter.

---

* These vary somewhat from airline to airline, so check first.

Foreign Travel

It is not so easy to get dogs admitted to other countries. Some countries will not allow dogs to come in at all; others have quarantine systems that are very nearly prohibitive. These are the countries that are rabies-free. Since there is one chance in thousands that a properly inoculated dog can contract and introduce the disease, they choose a course of strong resistance. As of this date, they are as follows: in the Caribbean, Anguilla, Antigua, Barbados, Guadeloupe, Montserrat, Martinique, Nevis, St. Kitts, St. Lucia, St. Vincent, Aruba, Curaçao, St. Martin, Virgin Islands, Bermuda Islands, Jamaica, Bahama Islands; Australia; in Europe, Faeroe Islands, Finland, Ireland, Norway, Sweden, United Kingdom, Iceland; in Asia, Japan and Taiwan; in Oceania, Fiji, Guam, New Zealand, American Samoa, Saipan. Papua New Guinea also claims to be rabies-free, but is not yet included on the Public Health Service's official list.

Many countries in the world do admit dogs on both a permanent and temporary basis, but they usually demand a certain amount of paper work. For this reason we urge you to make all foreign travel arrangements *well* in advance. Many countries will not accept the dog unless he is accompanied by two separate certificates, both the veterinary health certificate and the rabies vaccination certificate. Because the health certificate includes information about rabies inoculation, some countries require this form only. However, *it is the rabies vaccination certificate and not the health certificate that will be required for reentry into the United States*. The important thing is to know all the necessary requirements and follow them explicitly. The consulates of the countries will be able to help you with this in advance, but the best source in our experience is the airlines.

When you return to the United States, your dog will be inspected by a quarantine officer at the airport or port of entry. In addition to having his rabies inoculation certificate, he must be free of all evidence of disease, including such symptoms as emaciation, skin lesions, nervous system disturbances, jaundice or diarrhea. If he shows any of these symptoms, the quarantine officer may give the owner a chance to have the dog examined by a veterinarian, and on the basis of the latter's findings will decide whether the dog can be admitted or whether he must be quarantined. When an apparently healthy dog has been exposed en route to a sick or dead animal suspected of having a communicable disease, the dog must be tested, examined, held for the appropriate period of time and admitted only after he has been judged free of the disease in question. Dogs arriving in containers considered unsanitary by the officer in charge will not be admitted until the container is cleaned.

If the dog has not been vaccinated, he must be upon entry, and then quarantined for a period of thirty days. If he has been vaccinated less than thirty days prior to entry, he must be confined by his owner until a period of at least thirty days since vaccination has elapsed. Dogs arriving from quarantined areas or areas where there is a high incidence of rabies are subject to additional restrictions to be determined by the quarantine officer in conjunction with the Center for Disease Control of the Public Health Service.

Exceptions   If the agent in charge of dogs destined for laboratory research can demonstrate that rabies vaccination will interfere with research, these dogs are admitted. So are dogs arriving from countries designated rabies-free by the Public Health Service, as long as they have lived in the rabies-free country for at least six months. So are puppies less than three months old, with the proviso that they are confined by the owner until they are three months old, then vaccinated for rabies, and confined for an additional one-month period.

Herd Dogs   Dogs imported for the purpose of herding livestock are subject to additional restrictions imposed by the Department of Agriculture. A veterinarian will examine the dog upon entry for evidence of tapeworm. If the dog has tapeworm, he will be dewormed and quarantined for a period of two weeks.

Boarding Your Dog

There are many occasions when you will want to board your dog—not the least of which is so you can go on vacation without him. Many people feel guilty about this. Because of the pervasive fear that kennels are disease-ridden, parasite-infested and otherwise cruel institutions, you may be inclined to leave your dog with friends or neighbors instead of boarding him. In defense of kennels, we would like to tell you the story of Princess, the thousand-dollar dog.

Princess was a Maltese, not a show dog but a quality, sweet-tempered dog, loved and slightly pampered by her owners. When they were making their vacation plans, they decided not to take Princess along. They were afraid that she would get ill or be mistreated in a kennel, so they left her with a very close friend. Somehow the front door of the friend's house got left ajar, and

Princess made her escape. The owners were immediately notified and placed an ad in the paper promising a reward of $1,000 for her return. Within a few days she was returned, and the grateful owners paid the bounty. In addition, the young wife who had originally received Princess as a gift from her husband was so certain that her little dog had been traumatized by the unfortunate experience that she cut short her vacation and flew home to comfort the animal. The moral of the story is this: A good kennel never leaves the door open. Incidentally, Princess was the beloved pet of Mrs. and Mrs. Matthew Margolis.

The solution is to find a kennel you can trust. A good kennel should have the following qualities:

1. You should be allowed to inspect it at any time; a kennel that is proud of its condition and reputation will allow this.

2. When you inspect, you should make sure that the kennel and runs are clean, with no offensive doggy odor and no droppings in the runs.

3. The kennel should have both indoor and outdoor runs and *no cages*.

4. The kennel must have someone on duty seven days a week, twenty-four hours a day, and a veterinarian either present or on twenty-four-hour call.

5. The kennel should have twenty-foot runs; this length offers adequate space for exercise and is optimal for drainage.

6. The kennel should provide a good diet. Ask what the dogs are fed, and if it deviates much from your dog's regular diet, make sure that you are allowed to provide a supply of your dog's own food.

7. There should be adequate and regular exercise every day.

8. You should be allowed to visit your dog at any time. You may not want to, but it is nice to know that the choice is yours.

9. Above all, make sure that the kennel has health requirements. This means that every dog is required to have a valid rabies vaccination (within two and a half years for modified live-virus vaccine); and a valid DHLP shot (within one year). DHLP stands for distemper, hepatitis, leptospirosis and para-influenza or kennel cough. The para-influenza vaccination is not recommended for most dogs except when they are traveling the show circuit or boarding and therefore will be exposed to a large number of other animals. Kennel cough is airborne, and easily passed from one dog to another in the kennel.

Many people are afraid that their dogs will be unhappy in the kennel environment. This usually occurs when the dog is allowed to grow up without ever having the kennel experience. We advise that every dog be kenneled for a brief period of time after he receives his first rabies vaccination when he is about four or five months old. This first boarding experience is a practice run and ought to be enforced whether or not you will be away from home. At this young age, the dog learns to adjust to the kennel environment, and as long as the kennel is a healthy and friendly place, he will have no trouble staying in it later when you really need it.

State Regulations*

Alabama Requires a health certificate and rabies inoculation not more than twelve months prior to entry. Puppies less than three months of age are exempt from rabies inoculation. Dogs arriving from quarantined areas or areas where rabies is known to exist will not be admitted.

> State Veterinarian
> P.O. Box 336
> Montgomery, Alabama 36109

Alaska Requires a health certificate and rabies inoculation (killed virus not more than six months; modified live virus not more than twenty-four months prior to entry). The health certificate must state that the dog has not been exposed to rabies. Puppies less than four months old are exempt from rabies inoculation. Dogs arriving from quarantined areas will be admitted only by special permit obtained from the Alaska state veterinarian.

> State Veterinarian
> P.O. Box 490
> Juneau, Alaska 99801

Arizona Requires a rabies vaccination certificate stating that the dog has been vaccinated against rabies (killed virus no more than twelve months; modified live virus no more than thirty-six months prior to entry). Puppies less than four months old are exempt.

> State Veterinarian
> Room 419, 1688 W. Adams St.
> Phoenix, Arizona 85007

Arkansas Requires a health certificate and rabies inoculation not more than twelve months prior to entry. Puppies less than three months old are exempt from these requirements.

> Director, Arkansas Livestock &
>   Poultry Commission
> 2915 S. Pine St.
> Little Rock, Arkansas 72204

* Regulations are subject to change.

California   Requires a certificate of valid rabies vaccination (killed virus within twelve months; modified live virus within twenty-four months prior to entry). *No health certificate is required*, but this document is recommended, since the owner may find it useful if he travels by airline. The dog must be apparently healthy. Puppies less than four months old are exempt from rabies inoculation and certificate.

> State Veterinarian
> Chief, Bureau of Animal Health
> Division of Animal Industry
> 1220 N Street
> Sacramento, California 95814

Colorado   Requires a health certificate and rabies inoculation not more than twelve months prior to entry. The certificate must state that the dog has not been exposed to rabies. Puppies less than three months old are exempt from rabies inoculation.

> State Veterinarian
> 1525 Sherman St., Room 416
> Denver, Colorado 80203

Connecticut   Requires a health certificate. The certificate must state that the dog does not originate from a quarantined area, that he has not been exposed to rabies within a hundred days prior to entry, or that he has been vaccinated against rabies not less than twenty-one days nor more than six months prior to entry. A copy of the health certificate must be forwarded to the Commissioner of the State Department of Agriculture in Connecticut. Show dogs or dogs entering the state for a period of thirty days or less are exempt from these requirements.

> State Veterinarian
> Department of Agricultural and
>   Natural Resources
> State Office Bldg., Room 287
> Hartford, Connecticut 06115

Delaware   Requires a health certificate and rabies inoculation. The type of vaccine used and date of administration must be stated on the health certificate. Puppies less than four months old are exempt from rabies inoculation. Animals arriving from quarantined areas will not be admitted.

> State Veterinarian
> State Board of Agriculture
> Drawer D
> Dover, Delaware 19901

District of Columbia   Rabies inoculation is required within one year prior to entry. Health certificate is not required. (For the address of a state veterinarian, see the listing for Maryland or Virginia.)

Florida   Requires a health certificate stating that the dog is free from infectious or communicable disease, did not originate within an area under quarantine for rabies, and has not been exposed to rabies within a hundred days prior to entry. Dogs who cannot comply with the above must be accompanied by a health certificate stating that the dog has been inoculated against rabies not more than six months prior to entry. Show dogs are exempt.

State Veterinarian
Director DAI
328 Mayo Bldg.
Tallahassee, Florida 32304

Georgia Requires a health certificate and rabies inoculation within six months prior to entry. Puppies less than three months of age are exempt from rabies inoculation. Dogs arriving from quarantined areas or areas where rabies is known to exist will not be admitted.

State Veterinarian
19 Hunter St., S.W.
Atlanta, Georgia 30334

Hawaii All dogs are quarantined for a period of a hundred and twenty days (four months). No exceptions are granted. Immediately upon arrival, the dog is transported by a quarantine inspector to the quarantine station on Honolulu. A registration fee of $10.00 plus a $2.45 per day maintenance fee (grand total of $304.00) must be paid in advance or upon arrival to: Department of Agriculture, P.O. Box 5424, Honolulu, Hawaii 96814. For details on quarantine write to:

Hawaii Animal Quarantine Station
99770 Moanalua Rd.
Honolulu, Hawaii 96701

Special cottages are available to guide dogs and their masters at a rate of $1.95 per day. Space may be reserved two to three weeks in advance of arrival through the Department of Agriculture in Hawaii.

State Veterinarian
Chief, Livestock Disease Branch
1428 S. King Street
Honolulu, Hawaii 96814

Idaho Requires a health certificate and rabies inoculation (nervous tissue vaccine within six months; chick embryo vaccine within twenty-four months prior to entry). Puppies less than four months of age are exempt from rabies inoculation. Dogs arriving from quarantined areas, or from within a fifty-mile radius of areas where rabies is known to have existed within the last six months, will not be admitted. Puppies less than four months of age arriving from quarantined areas will be admitted with a special permit to be obtained from the Bureau of Animal Health.

Chief, Bureau of Animal Health
716 Idaho St.
Boise, Idaho 83702

Illinois Requires a health certificate issued within thirty days, and a rabies inoculation (killed virus within six months; modified live virus within twelve months prior to entry). Puppies less than sixteen weeks old are exempt from rabies inoculation. Performing dogs, show dogs, and dogs consigned to hospitals are exempt. Dogs arriving from quarantined areas will not be admitted.

> Division of Meat, Poultry and
> Livestock Inspection
> Emerson Bldg., State Fairgrounds
> Springfield, Illinois 62706

Indiana Requires a health certificate issued within thirty days prior to entry, and a rabies inoculation within twelve months prior to entry. Puppies less than three months old are exempt from rabies inoculation. Dogs exposed to a rabid animal within the last twelve months prior to entry will not be admitted.

> State Veterinarian
> 700 N. High School Rd.
> Suite 200
> Indianapolis, Indiana 46224

Iowa Requires a health certificate and rabies inoculation (modified live virus, chick embryo vaccine according to the U.S. Public Health Compendium for Rabies Vaccine; all other licensed vaccines at intervals recommended by the manufacturer and approved by the U.S.D.A.). Puppies less than four months old are exempt from rabies inoculation. Performing dogs and show dogs are exempt from all requirements.

> Chief, DAI
> State Capitol Bldg.
> Des Moines, Iowa 50319

Kansas Requires a health certificate stating that the dog is free from symptoms of any communicable disease, that the dog has not been exposed to rabies, and that the dog has received a rabies inoculation (killed virus within twelve months; modified live virus within twenty-four months prior to entry). Puppies less than three months old are exempt from rabies inoculation.

> Livestock Commissioner
> Kansas Department of Agriculture
> 535 Kansas Ave., 7th Floor
> Topeka, Kansas 66603

Kentucky Requires a health certificate and rabies inoculation (killed virus not more than twelve months; modified live virus not more than two years prior to entry). Puppies less than four months of age are exempt from rabies inoculation. Show dogs entering for a period of ten days or less are exempt from health certificate requirements. Dogs arriving from quarantined areas, or areas where rabies is known to exist, will not be admitted.

> State Veterinarian
> 635 Comanche Trail
> Frankfort, Kentucky 40601

Louisiana Requires a health certificate and rabies inoculation (killed vaccine within one year; chick embryo vaccine within twenty-four months prior to entry). Puppies less than two months old are exempt from rabies inoculation requirements.

> State Veterinarian
> P.O. Box 44003, Capitol Station
> Baton Rouge, Louisiana 70804

Maine   Requires a health certificate showing that the dog has been vacci-nated against rabies within the last two years prior to entry. Any dog six months or older has ten days in which to obtain a license. All other import regulations have to do with dogs shipped into the state for resale. Dogs less than six months old are exempt from rabies inoculation.

> Division of Animal Industry
> State Office Bldg.
> Augusta, Maine 04333

Maryland   Requires a health certificate approved by your state veterinarian, stating that the dog is free from symptoms of infectious and contagious disease, that the dog does not originate from an area under quarantine for rabies, and that the dog has received a rabies inoculation (killed vaccine within twelve months; modified live virus within three years prior to entry). Puppies less than four months of age are exempt from rabies inoculation. Show dogs are exempt from health certificate.

> State Veterinarian
> DAI, Animal Health Section
> Symon's Hall, Room 220
> University of Maryland
> College Park, Maryland 20742

Massachusetts   Requires a health certificate and rabies inoculation within twelve months prior to entry. Show dogs are exempt.

> Division of Animal Health
> Leverett Saltonstall Bldg.
> 100 Cambridge Street
> Boston, Massachusetts 02202

Michigan   Requires a health certificate, a copy of which must be endorsed by the state veterinarian of the state of origin and sent to the state veterinarian of Michigan. Rabies inoculation is required within six months prior to entry if the dog comes from a point within a fifty-mile radius of an area where rabies is known to have existed within the past six months. Any such dog is also subject to a sixty-day quarantine at the discretion of Michigan's commissioner of agriculture. Dogs in transit and show dogs are exempt.

> State Veterinarian
> Animal Health Division
> 5th Floor, Lewis Cass Bldg.
> Lansing, Michigan 48913

Minnesota   Requires a health certificate and rabies inoculation. The health certificate includes the usual information plus the date of rabies inoculation, the product name, serial number, and the manufacturer's name. The date of the rabies inoculation must be within the required immunity period for the type of vaccine used. A copy of the health certificate must be sent to the Minnesota Livestock Sanitary Board by the state veterinarian of the state of origin. Performing dogs, show dogs, and dogs entering a veterinary facility for treatment are exempt.

> Secretary and Executive Officer
> Livestock Sanitary Board
> 555 Wabasha St., Room 300
> St. Paul, Minnesota 55102

Mississippi   Requires a health certificate and rabies inoculation within six months prior to entry. Puppies less than three months old are exempt from these requirements. Dogs arriving from quarantine areas or dogs who have been exposed to rabies will not be admitted.

> State Veterinarian
> 2431 North West St.
> P.O. Box 4389
> Jackson, Mississippi 39216

Missouri   Requires a health certificate issued within fifteen days of entry, and rabies inoculation (killed virus not more than one year; modified live virus not more than twenty-four months prior to entry). Puppies less than four months old are exempt from rabies inoculation. Performing dogs, show dogs, and dogs brought into the state for breeding purposes are exempt for thirty days as long as they are kept on leash in public places.

> Department of Agriculture
> P.O. Box 630
> Jefferson City, Missouri 65101

Montana   Requires a health certificate stating in addition to the usual information that the dog has been vaccinated against rabies in accordance with procedures recommended in the latest version of the U.S. Public Health Compendium for Rabies Vaccine. Puppies less than three months old are exempt from rabies inoculation. Dogs arriving from quarantine areas will not be admitted unless accompanied by a permit from the state veterinarian of Montana.

> State Veterinarian
> Animal Health Division
> Department of Livestock
> Capitol Station
> Helena, Montana 59601

Nebraska   Requires a health certificate valid for thirty days from the date of the examination. Requires rabies inoculation (killed virus not more than one year; modified live virus not more than two years prior to entry). Unvaccinated dogs must be vaccinated within thirty days. Puppies less than four months old are exempt.

> State Veterinarian
> Bureau of Animal Industry
> 301 Centennial Mall South
> P.O. Box 94787
> Lincoln, Nebraska 68509

Nevada   Requires a health certificate and rabies inoculation (nerve tissue vaccine within twelve months; modified live virus within twenty-four months prior to entry). Puppies less than four months old are exempt from rabies inoculation. Dogs in transit and show dogs are exempt. Dogs arriving from quarantine areas or dogs who have been exposed to rabies will not be admitted unless a special permit is obtained from the director of the Division of Animal Industry.

> Director, DAI
> P.O. Box 11100
> Reno, Nevada 89510

New Hampshire   Requires a health certificate for all dogs brought into the state for *resale*, and no puppy shipped into the state for sale or resale may be less than eight weeks old. All dogs are required to have a rabies inoculation (killed vaccine within one year; modified live virus within thirty-six months prior to entry). Puppies less than three months of age are exempt from rabies vaccination, but must receive a vaccination within thirty days after reaching the age of three months. Dogs arriving from quarantined areas or areas where rabies is known to exist will not be admitted.

> State Veterinarian
> H.H. DAI
> Park Plaza
> 85 Manchester St.
> Concord, New Hampshire 03301

New Jersey   Requires a health certificate. The certificate must state that the dog is free from rabies and other communicable disease, and if the dog has been vaccinated, the type and date of vaccination. Upon arrival the owner must forward the health certificate to the board of health in the district where the dog is located, which will then forward the certificate to the State Department of Health. Show dogs or dogs used for breeding purposes are exempt.

> Division of Animal Health
> Department of Agriculture
> P.O. Box 1888
> Trenton, New Jersey 08625

New Mexico   Requires a health certificate and rabies inoculation within one year prior to entry. Show dogs are not exempt. Puppies less than three months old are exempt from rabies inoculation. Dogs arriving from quarantined areas will not be admitted.

> State Veterinarian
> New Mexico Livestock Board
> P.O. Box 2048
> Albuquerque, New Mexico 87103

New York   Requires a health certificate issued within seven days of entry and stating that there is no evidence of infectious or contagious disease including external parasites and fungi, and that to the best of the veterinarian's knowledge the dog has not been exposed to such disease. A copy of the certificate must be forwarded to the director, Division of Animal Industry. Dogs in transit, dogs brought into the state for temporary residence and show dogs are exempt from the health certificate requirement, as long as they are properly restrained and under the immediate control of the owner or custodian.

> Director, DAI
> Bldg. #8, State Campus
> Albany, New York 12235

North Carolina   Requires a health certificate and rabies inoculation within twelve months prior to entry. Puppies less than four months old are exempt from rabies inoculation. Show dogs are exempt. Dogs arriving from quarantined areas will not be admitted except at the discretion of the state veterinarian of North Carolina.

> State Veterinarian
> 370 Agriculture Bldg.
> P.O. Box 26026
> Raleigh, North Carolina 27611

North Dakota   Requires a health certificate and rabies inoculation (killed virus within one year; modified live virus within two years of entry). Puppies less than four months old are exempt from rabies inoculation. Show dogs are exempt. Dogs arriving from quarantined areas will not be admitted, and the health certificate must state that the dog has not been exposed to rabies within a hundred days of entry. Hunting dogs must be accompanied by a health certificate stating that the dog has been immunized against rabies not less than thirty days prior to the date of entry.

> State Veterinarian
> North Dakota Livestock
>   Sanitary Board
> State Capitol Bldg.
> Bismarck, North Dakota 58501

Ohio   Requires a health certificate and rabies inoculation (within twelve months prior to entry or within thirty-six months prior to entry if rabies vaccine used is approved for this same interval by the Rabies Subcommittee, Animal Health Committee of the National Research Council of the National Academy of Science). Puppies less than six months old are exempt from rabies inoculation.

> Ohio Division of Animal Industry
> Room 702, 65 S. Front St.
> Columbus, Ohio 43215

Oklahoma   Requires a health certificate and rabies inoculation (nervous tissue vaccine within twelve months; modified live virus within twenty-four months prior to entry). Puppies less than four months of age are exempt. Dogs who have been exposed to rabies or dogs arriving from quarantined areas will not be admitted.

> Director, DAI
> 312 N.E. 28th St.
> Oklahoma City, Oklahoma 73105

Oregon   Requires a health certificate and rabies inoculation (killed virus not more than six months; modified live virus not more than thirty-six months prior to entry). Puppies less than four months old are exempt from rabies inoculation unless they originate from a quarantined area. Dogs arriving from quarantined areas will be admitted only by special permit obtained from the Oregon state veterinarian.

> State Veterinarian
> Animal Health Division
> 635 Capitol Street, N.E.
> Salem, Oregon 97310

Pennsylvania   Requires a health certificate and rabies inoculation (killed virus within one year; modified live virus within three years prior to entry).

The name of the vaccine, date of vaccination, and manufacturer must appear on the health certificate. Puppies less than twelve weeks of age are exempt from rabies inoculation. Dogs arriving from quarantined areas or who have been exposed to rabies within the last hundred days prior to entry will not be admitted.

> Director, DAI
> 2310 N. Cameron St.
> Harrisburg, Pennsylvania 17120

Rhode Island   Requires a health certificate and rabies inoculation (killed virus not less than thirty days nor more than six months; modified live virus within two years prior to entry). Puppies less than four months old are exempt. Dogs arriving from quarantined areas, or areas where rabies is known to exist, will not be admitted.

> Chief, Division of Animal and
>   Dairy Industry
> Room 207, Health Bldg.
> Davis St.
> Providence, Rhode Island 02908

South Carolina   Requires a health certificate and rabies inoculation not more than twelve months prior to entry. Dogs arriving from quarantined areas or areas where rabies is known to exist will not be admitted. The health certificate must further state that the dog has not been exposed to rabies.

> Director, Livestock-Poultry
> Health Department
> P.O. Box 218
> Elgin, South Carolina 29045

South Dakota   Requires a health certificate and rabies inoculation within the last twelve months prior to entry. Puppies less than three months of age are exempt from rabies inoculation.

> State Veterinarian
> S.D. Livestock Sanitary Board
> Sigurd Anderson Bldg.
> Pierre, South Dakota 57501

Tennessee   Requires a health certificate and rabies inoculation within one year prior to entry. Show dogs and puppies are not exempt. Dogs arriving from quarantined areas will not be admitted.

> State Veterinarian
> P.O. Box 40627, Melrose Station
> Nashville, Tennessee 37204

Texas   Requires a health certificate and rabies inoculation within twelve months prior to entry. Puppies less than four months of age are exempt from rabies inoculation.

> Executive Director,
>   Texas Animal Health Commission
> 1020 Sam Houston State Office Bldg.
> Austin, Texas 78701

Utah   Requires a health certificate and rabies inoculation (killed virus within twelve months; modified live virus within twenty-four months prior to entry). The date of the vaccination must be given and the name of the product used. Puppies less than four months old are exempt from health certificate and rabies inoculation.

> State Veterinarian
> 147 North 200 West
> Salt Lake City, Utah 84103

Vermont   Requires a health certificate and rabies inoculation, modified live virus within twelve months of entry. Puppies less than four months old are exempt from rabies inoculation. Dogs arriving from quarantined areas will not be admitted.

> Livestock Division
> 116 State St.
> Montpelier, Vermont 05602

Virginia   Requires a health certificate issued within ten days of entry, and a rabies inoculation within one year prior to entry. Puppies less than four months old are exempt from rabies inoculation. Dogs in transit or dogs brought into the state by a person who intends to make his residence in Virginia are exempt from rabies inoculation. Dogs arriving from quarantined areas or areas where rabies is known to exist will not be admitted.

> State Veterinarian
> Division of Animal Health
>   and Dairies
> Suite 600, 823 E. Main St.
> Richmond, Virginia 23219

Washington   Requires a health certificate stating that the dog is free of contagious and infectious disease and has been inoculated against rabies according to U.S. Public Health Department regulations and standards at the time of entry.

> State Veterinarian
> Division of Animal Industry
> 406 General Administration Bldg.
> Olympia, Washington 98504

West Virginia   Requires a health certificate and rabies inoculation not more than twelve months prior to entry. Dogs arriving from quarantined areas, or areas where rabies is known to exist, will not be admitted. A copy of the health certificate must be forwarded to the state veterinarian.

> Director, Animal Health Division
> Room E-102, Capitol Bldg.
> Charleston, West Virginia 25305

Wisconsin   Requires a health certificate stating that the dog has received a valid rabies inoculation, and that the time for revaccination has not expired prior to entry. Dogs less than six months of age are exempt from health certificate and rabies inoculation.

> State Veterinarian
> Animal Health Division
> 801 W. Badger Rd.
> Madison, Wisconsin 53713

Wyoming Requires a health certificate and rabies inoculation within twenty-four months of entry. Puppies less than four months old are exempt from rabies inoculation. Dogs arriving from quarantined areas will not be admitted.

> State Veterinarian
> Livestock Board
> State Office Bldg. East.
> Cheyenne, Wyoming 82002

THE AGING DOG

Old age varies in a dog, depending on the breed and also on the individual. Fifteen years is not an unusual life span for a poodle. The smaller breeds may live even longer. But an eight- or nine-year-old Great Dane or St. Bernard is already an old dog.

Dogs don't just get old and die. Like human beings, they often die slowly, and it is your responsibility to see that your dog makes the transition as comfortably as possible. With the advice and help of your veterinarian you will be able to care for the animal and provide him with the right medications. These are things to watch for:

Eyes

There may be a discharge from the eyes. If there is, clean around them with boric-acid eyewash. Check with your veterinarian to find out if further medication is required.

Older dogs can also get cataracts. You may notice a kind of hazy grey to the interior of the eye. This is not a true cataract; it's just a change that occurs in the older animal and never really bothers him. But if you see it and have a question about it, you should have the veterinarian look at it to determine whether it *is* a cataract.

If it is, the dog may eventually go blind. This is not a disaster. A dog can live a normal life even without sight. If he is allowed to maintain his established routine, stays in his own environment and knows where things are, he will remain safe and content. The owner should take certain precautions: he should not move the furniture around, and he should be prepared to protect the dog when he goes outdoors—keep him away from stairs and from moving automobiles, which he will not be able to see.

Ears

Many older dogs begin to lose their hearing simply in the process of growing older. You will notice that the dog does not respond as quickly to sound as he used to. You may come up on him from behind and surprise him. If he is deaf, or partially deaf, you must protect him just as if he were losing his eyesight, keeping him away from traffic and other dangerous situations in which he would need to be able to hear in order to protect himself.

Nose

The dog's sense of smell may deteriorate to a degree. This can be detrimental to his appetite. Dogs don't have much sense of taste; it's mostly the sense of smell that attracts them to their food. If the dog can't smell, he may become finicky about eating. Watch his diet and try to tempt him.

Skin

Skin problems are very common in older dogs because their metabolism isn't as good as it once was. The dog may have a dry, dandruffy or dull hair-coat. He may develop a rash. Certain shampoos are helpful in controlling the problem, and supplementing his diet with oils and vitamins may help. There are also geriatric vitamins that contain male and female hormones to improve the general function of the animal's body. These are available only on a vet's prescription.

Muscular-Skeletal System

Arthritis in the hip, shoulder and wrist joints is fairly common among older dogs. Breeds that suffer from patellar luxation all their lives are especially susceptible to arthritis in the stifle or knee. The arthritic dog is not in severe pain most of the time; like human beings with arthritis, he learns to live with a certain amount of discomfort. He may be stiff when he wakes up in the morning, or he may develop a limp. Often a little aspirin will help him over the bad spots, and he'll be able to live a normal happy life. Check with your veterinarian for the proper dosage, and if the pain becomes severe, the veterinarian may be able to prescribe other, stronger medication.

Heart

Dogs do not have heart attacks the way human beings do, so you aren't likely to find your animal in a state of sudden cardiac arrest. You should be prepared, however, to notify the doctor of any cardiac symptoms, such as shortness of breath. Don't wait until the animal is coughing at night and can scarcely breathe.

Kidneys

You have probably heard about the popular high-protein diets recommended for people who want to lose weight. If you go on a high-protein diet, you are required to drink eight glasses of water a day. There is a reason for this. The kidney is the organ that excretes protein nitrogens. A high-protein diet puts an extra load on the kidneys, and consequently they need more water to do the job.

The kidneys decide which substances to reabsorb and which to throw off in the urine as waste. As a dog gets older, his kidneys may deteriorate until they can no longer reabsorb and throw off substances effectively. If an older dog begins to drink and urinate more frequently, his kidneys may be having a difficult time eliminating body wastes. Notify your veterinarian immediately. Since these are also symptoms of other diseases, the veterinarian will have to perform laboratory tests to determine the actual source of the problem. If it is the kidneys, a low-protein diet may be helpful.

Hot and Cold

The older dog has to be pampered. He, like the puppy, is more sensitive to heat and cold. Even if he is used to sleeping outdoors, you may have to bring him inside because he needs additional warmth and shelter.

Diet

As the dog begins to lie around more, his daily meal should be reduced to prevent obesity, which would put an extra strain on his heart, muscles and bones. If the dog has a special problem, the veterinarian may adjust his diet. Otherwise there's no need. However, since he doesn't need as much protein as a younger animal, because he's not building bone and muscle tissue, it can't hurt to put him on one of the commercial diets recommended for older dogs.

Water

Whether or not his consumption of water increases, the older dog should have access to water at all times, especially during hot weather. An eight- to ten-year-old dog may begin to have housebreaking problems again, but this is not from drinking more water but simply because he is no longer able to hold his urine. You can't expect him to go twelve hours any more; you will have to walk him more frequently.

Exercise

Sudden, hard exercise can be harmful, especially for the older dog. See that he has enough every day, with no sudden spurts.

The Last Goodbye

Eventually your dog will die. He will either die naturally or he will reach a state where the level of deterioration is so great, the pain he suffers so intense or the amount of treatment required so expensive that you can no longer afford to keep him alive—either practically or emotionally. You will probably know before your veterinarian when this moment arrives. In any case it is a decision you will have to make yourself, and it's not an easy one.

When the decision is made, you may feel relieved. But once the dog is gone, you'll feel sad. This is the way things ought to be. If you have a child, he will probably feel it even more acutely than you do. Let him mourn. Don't try to distract him. Above all, don't tell him not to cry. He is learning about one of the most important parts of life—death. Some people believe that they "can't go through it again," but this is really not true. You may want to wait before you replace the dog. But the wonderful thing is that the process of buying a puppy, rearing him, playing with him, training him and loving him can be repeated.

DOGS FOR SPECIAL PURPOSES

Sometimes a dog owner will find himself stuck with a dog who doesn't seem to do anything right. He may not understand that the particular breed was designed for a special purpose and was therefore bred for certain quirks of temperament. The following section describes some of the very special reasons for which certain dogs have been bred. It may help you understand your dog better. It may even give you some new ideas about him.

SHOW DOGS

One of the most popular reasons for buying a dog is to show him. Showing can be fun, but it also is apt to be expensive. It requires portable equipment, up-to-date health certificates, plane fare, train fare and plenty of gasoline for the family car. The Professional Handlers Association (PHA) recommends heartworm checks and DHL inoculations every six months—twice as frequently as for the family dog.

If you hire a professional handler, the costs increase, although the results are more certain because after years on the show circuit he knows the judges, what they expect of him, and how to prepare his dogs. Expenses for a handler include: $200 retainer fee, food and board for the dog, insurance, pickup and delivery at the airport, bathing and grooming, handling of stud services (if you so choose),

Rings at Santa Barbara Kennel Club show, 1978.

a fee of $35 to $50 per dog per show, and bonuses for wins. It may take one to four months and cost $500 to $2,000 to get a good dog his championship. A multiple-group or best-in-show winner may cost his owner $25,000 in one year.

Yet there are plenty of people with moderate incomes who show dogs. If you decide to show your dog yourself, you may be able to cut some corners, but you must be prepared to spend a considerable amount of time and effort preparing the dog and learning some of the tricks of the trade yourself.

You'll have to learn all about the breed standard, qualifications and *disqualifications*, entry forms, equipment, grooming and practical considerations such as how to show in foul weather. You'll need to know the rules and manners of the ring and all the special techniques that a handler would use to show your dog off to his best advantage. It's also a good idea to visit as many shows as you can and closely observe the dogs that win. For more information, contact the Owner Handler Association (OHA, 61 Tara Drive, Roslyn, New York 11576; telephone: 516-626-0004).

Showing can be a tremendous source of pleasure to both you and your dog. It is a sport with its own rules and regulations, and the thrill of competition. Many people show their dogs just for the fun of it, because they enjoy the environment and the excitement. The

Sporting group in the ring, Westminster Kennel Club, 1979.

dog enjoys it too. He struts through his hour in the ring with all the flair of a great actor performing Shakespeare. If he wins, he wallows in the praise and attention he receives for a job well done.

There is an added advantage in the fact that once a dog becomes a champion, his value—and that of his offspring—increases. Still, you may not ever make up for the cost of showing, subsequent stud fees or the expense of raising pups, but you will have the satisfaction of helping to improve the breed. Champions mated with champions usually produce champions, representatives of the breed that most nearly approach the standard or ideal. That's really what the American Kennel Club is all about.

The Rules

To qualify for entry in an AKC-licensed or member show, the dog:

1.   Must be registered either individually in the AKC Stud Book or as part of an AKC-registered litter. To be registered, a dog must be pedigreed and a member of an AKC-recognized breed.

2.   Must be entered in his owner's name, and the owner must be in good standing with the AKC.

A Komondor stands for examination in the show ring.

Oak Tree's Irishtocrat, an Irish Water Spaniel, wins Best in Show, Westminster, 1979.

3. Must be entered with appropriate forms correctly filled out, submitted before the closing date, and accompanied by the proper fee.

4. Must be whole. He cannot be blind, deaf, lame, spayed or castrated. The male must have both testicles in the scrotum. Surgical or chemical intervention to improve his appearance or alter his coat color is not allowed, except for removal of dewclaws, ear-cropping and tail-docking as required by the standard for certain breeds, although dogs with cropped ears are not eligible to compete in states where that operation is against the law.

5. Must be free of infectious diseases and from *exposure* to distemper, hepatitis or leptospirosis within thirty days of the show.

There are six basic types of shows held under the auspices of the American Kennel Club.

1. A *member* show is held by a club that is a member of the American Kennel Club. Championship points may be awarded.

2. A *licensed* show is held by a club not a member of the AKC, but which has been given license by the AKC to hold the show. Championship points may be awarded.

3. A *restricted entry* show is either a member or licensed show with restrictions placed on the entries as permitted by the AKC. Championship points may be awarded.

4. A *specialty* show is held by a specific breed club. Championship points may be awarded to dogs of that breed only.

5. An *American-bred specialty* show is given by a member club for a specific breed, and entries must all have been bred in this country. Championship points may be awarded.

6. A *sanctioned match* is held by a club sanctioned by the AKC to do so. Championship points are *not* awarded. The match is considered an informal event, and often serves as a training ground for both inexperienced dogs and handlers.

For additional information, write the American Kennel Club, 51 Madison Avenue, New York, New York 10010; ask for "Rules Applying to Registration and Dog Shows."

Caring for a Show Dog

Grooming   The show dog has an ongoing affair with brush and clippers. The more difficult breeds (like the terriers) take an experienced groomer eight to ten hours a week of brushing and plucking. Even the short-coated breeds must not be neglected if you expect them to win.

Training   The dog must be willing not only to pose and trot but to stand perfectly still while handled by a stranger. He must also learn to relieve himself in special pens provided at shows for this purpose, and he must learn to live comfortably in a crate for long periods of time.

Diet   The dog must be maintained at optimal weight, which is a very individual matter with show dogs. Since all show dogs are under stress, their nutritional needs are more demanding. But diet control is also a very effective method of camouflaging the dog's physical faults. In some cases, they will be less apparent if the dog is on the thin side—in other cases, on the heavy side. However, he should never appear either gaunt or fat, and his muscles should never be allowed to go lax.

Obedience Trials

The purpose of obedience trials, according to the American Kennel Club, is to "demonstrate the usefulness of the pure-bred dog as a companion of man." While all entries must be pedigreed, this is one case where temperament cannot be sacrificed to good looks.

Originally, the obedience ring was merely a gate attraction to increase attendance at dog shows. The theory was that while the neophyte might be unclear as to what was going on in the conformation ring, since he didn't know what the judge was looking for, he was sure to be excited by a dog who cleared a jump with a dumbbell in his mouth. The first obedience competition, held in Mount Kisco, New York, in 1933, proved the theory true. The event drew great crowds and was enthusiastically received by the press. Ever since obedience trials have sold tickets to what might otherwise be an indifferent segment of the public.

The degrees to be earned are CD (companion dog), CDX (companion dog excellent), and UD (utility dog), the coveted Ph.D. for dogs. A T is sometimes attached to the last, which means a tracking degree has been earned as well. Utility dogs are qualified to compete for a title certificate, O.T.Ch., obedience trial championship.

Poodles have always been obedience-trial favorites because they respond so well to training.

But even toys make good obedience candidates, as this little Pomeranian demonstrates.

The rules are the same as those for the conformation ring, with a few exceptions:

1. Since the ultimate goal is not to breed but to perform, spayed bitches and castrated or cryptorchid males* are allowed to compete.

2. A bitch in season may *not* compete.

3. Any dog that tries to attack a judge, handler or another dog in the ring is immediately disqualified.

For more information, write to the American Kennel Club and ask for "Obedience Regulations."

If you have your eye on the obedience ring, don't wait for a six-month-old puppy; conformation faults—even major ones—will not disqualify a dog here, but a faulty temperament and improper socialization will almost certainly result in disappointment and failure. Get a seven- to eight-week-old puppy of the breed you like best. Consult our temperament test, choose a responsive, outgoing puppy, care for him lovingly, socialize him, train him diligently, and he'll paper your walls with certificates. (You can also find private or group classes in obedience training just about anywhere in this country.)

Junior Showmen

Junior showmanship originated in 1920 when Leonard Brumby, Sr., got the idea that handling dogs was something children should have the chance to do. But it wasn't until 1971 that junior showmen were officially sanctioned by the AKC. At first, boys and girls competed separately, but soon it became clear that in this sport sex was a purely arbitrary distinction.

Today, classes are divided according to age and experience: Novice A and Novice B for ten- to twelve-year-olds and thirteen- to sixteen-year-olds who have never won a junior showmen competition; Open C and Open D for ten- to twelve-year-olds and thirteen- to sixteen-year-olds who have. First-prize winners of open classes are working for eligibility to compete at Westminster.

The purpose of junior showmanship is to test the child's ability to handle, and judges base their decisions on the junior's ability to gait and pose his dog. Conformation of the dog is not at issue, but it must be noted that some of the most successful juniors have been "helped" by winning dogs. A dog with plenty of experience in the

---

*Cryptorchid: unilateral, with one undescended testicle; bilateral, with two undescended testicles.

show ring imparts his own confidence to the handler and makes the competition less formidable.

The dog

1. Must be eligible to compete in the conformation or obedience ring but need not be entered in either to compete in the junior category.

2. Must be owned or co-owned by the junior handler or a close relative.

3. Must be of the appropriate breed in a specialty show.

The bitch in heat is allowed in the ring in junior showmanship, but naturally requires more handling finesse. There are products available made specifically to mask the odor and deceive the male. The junior should consult a vet who will help him choose the product that works best on his animal. However, if such precautions fail, the junior should retire his dog from the ring before he—or she—gets in serious trouble.

Ring conduct, rules and appropriate dress are all important considerations. For more information consult your local all-breed or specialty club.

COURSING DOGS

Lure coursing or simulated hunting was established in 1972 by the American Sighthound Field Association. Breeds allowed to run are: Afghans, Borzois, Greyhounds, Ibizans, Irish Wolfhounds, Pharaoh Hounds,* Salukis, Scottish Deerhounds and Whippets, all of which follow their quarry by sight. All entries in competition must be registered by a recognized organization, such as the American Kennel Club, the National Greyhound Association or a foreign registry recognized by the American Kennel Club. Since the purpose is to "preserve and further develop the natural beauty, grace, speed and coursing skill of the sighthound," the "recognized system" of accepting only registered dogs maintains the integrity of the breeds.

Lure coursing is not the same as racing. In a race, the dogs run either an oval or straight track and are timed, and the winner is the first to cross the finish line. In coursing, the dogs run in trios over an open course of some 1,000 to 1,500 yards after a lure (usually a

---

*Although Pharaoh Hounds are not yet recognized by the AKC, they are a well-established breed, so an exception was made in this case.

Salukis being released from the gates at a lure course.

Whippets running in an open stake.

shredded white plastic bag with or without fur attached to it), and are judged by two judges on enthusiasm, agility, skill in following the lure, and speed. To a small degree the lure course also tests the dog's endurance.

There are several different types of stake. The open stake is run by dogs and bitches* of a single breed, who may or may not have won before. The field champion stake is restricted to champions of record of a given breed. In a mixed stake, different breeds compete against one another. The ultimate goal for a coursing dog is the title of lure courser of merit. There are no stakes for this title; it is awarded on the basis of a specific number of points and types of placement accumulated in field champion stakes.

Training equipment is minimal. You need only a slip lead—a large piece of leather, part of which is a thick collar with two rings, one on either end, and a lead strung through the rings in such a way that when one end of it is released, the collar opens and the dog is set free—a place to train the dog, and a lure machine. As the popularity of the sport increases, this last difficulty will be easier to overcome, and most sighthound breed clubs will run practice sessions.

Lure coursing is one of the less expensive dog sports. Clubs provide the blankets in which the dogs run, but you may want to have a crate or exercise pen for your dog when he is not running and a blanket to shade him from the heat, since most coursing breeds are prone to heat prostration. If you plan to attend a two-day course, you will have the cost of an overnight stay, although in many cases other coursing enthusiasts put up out-of-towners, or at least supply a driveway where you can sleep in your car or camper. Entry fees average from $5 to $8, with higher fees typically charged in the Midwest and East, where the sport is less common and less well attended.

"Training classes" are available in some areas of the country but are usually just lure practices done in conjunction with a sighthound club. Since chasing the lure is what the sighthound is bred for, you don't really have to teach him; just set him free on a lure course and encourage him to heed his natural inclination, which is to chase anything that moves. Training should begin as early as possible. You can start in your living room by teasing your eight-week-old puppy with a rag to get him used to the idea of chasing something.

Basic obedience is not a prerequisite to lure-course training but does not conflict with it either. In fact, many coursing dogs have earned obedience degrees.

The coursing dog, if properly trained, makes an excellent house

*Bitches in season are not allowed to compete.

pet. The worst problems that occur have to do with temperament. The dog must be ambitious, competitive, spirited, outgoing and responsive, but at no time can he be aggressive in the sense of attacking another dog. This is severely penalized by either dismissal from the course or disqualification. On the other hand, aggression should not be confused with the excitability typical of the more high-strung dogs like Whippets. Sometimes these dogs become so excited by the sound of the lure machine that they bark, flip in the air and may even bite the handler, if his fingers get in the way. This sort of behavior occurs only when the dog is waiting to run, however; under normal circumstances he will be as well-mannered and quiet as you please.

A shy temperament can also cause problems, especially if the shyness is partially at least the result of being tied up or fenced in most of the time. Any coursing dog who lives a restricted or confined life between trials may need special encouragement and praise to chase the lure. If the dog genuinely doesn't want to run, for whatever reason, give up the idea. After all, the sport is for the pleasure of both owner and dog and should not be forced on either party.

Dr. Jerry Steingard runs his Alaskan Huskies in a seven-dog race.

GRIT PHOTO

Any racing dog's feet require special attention. Burs and little pebbles can get caught in the pads, which must be examined carefully after every run. In California, where coursing is a popular sport, foxtails are common. These little yellow stickers are extremely dangerous, for they can get caught in the dog's foot, or anywhere else for that matter, work into the pads and legs, into the eyes or the head, even into the ear canals, and cause an amazing amount of damage. Therefore, the owner should go over his dog's head, body, legs and feet thoroughly whenever the dog is allowed to run in areas where foxtails are indigenous. The dog's nails should also be kept clipped to prevent him from tearing them off.

Greyhounds alone sometimes present a serious problem because many of them will run until they are forced to stop. If the owner allows his competitive spirit to overtake his interest in the dog's welfare, he may allow his dog to "run his back off"—that is, to tear the muscles of his back, an almost always fatal situation.

For more information write to:

President, ASFA
Mr. Arnold Ross
4333 Mt. Jeffers Ave.
San Diego, California 92117

SLED DOGS

There are three popular misconceptions about sled dogs: first, that the sled dog is always a Siberian Husky; second, that the sled dog is a snarling, vicious, aggressive creature; third, that sled-dog trainers abuse their dogs and the sport is therefore cruel. Sled teams include everything from the northern breeds—purebred Siberians and Samoyeds—to Irish Setters, Dalmatians, Foxhounds and Walker Coonhounds. The great majority, however, are not pure anything, but rather Alaskan Huskies, who are crossbreeds, usually about three-quarters Siberian mixed with hound for speed and endurance. The most popular size is a dog who stands about 24 inches at the shoulder and weighs 50 pounds. Occasionally a 60-pound dog is used, but too many on one team slow it down. This rules out Malamutes, used primarily today in weight-pulling contests or freight races, in which the dogs pull a load.

As for being snarling and vicious, nothing could be farther from the truth. These dogs are loving, happy and outgoing if somewhat high-strung and excitable. The leader may even be a little nuts but never vicious. And far from being abused, sled dogs are kept in tiptop physical condition. They are well fed, usually on controlled diets, checked out by a veterinarian, and well exercised to keep their muscles in rock-hard condition. Trainers teach the dogs with kindness, since the last thing a trainer wants is to produce a miserable, cringing creature who is unwilling or afraid to run. It is a tribute to the superb care these dogs receive that one member of the winning team in the 1978 1,049-mile Iditarod race from Anchorage to Nome in Alaska was twelve years old.

There are four types of "sprint" races: the unlimited class, in which the team is composed of seven to sixteen dogs and distances range from twelve to thirty miles; the seven-dog class, in which teams are composed of four to seven dogs and distances range from seven to twelve miles; the five-dog class, in which teams are composed of three to five dogs who run from five to eight miles; and the three-dog class, teams composed of two to three dogs who run from three to five miles. In addition to these races, long-distance races are becoming increasingly popular. Races of 250 to 300 miles are run regularly in Michigan, New Hampshire and Alaska, where the race along the recently resurrected Iditarod trail, which the gold miners used, is now a yearly event.

The International Sled Dog Racing Association has established rules to govern the safety of both team and driver. Races are canceled if conditions are too severe—too much ice, which may cause injury, or very hot weather, which can dehydrate the dogs. A veterinarian is present at each event. In long races like the Iditarod, dogs are examined at checkpoints, and if the veterinarian feels his condition warrants it, a dog may be removed from the team. The driver (musher) will in fact often unhitch a dog during a race and carry him the rest of the way on his sled in the "dog bag."

The team itself is composed of one or two lead dogs followed by "point dogs," who are in turn followed by a series of "swing dogs," with "wheel dogs" harnessed right in front of the rig or sled making up the rear. Dogs must be anxious to go, able to take some pressure, so excited by running that they won't give up, and not afraid of crowds. A dog must never be a fighter. Males and females are equally useful, each with its own strong points. The female gets in racing condition faster than the male, but the male is stronger and doesn't come into season. Females may or may not be spayed depending on whether or not the owner wants to breed. As far as working ability goes, there is no advantage either way. A female in heat may run on a team with males, who are very often able to tolerate her condition.

This seems to depend more on the bitch's behavior than on that of her teammates.

Lead dogs present their own particular problems, the most obvious being that a good lead dog is hard to find. Dr. Jerry Steingard, vice-president of the International Sled Dog Racing Association, estimates that it may take many litters, sometimes hundreds of dogs, before a breeder will come up with leader material. The leader has to want almost desperately to run, must have an excess of nervous energy, must be willing to stay ahead, and must be able to take pressure. In other words, if a musher yells at him in the middle of a race, the dog can't cave in. The leader is the only dog who is really trained in commands, although the other dogs will learn from him (or her, since some of the best leaders have been bitches).

Training begins when the puppies are three months old: they are allowed to run about a half a mile with the team, then returned to the truck. When the puppy is about seven months old, he is hooked up behind a good leader. Eleven- to twelve-month-old puppies may run in five-mile races, but seldom in longer ones. Putting too much pressure on a young dog will ruin him forever. The important thing is to work him with more experienced dogs who can impart their enthusiasm. The young dog must get used to pulling and tugging, and he must learn not to get tangled up in the lines. For this reason, experienced mushers will chain their dogs outside, a practice that other sporting-dog enthusiasts may think barbaric. The fact is, the dogs don't seem to mind it; they get used to the weight of the chains on their necks and learn not to get tangled up with each other. Training is usually a year-round affair, with dogs being harnessed to wheeled training rigs during the warmer months. Training in very hot weather is not healthy for the dogs and is kept to a minimum, with the musher taking his dogs out in the very early morning hours while the air is still cool.

Basic obedience is a matter of controversy among mushers. Some teach it and some don't, believing that it creates a dog who's always waiting for a command. Those who are opposed to the idea want their dogs to "go all the time." Emphasis is placed on the two commands "Take it easy" (slow down) and "Pick it up" (go faster), with less emphasis on "whoa," which of course means stop and is the least important thing for a sled dog to do.

Equipment includes a wheeled training rig, harnesses, lines, a racing sled, and a truck (car or trailer) for transporting the dogs. Equipment may be purchased from outlets that advertise in sporting-dog or sled-dog magazines, although sooner or later mushers learn how to make their own lines and harnesses, and some of them even make the rigs and sleds. This reduces the amount spent on upkeep, which is already high enough, including the cost of a kennel full of dogs, the kennel itself, food and other maintenance expenses, and traveling to the Far North if the musher doesn't already live there (mushing is now a popular sport in forty-two states). Some very excellent professional and winning drivers are sponsored by large companies.

Dogs are fed special diets of meat, meal and fat, with the proportions varying depending on the season. Tested and recommended by expert mushers for the racing season is a diet of 75 percent meat and 25 percent meal with additional fat—pork fat being a strong favorite. During the summer, meat may be reduced to 50 percent and meal elevated to the same level. Commercial diets are considered acceptable as long as the dog is used to the feed.*

Grooming seems to be a matter of little concern. Some mushers, in fact, never groom their dogs at all, although they spend a great deal of time going over them, examining them and taking them to the veterinarian. Special medical problems include fractures, muscle pulls and worms, especially during the running season when the team is exposed to a large number of strange dogs. Most mushers have the dogs examined by a vet every six months and have the stools checked even more frequently. On the other hand, these dogs are in the excellent condition of trained athletes. When a dog begins to lose stamina, he may be switched to a team that runs shorter races. Feet, as with all racing dogs, present special problems. Some mushers toughen the feet by running their dogs in sand. Sled dogs often wear little boots to protect their feet from ice which cuts the pads. Cut pads are frequent and must be treated at once before they become serious and the dog goes lame.

The sled dog is an excellent house pet, although many are kenneled outdoors for almost all their lives. They are wonderful with children and not at all protective. They do tend to howl, however, so they are not recommended as city pets unless they are trained out of the habit. Some owners, we are told, have the vocal cords removed, but we are strongly against this procedure. Besides, it is a temporary measure; the cords grow back after three years.

For more information write:

International Sled Dog Racing Assocation
460 South 43rd
Boulder, Colorado 80303

---

*Eskimos traditionally fed their dogs fish, sometimes raw, which created thiamine deficiencies. Fish, of course, is an excellent high quality source of protein, but must be served cooked.

EARTH DOGS

The American Working Terrier Association sponsors "earth trials" for terriers—to "preserve the natural instinct of the working Terrier." Terriers are a feisty group, originally bred for varmint hunting, with an aggressive streak that serves them well against rats and other such fighters. In these trials, the terrier is sent to earth—i.e., down a tunnel—and in order to score points he must put up a fierce show when he meets his opponent at the end. Eligible entries include any working terrier capable of running an earth nine inches deep. Except for Dachshunds, dogs from the other groups are ineligible, including mixed breeds and toys, even those called terriers, like the Yorkie. The bitch in heat is also ineligible, since her strong enticing odor would interfere with the artificial scent trail that leads to the tunnel—not to speak of what she might do to the males present.

At each trial, the earths are constructed with the quarry, a black-and-white hooded rat, planted in a cage at the end of each tunnel. The dogs run in three classes. The *novice* runs a ten-foot tunnel. He is allowed to enter and leave several times before he reaches the quarry, but if he takes more than one minute to get there, he loses points. He may also receive encouragement from his handler, but the more he needs to be encouraged, the more points he loses. When he arrives at the end of the tunnel, he is expected to "work" the quarry—to bark, whine, lunge and bite at the cage. Once the fuss is over, so is his part in the contest. *Open* and *certificate* entries run a thirty-foot tunnel and must reach the quarry in *half* a minute. The handler may not encourage them. Dogs are scored on the time it takes to reach the quarry (30 seconds = 50 points), with a "certificate of gameness" awarded to the open entry only, if he scores 100 percent of his points. Once he earns a certificate, the dog may *only* run in certificate classes.

These trials are still strictly backyard stuff, not yet sponsored by the AKC, and held on rent-free trial grounds with all expenses kept to an absolute minimum. Whoever decides to post a trial is responsible for handling all the details—establishing the dates with the AWTA well in advance, organizing a committee, getting a judge, providing accommodations for him, finding a trial ground (rent-free) where he and the other members of the committee will be allowed to build the earths, and purchasing the rats—only the hooded rat is acceptable quarry, and he may be purchased or ordered from a pet shop. If you are interested in organizing a trial or training your terrier to run to earth, write to: Patricia Adams Lent, Trial Secretary, Dogwood Cottage, RD2, Box 38A, Franklinton, North Carolina 27525.

WATER-RESCUE DOGS

This is a job for Newfoundlands only—and if you live near the water and love this big black bear of a dog, you ought to consider the possibility of training one for this. Official rules allow only New-foundlands to enter competitions and win water-rescue degrees. In fact, the whole idea of water rescue was resurrected by the NCA (Newfoundland Club of America) in 1972. The NCA wanted to plug the Newfoundland back into his history.

The Newf began as a fisherman's dog and helped with the nets. Ultimately his fame spread when he applied his talents to other areas. He is a dog whose whole physical presence (average height, 28 inches; weight, 150 pounds; deep chest, broad back and massive bone structure) embodies strength, and this combined with intelli-gence, a sweet disposition and love of water led naturally to the job of rescue work. He learned to carry lifelines to sinking ships and retrieve men, women and children from the wet jaws of death.

Water tests are divided into two categories, junior and senior divisions. In the junior division, the dog must learn basic obedience off-lead according to AKC obedience regulations, with emphasis on

Kestrel, a Newfoundland, performs the "take a line, tow a boat" exercise.
JUDI ADLER

Kestrel leaps into the water to retrieve a bumper thrown by her handler. JUDI ADLER

Kestrel dives from a dock.

Kestrel delivers a life ring to aid a drowning victim.

precision and the handler's ability to maintain control. The dog must retrieve an object from the water and a boat bumper at the end of a thirty-foot throw; deliver a line to a steward planted seventy-five feet away; and tow a boat for no less than fifty feet. In the senior division, these basic skills are honed and developed to the actual job of water rescue. The retrieving and towing tasks are made increasingly difficult. The dog must carry a life ring to a capsized boat, rescue a person who has fallen from a boat, and retrieve an object from deep water.

The Newfoundland is proof that retrieving is a generalized char-acteristic, not limited to bird dogs. It is interesting that while the bird-dog experts tend to wait until the dog is mature before they teach him to retrieve, Newfs get their first taste of water work when they are eight to ten weeks old and are constantly encouraged to play in the water and retrieve. Retrieving comes naturally to them, but part of that "naturalness" may have to do with the fact that they have a go at it so early. The "critical period" for retrieving, according to Scott and Fuller, who studied and compared five breeds, is when the dog is *nine weeks old*.

Problems

This big, burly creature is a great family dog, but because of his size and strength, he requires exercise and obedience training even if you don't intend to use him for rescue work. If you *do* intend to work him, you must of course spend the necessary hours in training. Group training is recommended because many of the exercises need several people and expensive water equipment, including life jackets, rings, lines and a boat. Also, group experience tends to reinforce the basic goal—to prepare the dog for a difficult task demanding his astute attention to the handler and willingness to respond instantly to command. The Newf is not by nature a businesslike dog. He is affable and playful, and loves nothing better than a lengthy swim. These qualities must be indulged and encouraged and at the same time directed toward the job at hand.

HUNTING DOGS

There are two kinds of hunter in this country, the man who hunts with his gun, and the man who hunts with his dog. Those who use a dog swear that "Once you've tried it, you'll never do it the other way again." To the man who hunts with his dog, the gun is secondary. His primary interest is not the kill but his dog's performance; his ability to chase a rabbit, sniff out a bird, hold a point, retrieve and accomplish any number of other related tasks. The relationship here between man and dog is a very close one, based on years of working side by side in the brush or field.

There are three categories of hunting dog: the blue-blooded bench dog, the personal hunting-companion dog and the field-trial dog with field-trial champions in his background.

An English Springer Spaniel bred for the field.

The Bench Dog

Veteran trial buffs claim that bench enthusiasts have been responsible for ruining a good many hunting dogs, and they're probably right. Originally, the show breeders claimed that good conformation was a corollary to good performance, and they established their shows on that basis. But as time passed, bench and field became more and more separate. Many of the breed people never actually hunted, so they didn't really know what kind of dog the hunter needed. They developed their own beauty standards, often quite different from the standards set up by trial enthusiasts. As a result, bench and trial champions don't even look much alike today. It is still possible for a dog to win a dual championship, but it's a rare dog who can pull it off.

The Personal Hunting Companion

This dog has no technical qualifications beyond the fact that he does his job. We know a man in California who owned several such dogs. They were curs rescued from the gutter, all of them smart as bandits and trained by the boot. We don't recommend the last technique as a training method; the point is, even a mixed breed has his uses if you take the trouble to harness his strengths. In all fairness, however, the pedigreed pup with proven ancestry is a more reliable choice.

The Trial Dog

The purpose of the field trial is "to demonstrate the progress made in breeding for practical use." *Sanctioned* trials are informal events where dogs compete to gain experience for *member* and *licensed* trials, where championship points may be awarded. The trial dog competes for either amateur field champion or field champion. The "amateur" in the title refers to the handler, not the dog; an amateur is a person who has not for a two-year stretch or longer trained or handled dogs for money. The division of trials into amateur and professional categories gives the dogs an equal opportunity to show their stuff without human competence or incompetence, as the case may be, interfering with judgment.

The AKC sponsors pointing breed trials, retriever trials, spaniel trials, Beagle trials, Basset Hound Trials and Dachshund trials. Each follows a specific format, and procedures, wins and the awarding of titles vary as much by breed as by type of trial. For example, an English Pointer can win the title of champion in the pointing category when he acquires the appropriate number of points. But the versatile dogs like German Shorthaired Pointers and Weimaraners don't qualify as champions in the pointing category until they have passed water and retrieving tests. All such additional requirements have been established to protect the differences among breeds.

Entry rules and qualifications are essentially the same as rules of the show ring; again, consult the American Kennel Club and ask for the following publications:

1. "Registration and Field Trial Rules and Standard Procedures for Pointing Breeds, Dachshunds, Retrievers, Spaniels."

2. "Standing Recommendations of the Retriever Advisory Committee."

An English Springer Spaniel
stretching for a retrieve.

Anxious to capture the prize, he gets
a mouthful of feathers.

Returning from a water retrieve.

3. "Beagle Field Trial Rules and Standard Procedures."

4. "Basset Hound Field Trial Rules and Standard Procedures."

Selecting a Breed

Nothing predetermines your choice of a hunting breed more clearly than what you ultimately intend to do with him. If you want to show him, you choose according to your living conditions, life style and personal taste. If you live in the country or suburbs and can offer the dog four or more hours of vigorous exercise a day, just about any breed will do. If you live in an apartment, you must consider the fact that bird-dog puppies are bred for the qualities they need to succeed in the field. High on the list of temperament traits is a goodly amount of nervous energy combined with a stubborn streak several yards long. These qualities are called spirit and stamina in the field, but they can produce mayhem in the confines of an apartment. For quail, such a dog may have a mouth as soft as silk, but show him the upholstery, and his mouth goes hard.

There are several among the hunting breeds, however, that adapt nicely to apartments. Cocker and Springer Spaniels are easy to contain. Beagles, Bassets and Dachshunds are loving, affectionate, and tend to be good with both children and furniture. Golden and Labrador Retrievers are superb in any situation. Both are used as guide dogs, and the black Lab has been used for mine and narcotics detection. These types of specialized training indicate a high degree of adaptability. As for pointers, setters, and versatile gun dogs—the rule is, if you show them, you train them, so they're not likely to ruin your furniture more than once.

If you intend to hunt your dog or get him his championship in the field, you must choose your game before you choose your dog. Find out what kinds of trial are held where, and even more important, what types of game are available to you and your dog for practice. There's not much point in owning an English Pointer if you'll have to train him on ducks. Ducks are for retrievers, and while a pointer may get the hang of it after a while, you can be sure he'll never excel, and he could drown both of you in the process.

Bird dogs include pointers, setters and spaniels for the uplands, retrievers for the lowlands, and versatile hunting dogs for either. English Pointers and English Setters are fast, wide-ranging dogs; for years they have been vying for the lead in pointing-trial wins, and in general they work best with the man on horseback. Spaniels were

A Golden Retriever goes out on a blind. He has seen one bird fall but must ignore it, take direction from his handler and go to another bird that he has not seen.

A Golden Retriever does some fancy field work.

developed long before guns had any range to them, so they are content to stick close and make excellent foot companions. The versatile dogs, as their name implies, were developed as all-purpose dogs for the man who wished to hunt several types of game, couldn't afford more than one dog, and didn't own a horse. They tend to be close-ranged and not so speedy.

Hounds are used mostly on small game in this country. Beagles and Bassets are highly favored rabbit dogs, but Dachshunds are perhaps the most interesting of the rabbit dogs. We think of them primarily as house pets, but Dachshunds hunt in pairs or packs in trials sponsored by the AKC and win points by running live cottontails to earth. For coons, of course, the indigenous Coonhound is best. While we think of coon-hunting as primarily a Southern fancy, coon-hunting clubs are sprinkled liberally throughout the country—as far west as Illinois and as far north as Michigan. For more information, write to the United Kennel Club, 321 West Cedar St., Kalamazoo, Michigan 49006.

Bird Dogs   For a personal hunting companion, ignore a field-trial background. Buy a dog whose mother, father and grandparents hunted. A foot dog should be close-ranging and slow enough for you to keep up with without dying of heart failure. In this case, pedigree may not give you the answers, so don't be embarrassed to ask the breeder personal questions such as "Did you hunt with this dog's mother?"

For a trial dog, of course, you have to study his papers. He should have field champions among his close relatives—mother, father, grandparents. Avoid the pup with bench champions in his near background, unless his parents also won in the field. Obedience titles may indicate that the dog is descended from good temperament and is trainable in the field and for the trials—with the exception of tracking degrees. A dog who tracks follows ground scent, and a good bird dog hunts by airborne scent. If a dog tends to hunt with his nose to the ground, he is accused of pottering, which is considered a grievous fault. While tracking is technically considered learned behavior, some dogs seem to have an inclination to work this way, and it's best to avoid them.

Rabbit and Coon Dogs   Here the bench, trial and practical hunting dog seems to be less at odds with each other. If you want a hunter of any sort, however, make sure there's plenty of hunting in his background. For trial dogs, always choose pups with champion blood.

Training

This takes many hours of effort in most cases, beginning when the dog is quite young (eight weeks) and continuing through his second year (or longer) when he is considered "finished." If you want to avoid part or all of the training process, you can buy a "started" or even "finished" dog, but expect to pay accordingly and buy only from a trainer with a good track record. Otherwise you may run into one of the special training problems that hunters confront. These are the worst:

1. *The gun-shy dog.* The problem is usually caused by improper introduction to gunfire. Little can be done about it.

2. *The dog with a hard mouth.* Either he got it from improper training, or he was born with it. Various methods have been used to ameliorate the problem, including dummies embedded with little spikes. Sometimes the technique works. In other cases, it's not worth the effort.

3. *The retriever who's afraid of water.* Some retrievers take to water naturally. Others have to be gently urged. Never throw one in. The terror that may result from such impatience on the part of the owner can leave permanent mental scars.

Diet

The idea that a dog should hunt hungry is largely a hoax. If he does, he will tire too easily and will find it difficult to perform efficiently. Remember, he is not hungry for the kill; he, like you, is hungry for adventure and excitement. When the season is on, the dog works hard and needs extra calories. In addition, he may need a change in schedule. Instead of the traditional morning feed, he may need several small meals spaced throughout the day, beginning with a light breakfast and ending with a final supper an hour or so after he returns from the field.

Off-season, his caloric intake should be reduced to accommodate the amount of daily exercise he receives. Hunting dogs tend to have excellent appetites, sometimes to the point of overeating. You, as owner, must make a firm assessment of your dog's nutritional requirements and stick to it.

After Care

After the hunt when your bones ache and you feel so tired you can hardly lift your feet, you still have one more job to do. You have to take care of your dog. Go over him carefully for ticks, lice and other external parasites. Remove burs and thorns, and give him a careful and thorough brushing. Finally, make sure that he is comfortable, relaxed and well fed. Then, and only then, can you take the time to pamper yourself.

Accidents

All care must be taken to make sure the shot falls in the right place. Also, beware of the other man in the same wood! A dog moving through the brush can easily be mistaken for the mark, especially if he is small or blends with the scenery.

If the area is particularly wild, you must guard your dog against attacks by wild animals. A big cat can rip a dog's belly open with one swipe of the paw, and a bear can literally remove a dog's head from his shoulders. Sometimes the hunted can inflict damage—the coon, for instance, with his sharp claws and teeth.

Dogs with long, brush-like tails that can be caught in bushes or snagged by thorns have a particular problem. It's difficult for a tail injury to heal because it is constantly aggravated and exposed during the hunting season. In such cases, it's best to devise some method of protection.

The Bitch in Season

This is less of a problem than you might think unless it interferes with her desire to hunt. If you own more than one dog and intend to hunt with several of them, consult your veterinarian about sprays and pills that effectively mask the odor.

Be warned, however, that the bitch in season is not permitted to run in *member* or *licensed* field trials except in specified stakes where males will not run the same ground until the next day.

One alternative is to spay, but then you can't breed the bitch, and if she's of champion blood, you will probably find the very thought distasteful. Spayed bitches are allowed to run in *all field trials*, except for Bassets and Beagles, who cannot qualify for AKC member or licensed trials if they are spayed.

POLICE / WAR DOGS

First and foremost among the dog's special talents is his ability to distinguish scents. Laboratory tests have established the fact that the dog is so sensitive to human smell that he can even distinguish between identical twins—by scent alone. To a dog, the scent of a man's sweat is his own unique calling card and as readily identifiable as a fingerprint is to a skilled detective. Man has made use of this fact without special laboratory knowledge for centuries. Tracking dogs have located criminals with such accuracy that their work has resulted in literally hundreds of arrests. It is a testament to the dog's reliability that his evidence stands up in court.

The Bloodhound is, of course, the classic case. Movies and books have glamorized this canine professional to the point where the very thought of a Bloodhound on the trail strikes terror. This is, however, an inaccurate picture. The Bloodhound is single-mindedly interested in the chase. Once he has tracked down the fugitive, he closes in for the kiss, not the kill. For him, the game is over, and he needs only the praise of his handler to keep him hot for the next one. He is a sweet-tempered, lovable, affable, somewhat delicate creature with an excellent nose—completely useless for crowd control or attack work, both of which require a more aggressive nature.

Tracking ability has been used extensively in warfare, until recently in the classic sense, with dog and handler working as a team, and the handler actually serving as the primary tracker. In the guerrilla warfare in Vietnam, the dog's performance was considerably extended. American bases were being subjected to one- and two-man attacks, and it was hopeless to pick off the enemy one by one. Black (to prevent their being seen at night) Labrador Retrievers were therefore used as "stalkers."

These Labs were off-leash trained so that handlers could follow at a distance and not subject themselves to possible enemy capture. The ultimate adaptation was to embed an electronic device in the dog's harness, which made it possible to monitor his location by helicopter from a distance of several miles. The object was to stalk infiltrators back to their original headquarters. There the dog would lie down, indicating the presence of the enemy camp, and American troops would attack and destroy the heart of enemy operations.

Additional experimentation proved that dogs could be used for other purposes. A major source of demoralization among American troops was the "surprise" effect of booby traps, false tunnels and sudden mine explosions. These enemy devices were often considered a fate worse than death, not only because of the terrible injuries they

One of the Santa Monica police force's dogs helps to apprehend a criminal.
(*Photograph courtesy of the Santa Monica Police Force*)

inflicted, but also because the "attack" was totally unpredictable. Like a snake without a rattle, the enemy would strike without warning, leaving the soldier maimed, dismembered, desexed, blinded, or with permanent brain damage.

In an effort to counteract the situation, another dog-based system was established to train dogs to detect mines, traps and tripwires. Again, the unique canine scenting ability was called into play. Not only was the dog trained to scent out man-laid traps, he was sensitized to the smells of different explosives. The system proved more reliable and effective than any mechanical device.

A civilian adaptation of the canine mine detector is the police dog who is used for bomb detection. Dogs are estimated to be more than 95 percent reliable and twenty times as fast as human beings at locating bombs. In cases where a bomb squad is working against a ticking clock, such speed and accuracy are of inestimable value.

In addition to bomb detection, police dogs are used for search, attack and capture; crime prevention on the street (including crowd control); and narcotics detection. The last case is another innovation that came from Vietnam, where heroin addiction had become an increasingly severe problem among American soldiers. Before the problem could be attacked, a system had to be devised whereby the drug could be identified and users could be isolated. Although heroin is nearly scentless to humans, dogs are capable of detecting it.

Subsequently, dogs were used to help break up a smuggling ring in Southeast Asia; heroin was being sewn into the bodies of American casualties, who were then flown back to the United States. D-dogs (as these detector dogs are called) have since helped fight the battle against smuggling, particularly at the Mexican border. A dog can inspect an entire car in a minute and sniff out stashes of marijuana, hashish and other drugs concealed beneath layer upon layer of hard and soft surfaces and camouflaged by the conflicting odors of food, baby powder or even black pepper.

Selecting a Breed

The Mastiff was the first type of war dog. Developed initially as protectors of the flock, these dogs had size, strength and a guarding instinct that made it easy for the ancient Romans to convert them into fierce fighters. Boxers were developed in Germany for border patrol. German Shepherds and Doberman Pinschers have been long-term favorites among U.S. Army and police personnel because they combine strength with speed, stamina and easy trainability. More recently, the black Lab has joined their ranks.

Dogs used for offensive and defensive maneuvers must be protective and have the capacity for aggression. German Shepherds are usually used for attack and capture because they are easy to obtain, have strength, speed and endurance, and are not reluctant to use their teeth if they have to. These dogs are trained to follow the orders of one master, to attack on command, and not to hesitate at the sight or sound of a gun. Nevertheless, when not on duty the police dog is friendly to strangers and walks peaceably among everyday pedestrians.

Shepherds and Labs have both been used successfully by the Army for various kinds of detection tasks. Since his job is merely to sniff out trouble, all the D-dog needs is a good nose, a lively interest, determination and a high degree of trainability. He does not have to be aggressive. In fact, it is better if he is not. U.S. customs officials have used Golden and Labrador Retrievers, Spaniels and even Border Collies to do the job.

Selecting the Individual

Again, it depends on the goal, but generally speaking, the police war dog has to be medium to large in size and sturdily built, with stamina, endurance, a tracking temperament and a responsive personality; he must also be intelligent, capable of an independent decision, stable, outgoing, and in some cases, protective. This is a stiff order, and most dogs, even of the appropriate breeds, are disqualified from training programs on the basis of physical inadequacies alone.

Males and females are equally effective prospects.

Training

Since the police dog is usually an adaptation of the war dog, or vice versa, training for both types of work is nearly identical. It is long and arduous for both the dog and his handler, who has the job of keeping training sessions interesting and fun. If the dog gets overtired, he begins to make mistakes, which can turn into permanent bad habits. Since older dogs make fewer mistakes and pay attention for longer periods, puppies are not accepted into training programs until they are at least eight months to a year old.

A police dog in pursuit training, learning to go through a tunnel. (*Photograph courtesy of the Santa Monica Police Force*)

The major problem with all war- and police-dog training is the amount of follow-up necessary to keep dogs working at peak efficiency. The dogs don't forget; they just get bored. The dog considers most aspects of police work a kind of game. Tracking is a perfect example. The dog requires a large number of successful finds to serve as positive reinforcement. If he searches and fails to find, this is punishment, and he rapidly begins to lose interest. D-dogs used at the border for narcotics detection must be constantly revitalized by their handlers, who keep a private stash of drugs for this purpose.

The problem of follow-up is the real reason why most dog-based Army and civilian programs are eventually abandoned. Initially these programs are established by highly dedicated people who are willing to devote most of their time and energy to the development of training techniques. All improvements are based on close field observation and careful experimentation. But when the system is turned over to second-string officials, it ultimately caves in.

In police-dog training, the dog learns to leap high hurdles. This will help him later when he is confronted by fences. (*Photograph courtesy of the Santa Monica Police Force*)

Care

These dogs are under almost constant pressure. Diet must be adjusted to the workload. The police dog in particular needs extra calories in protein and carbohydrates to keep him going all day on his beat.

Typically, he lives with his policeman partner and family, who must make sure he has a quiet place to rest at night. Since he works so hard, he needs sleep badly and will be unfit the next day if he doesn't get it. But because he is so highly trained, he'll be up and down all night unless his sleeping area is insulated from strange noises, visiting neighbors, voices, doorbells, or any of the myriad distractions that put him instantly on red alert. The policeman's family must be willing to accept the presence of the dog and able to meet his special needs. For this reason, the family is as important to any dog-based program as the policeman himself.

GUARD DOGS

A bird dog trains with his nose buried in feathers, a guard dog with his teeth buried in a padded sleeve. The classic guard dog is a dog who has been trained to hunt men. He has a hard mouth, a fierce and dangerous bite, and an aggressive attitude. He is trained to recognize and respond to certain stimuli. The response is accurate and predictable as long as he is under the handler's control, which does not mean that he attacks only on command. A dog who attacks only on command serves no purpose if you are asleep or absent at the time of a burglary. The guard dog learns to attack with or without command in the presence of what he recognizes as a threat to himself, his owner or his owner's property. He is not mean. On the contrary, an effective guard is an animal with a sweet, loving, even and responsive temperament whose wits have been sharpened by intensive training.

Training

Guard-dog training is neither abusive nor harsh. An abused dog learns to cower and cringe, which is exactly opposite of what is wanted in a guard, who should be proud, outgoing and thoroughly dependable. Training is based on the game principle. The trainer agitates the dog until the latter responds aggressively; at this point the trainer retreats and allows the dog to "win." As training progresses, the dog is placed in increasingly difficult situations, the agitation becomes more intense, and the dog's response more fierce and aggressive. The important point is that the dog *always wins*, which increases his courage and confidence. He learns to *expect* to win, and winning is the reward toward which he directs all his efforts. Most dogs enjoy guard training and look forward to the daily sessions.

The end result can of course be extremely dangerous. Every law-abiding citizen in this country has the right to carry a gun, and we could say he also has the right to own a guard dog. But if you walk around with a loaded pistol in your belt, you have to take responsibility for it, and the same is true if you walk around with a trained guard dog. The following precautions must be observed:

● You must be trained as thoroughly as the dog. Otherwise you will not be able to control him effectively.

● Both you and the dog should be trained by a professional guard-dog trainer. Training is dangerous, so if you're going to get it, get it from a pro. Beyond that, since in order to develop the dog's "attack" instinct the trainer "agitates" the dog, you as owner-trainer should not act as the agitator. If you do, you are likely to become your dog's worst enemy.

● The dog does not have the same subtle judgment as his human master; he will respond to the appropriate stimuli even if it happens by accident. A small child, for example, who suddenly decides to bop the dog on the nose has provided the stimulus for attack action. Therefore the owner must be constantly aware of his dog's potential and must be prepared to act accordingly. This is not altogether relaxing. It means more than usual supervision, and whenever the dog makes a public appearance, he must be on-leash at all times.

● The dog must periodically undergo retraining, which is expensive and time-consuming.

For these reasons, if you want to own a guard dog, you must be prepared to spend time, money and effort in training and subsequent care and use of that dog. If you are willing to do the job right, you will have a wonderful dog worth a great deal of money in terms of training and utterly priceless as far as intelligence, temperament, companionship and security are concerned. But most people are not willing to spend that much time, money and effort. For these people there is an alternate solution—which is considerably safer for the average pet owner.

Home Protection

So far we have talked about the "classic" guard dog who undergoes rigorous training and is expected to respond instantaneously to certain kinds of stimuli. Actually, many types of dogs can be considered guards: dogs that bark; dogs that bark and growl; dogs that bark, growl and bite; and dogs that attack. We have found that when most people talk about wanting a guard dog, they are not really interested in a dog who will bite or attack. They want a dog who will protect them but will not inflict injury on anybody else. The thought of dog bites and possible court action is too risky.

A dog who barks and growls when he or his owner is threatened or when an intruder breaks into the house is just about all that is really needed in the way of protection. Most intruders, if they have their wits about them, will not try to get past such a dog—primarily because they don't know whether or not he will bite.

We classify a dog who barks and growls at the appropriate stimulus as a *home protector*, and strongly recommend this type of training for anyone who feels he has need of extra security. There are no unpleasant consequences to the ownership of such an animal. On the contrary, he lives most of his life as a loving and affectionate pet who has learned when and how to make his presence known. He is something like a living burglar alarm with the advantage of intelligence, which means that his wires cannot be disconnected by a clever thief.

The Breed

Almost any breed with a good mouth will do. The Basenji is of course out, for he is barkless, producing at best an unreliable wail. Even small dogs, however, are threatening behind closed doors, especially small dogs with deep voices. The Dachshund, for example, has a deep, threatening voice and sounds much bigger than he actually is if you can't see him. All terriers are aggressive and noisy. Hunting dogs are superbly throaty, and hounds—phlegmatic and peaceful by nature—strike terror in many hearts with their musical and prolonged bays.

Of course, the larger, more typical guard breeds—the German Shepherd, Doberman Pinscher, Great Dane, St. Bernard, Great Pyrenees, Bouvier des Flandres, Standard and Giant Schnauzer, Belgian Sheepdog, Boxer and Briard—offer an extra measure of protection by virtue of their threatening appearance. These dogs often appear to have blood on their teeth even when they are smiling—especially to a nervous burglar.

The Temperament

More important than breed is temperament, particularly if you own one of the larger, more typical guard breeds and want to give him any form of protective training. Like any form of specialized training, guard training tends to improve the character of the dog, but if you want to minimize the risks—even if he is merely a barker and growler—you ought to start with a sweet-tempered creature. A home protector should be loving, outgoing and happy. He may be slightly nervous, even stubborn in nature, as long as he is basically responsive and well-mannered. A shy dog must never be trained to bark, growl and especially bite. Aggression in the shy dog is the result of fear, not sharpened wits. If this type of aggression is encouraged, the result will be an undependable creature. Similarly, the aggressive dog should not be taught home protection. Every effort in training such a dog must be directed toward eliminating his nasty tendencies.

There is only one real problem with the home protector: he is bullet-bait for a professional robber. Unlike the attack-trained dog, he cannot stop a man with a gun.

HERD DOGS

The herding instinct is a piece of the hunting instinct left over from the dog's wild ancestors. One of the wolf's special techniques is his method of driving a herd of deer or elk for miles and then cutting off an animal who is weak, old or young enough to be killed. Man, through selective breeding of the dog, has developed the herding instinct, the driving and circling ability, and has suppressed the urge to kill. Thus we have the herd dog, as useful today as he ever was, even though a large portion of our population has become urbanized. Some herd-dog owners are "hobby herders." Others make a serious living from their flocks and herds. Still others are primarily interested in the sheepdog trials, which offer a rigorous test of working ability, thus fixing and establishing working bloodlines.

The four basic types of herd dog—the shepherd, the drover, the livestock guarding dog and the all-round farm dog—all overlap to some degree, but for our purposes, it is useful to distinguish among them here.

Home inspection.
Couldn't adopt till
a Saturday.

o ~~Crown~~ get books

o ~~Hechts~~

o ~~Lab~~

PG Animal Shelter

PG (301) 499-2809

9³⁰ - 3³⁰ Sat

8311 Darcey Rd
Forestville, Md.

Ext 11B Pa Ave
Stay in split lane
come onto Forestville Rd
come 1½ mi to Darcey Rd (rt onto)

¼ mi on rt hand
side. (Will see a sign)

48 hr process ⟶

Ch. A Beau Venture of Rimwald, a Puli, keeps his flock together.

The Shepherd

The shepherd is, of course, the dog who herds sheep. This is considered the most difficult of herding tasks and requires specialized skills. The Border Collie is by far the most popular shepherd in this country today, and with good reason. Over the last several hundred years, with only a few temporary lapses, he has been bred solely for his working ability and herding instinct. Attempts to breed him for the bench and thereby fix his conformation and color are justly despised by serious sheep people. As a result, he is the only breed competent to run in the sheepdog trials, with the possible exception of the Bearded Collie—about whom more later.

The Border Collie is a medium-sized dog, usually some combination of black and white, although color is not considered important. He looks like a mutt and has often been mistaken for such. Actually, however, he is one of the most carefully bred dogs alive, a natural header, which means that he controls his flock by circling around them, and a natural worker, born with a desire to make himself useful. The novice Border Collie owner must be warned that too much confinement will make this dog most unhappy. He must herd something, and he will settle for ducks, chickens, goats, sheep, cattle or children.

Above all else, the Border Collie has a kind of mystical quality called "eye," the inborn ability to control the sheep with his gaze.

A Border Collie "eyes" some sheep.

A pair of Border Collies hold their flock.

Ch. Parcana Silverleaf Vandyke, a Bearded Collie, has been given the command "walk on," which means he is to walk quietly directly behind the sheep.

Vandyke uses his tail as a rudder while he makes a sharp turn. He is obeying the command "way to me," meaning to circle the sheep counterclockwise.

He crouches with his muscles bunched and his legs drawn underneath him and fixes the sheep with his eye, holding them in position. He may have too much, too little or just the right amount of eye. Too much eye or sticky eye makes the dog overbearing with sheep; too little or loose eye means the dog has poor concentration; a medium amount of eye makes him the most effective sheepdog in the world.

Second to the Border Collie in fame, and almost equal in ability, is the Bearded Collie, also a natural header, and probably the only other dog capable of competing successfully with the Border Collie in sheepdog trials. Most are not used for trial work, but they seem to exhibit the same natural abilities. Border Collie enthusiasts swear that the Border Collie is the only breed with eye, but Beardies work in nearly identical fashion, most showing some degree of eye, and some showing a great deal of it. The beardie is not prone to sticky eye, which is to his advantage.

The Drover

The drover is the dog who works behind the sheep or cattle and drives them forward. The natural heeler makes the best drover. The Corgi (both Cardigan and Pembroke) is a natural heeler with an innate instinct for driving the cattle forward by nipping at their heels. While it may seem surprising that such small animals can work such large stock, both size and build are actually to the Corgi's advantage; he can flatten himself against the ground when necessary and avoid being kicked.

The Corgi goes out with the cattle in the morning and loafs around with them all day, keeping the young ones from wandering off. In the evening he brings the cattle back and puts them in the barn or milking facility. The Corgi's area of particular expertise is the milk cow. While some breeds will drive the cow too hard, thus causing her to give less milk, the Corgi tends to work her gently.

Both the Beardie and Border Collie can be taught to drive cattle, and both have been used for this purpose. Today certain strains of Border Collies are used exclusively for cattle work, although shepherds consider these collies inferior because they lack the natural heading instinct, which is difficult to teach. The loose-eyed Border Collie works best as a cattle dog because eye, which is so effective in herding sheep, is useless on cattle, who do not respond to the dog's gaze.

The Corgi, known as the small dog with a big dog's personality, drives cattle by nipping at their heels.

The Livestock-Guarding Dog

Most sheepdogs have some protective instinct, but certain breeds have been specifically developed along these lines. The livestock-guarding dog is not properly a herding or driving dog. He does not shape and direct the movement of his flock but follows it and protects it from such predators as wolves, bears and thieves. Ideally he is raised with the animals that he will guard and becomes firmly attached to them. He is massive, stately and placid in temperament, warding off predators by his mere presence, although he gives an impressive show of strength and attacks fiercely if necessary.

The Komondor is being used extensively in this country as a livestock guard in Texas and Colorado, primarily because he can keep coyotes and other predators off the sheep without disturbing the ecology. Other breeds being studied for this purpose by the U.S. Department of Agriculture are the Great Pyrenees, the Kuvasz, and less well-known breeds, including the Turkish Karabash, Italian Maremma, and Yugoslavian Shar Planinetz.

The All-Round Farm Dog

The old-fashioned Scottish Collie and the German Shepherd are still useful companions and helpers in the farmyard, but neither has a highly developed herding instinct. The Australian Shepherd, on the other hand, will work cattle, sheep, horses and even poultry and can be used on farms, on ranches and in stockyards for moving herds from one place to another or through a chute, chasing away strays, and loading stock into trucks and trailers. The Australian Shepherd is born either a natural header or a heeler. He is also a protective dog.

Selecting a Breed

The primary consideration is the job you expect this dog to perform. If you are interested in sheepdog trials, the only sure candidate is a Border Collie; Beardies require an ambitious handler who is more intent on training than on winning. If you want a working shepherd, the Border Collie again ranks at the top of the list, closely followed by the Beardie, whose rugged coat makes him perfect for harsh climates or terrain. The Australian Shepherd is a good choice if you have a variety of jobs for the dog to do. The Komondor or Great Pyrenees are recommended for areas where livestock may fall prey to wild animals. The Corgi is a good cattle dog.

Breed temperament is also an important consideration. The shyest of sheepdogs is the Shetland or Sheltie. Although this delicate and beautiful creature has been converted into a bench dog, he still has a strong working instinct. Never headstrong, he requires close direction. In fact he cannot be left to work alone. This is fine if you enjoy spending hours in the field with your flock. Incidentally, the Sheltie is too shy and fragile to tolerate very young children; nevertheless, he makes a loving, obedient, clean and well-mannered house pet and adapts well to apartment life.

The Border Collie is more outgoing and capable of independent action. His two most valued qualities are his strong working instinct and his biddability. The latter means that he is willing to obey orders at all times. Intelligence is nice, but according to sheepdog experts it is not a prime virtue, since a highly intelligent Collie who will not follow orders is utterly useless for herding sheep. The Beardie tends to be less biddable than the Border Collie. He is not stubborn but is extremely independent, an admirable trait that makes him capable of working long hours with no direction. Nevertheless, he is difficult to control and sometimes becomes so intent on what he is doing that he simply does not hear his master's orders.

The Border Collie, the Beardie and the Corgi love children, but they can tend to be overbearing. Because they are born with the instinct to herd, they are inclined to herd children. According to

The Belgian Tervuren is a hard-working sheepdog, but he is not well known in this country.

one Corgi breeder, "We have small children, and ours do not mind being herded. In fact, the dogs have even pulled the pants off of them!" All three breeds are clean, easy to train and make excellent house pets, but the Corgi adapts best to apartment life. The Border Collie and the Beardie are energetic, need plenty of exercise and above all need and love to work.

The Komondor is an excellent and independent guardian of either flocks or home and property. He is deeply suspicious of strangers, and any prospective owner should be aware of this and be prepared to confine him whenever necessary. Although he is not a dog who will accept a stranger's pat on the head, he loves children and seems to know instinctively the differences between those who don't know any better and those who do. He is willing to take an inordinate amount of abuse from young children but is less tolerant with older children and adults. He loves to play, and because he is big and strong, he plays rough. His protective instinct is aroused when children fight in his presence, and he may interfere at the expense of children who do not belong to him. All children should be taught not to tease this dog. He is easy to housebreak and makes a good, clean house pet as long as he receives plenty of exercise and is obedience-trained. He is not recommended for apartment life.

The Great Pyrenees and Australian Shepherd both adapt well to either working conditions or the easy life, and both can be raised in apartments as long as they receive a moderate amount of exercise and the necessary amount of obedience training. Both make loyal and devoted pets for children.

Training

Herd-dog training requires an excess of patience and fortitude. These dogs cannot stand any form of brutality but respond quickly and easily to gentleness accompanied by firm authority. Many herd dogs

The Australian Shepherd is a versatile herd dog who both "heads" and "heels." He is also a delightful family dog.

show the herding instinct as soon as they are old enough to walk. Others do not develop the desire to work stock until much later, some not until they are a year or a year and a half old. Since it is impossible to teach this instinct to the dog, you must wait until he shows an interest of his own accord. Many late developers turn into excellent working dogs, so it is well worth waiting if your puppy comes from good working stock.

Basic obedience training can be initiated when the puppy is weaned. The commands "down" and "come" are essential, and the dog must be perfect in these before he is introduced to livestock. Young dogs may be started herding ducks and chickens, the former being considered the most easily managed of all flocks. Goats can also be managed by dogs, but since they tend to wander into the brush, the more heavily coated dogs make the best goat supervisors.

Special training problems can be divided into two categories: those that relate to the handler, and those that relate to the dog. The former are the more common and the harder to cure. The handler must himself be familiar with the ways of the stock that he wants his dog to work, must know the commands backwards and forwards, and must *never* be confused about which means what. He must also be patient, even-tempered, gentle and firm. Any roughness will ruin a herd dog.

All of the dog's incurable problems have to do with lack of

instinct, loose or sticky eye, lack of biddability, poor working ability, lack of desire, or poor temperament. A dog that is too shy or too aggressive will be hard to train and difficult to handle. Some herd dogs tend to be stubborn, which makes if difficult for the handler but is wonderful when it comes to sheep. It is interesting that a good dog handled poorly can be retrained by a competent trainer and turned into an excellent working animal.

CALLEA PHOTO

ABOVE: A ''loose-eyed'' Border Collie makes a great herd dog for cattle. Here one heads a cow in the other direction. BELOW: A Border Collie narrowly avoids a cow's hoof.

Diet

As with any dog, a well-balanced ration is required. The working dog is considered under stress and requires an increase in nutrients. If he works outside during the winter, his nutritional demands double. The owner must always remember to cut back when the weather turns warm, and a daily examination will determine whether he has enough fat on his bones.

Grooming

Oddly enough, the sheepdog with the most elaborate coat is the easiest one to care for. This is the Komondor. He is never combed or brushed. His coat is allowed to form into long cords, which are a permanent arrangement. The dog must be bathed when he gets dirty, but his coat is then wrung out with towels, and the cords are simply allowed to dry.

The Australian Shepherd also requires no special attention, only the usual brushing, occasional bathing and external parasite control. The Border Collie, German Shepherd and Corgi are about the same. The little Sheltie and the Scottish Collie both have long, glamorous silky coats that need extra brushing and careful checking for ticks and fleas, but both have natural hairdos which are easy to maintain.

The Beardie has a harsh outer coat and soft undercoat and requires thorough brushing, with extra attention paid to the soft hair behind his ears and elbow. If he works where there is thick brush, he must have all burs removed to prevent matting. The tender skin between his toes must be checked for foxtails and cheatgrass, which can work their way in and cause serious damage. Combing his feet with a fine-toothed comb is strongly recommended.

Medical

Among the less common breeds—the Border Collie, the Beardie, the Corgi, the Australian Shepherd and the Komondor—the incidence of genetic disease is rare. Occasionally hip dysplasia occurs in Beardies, the Aussie and the Komondor, and the Aussie once in a while has an eye defect, but this is far from usual.

Other medical problems occur because of the nature of the dog's work. Dogs who work cattle may get kicked. Dogs who work sheep and goats are subject to "butting," which is seldom serious physically but may cause emotional damage, especially to a young animal just starting out. The Great Pyrenees and Komondor are constantly exposed to danger if they are used as guard dogs, and do not mind it, but as a result they are inclined to get injured. One famous Komondor named Maggie, whose owner kept a diary of her training and development, suffered an injury so severe that she lost her left eye. To this day the owner does not know what wild animal inflicted the damage, but after three days of recuperation in the hospital, Maggie returned happily to her flock of goats.

There is also the chance that herd dogs may contract a disease from the animals they work. The most common of these are parasitic diseases—for example, tapeworm. Therefore it is always recommended that both dogs and livestock be kept healthy and clean. Periodic stool checks and immediate treatment of all parasitic diseases is essential. A working dog should have a veterinary examination no less than once every six months.

The Bitch in Season

If she works alone, the bitch in season creates no problem, but of course she must be confined if she works with males and you don't want her to get pregnant. Spaying is a controversial subject, some experts objecting to it altogether and others recommending it in order to get more use out of the bitch.

GUIDE DOGS

"The confident, self-assured independent image of person and guide dog lifts the dignity of blind people ..."
—EDWARD MEIER, CHAIRMAN OF THE BOARD, GUIDE DOGS BOOSTER CLUB OF AMERICA

The guide dog is imbued with the intelligence, devotion, courage and skill he needs to serve as the eyes for a human being who has no sight. If you think of the guide dog as a miracle dog, you are wrong. He is not. Everything he is, he owes to his breeding, rearing and training. But he represents everything that is most valuable, noble and moving in the relationship between dog and man.

Guide dogs no longer concern only the small number of people who employ them. They are of immediate interest to families with

When the guide dog learns to heel, he is taught to move a little ahead of his master, not exactly at his left side.

children who are willing to raise and teach basic obedience to guide-dog puppies. Those who believe that children know only how to be cruel to dogs should consider the proven fact that in the guide dog's development and training, it is ultimately the child who makes the difference.

When the guide-dog puppy is between eight and twelve weeks old, he goes home with a child between the ages of nine and nineteen. The next year of his life he spends with that child. The child raises the dog, teaches him basic obedience and loves him as only a child knows how to love—which is perhaps what accounts for the success of the puppy-raising programs. When the puppy is about fifteen months old, he is returned to the school, where he undergoes another five months or so of intensive training. Then he is paired up with a blind person, and master and dog are trained in tandem for an additional month. On graduation day, the child is invited to come and see the results of his work. It's a day he'll never forget, for the emotions of all run deep and strong.

Can guide-dog puppies be raised successfully by adults? Yes, but the percentage of success is not as high. The guide-dog schools in this country all work in conjunction with 4-H extension programs, and willing families with children are always in short supply. For more information contact your local 4-H club, or the guide-dog school closest to you.

The Seeing Eye, Inc.
P.O. Box 375
Morristown, New Jersey 07960

Pilot Dogs, Inc.
625 West Town Street
Columbus, Ohio 43215

Leader Dogs for the Blind
1039 Rochester Road
Rochester, Michigan 48063

International Guiding Eyes, Inc.
5431 Denny Ave.
North Hollywood, California 91603

Guiding Eyes for the Blind, Inc.
106 East Forty-first Street
New York, New York 10016

Guide Dogs of the Desert
P.O. Box 1692
Palm Springs, California 92262

Second Sight
109-19 72nd Ave.
Forest Hills, New York 11375

Guide Dogs for the Blind
P.O. Box 1200
San Raphael, California 94902

These schools prefer to place their dogs in the foster homes located in their own states, but Guide Dogs for the Blind has been able to place puppies in Nevada, Oregon, Washington and Colorado as well as California.

About the Dog

A guide dog from one of the nation's eight schools has been carefully bred, maintained on a nutritious diet, given excellent regular medical attention and is expertly trained. Each dog represents an investment of $4,000 to $5,000, yet the dog, harness and leash, training, and room and board during the month-long training period are provided to the blind student at either no cost or for a token fee.

Some schools prefer bitches because they prefer their temperaments and personal habits. Other schools show no preference for either sex, although in all cases the dog must be neutered unless it is to be maintained by the school for its breeding program. The original studies of guide dogs at Guide Dogs for the Blind in California did, however, indicate that the female tended to have a longer working life. While a guide dog usually works until it is eight to ten years old, a much greater percentage of females last until they are nine or older. When a guide dog retires, his master goes back to school to get a new dog.

The most common breed for guide-dog training is the German Shepherd. International Guiding Eyes has only Shepherds because they are adaptable to both hot and cold climates and seem to learn "intelligent disobedience" more quickly than other dogs. Other schools also use Labrador and Golden Retrievers. All three breeds have the proper size, coat and temperament and are available in large enough supply to supplement breeding stock.

Other breeds that have also been used include Rhodesian Ridgebacks, Standard Schnauzers, Vizslas, Weimaraners, Siberian Huskies, Norwegian Elkhounds, Bouvier des Flandres, Border Collies, Collies, Bernese Mountain Dogs, Belgian Tervurens, Alaskan Malamutes, Salukis, Doberman Pinschers, Dalmatians, English Setters, Boxers and mixed breeds. Boxers were used extensively in New Jersey until it was discovered that the Boxer's life span was generally shorter than the Shepherd's or Retriever's. The mixed breed has shown considerable success as a guide dog—as long as he looks impressive, preferably like a Shepherd or Retriever.

"One never knows," says Bud Maynard of Guide Dogs for the Desert, "when someone might mention to the person that he or she has a funny-looking dog, and believe it or not, all good work seems to stop from then on."

The right temperament is of course essential. A guide dog must be friendly to everyone, able to tolerate street noise and the confusion of crowds and to ride in cars and public transportation without getting carsick. He must be intelligent. Harold Pocklington of Leader Dogs estimates that the guide dog must have an intelligence at least equal to that of a seven-year-old child and be able to respond to a hundred verbal commands. Above all, the guide dog must be calm, even-tempered and adaptable, able to adjust quickly and easily to a variety of environments and situations.

More dogs are rejected from guide-dog programs for emotional than for intelligence problems, especially if they are too aggressive or protective, too shy, easily distracted, flighty, high-strung, inconsistent in attitude, nervous or panicky. The dog may show a lack of responsibility or may pull too hard on his harness. Dogs are usually rejected early in the program, although they may be rejected at any time if they show any of these problems.

Physically, the dog should be between twenty and twenty-four inches high at the shoulder, have a good coat that is easy to groom, and be in good health, with no evidence of hip dysplasia.

What He Does

The guide dog's main job is to see that he gets his master where he wants to go safely. He is trained to stop at curbs and go forward when his master orders him. He must learn to turn right and left on command, retrieve objects that his master drops, sit and stay on command, disregard the distraction of other animals or people, and guide his master around obstacles and through crowds. He must also learn to disobey a command if he sees a danger that his master doesn't sense. For instance, if his master commands him to cross a street and he sees an oncoming car, the dog will not go forward. He will wait until the car is safely past.

Aside from this last, which is called "intelligent disobedience," the guide dog is completely subject to the will of his master. The master knows when street lights change because he is able to hear the flow of traffic. The master is the one who thinks and instructs. The dog guides the master to safety. This is why master and dog are referred to as a team.

How He Is Trained

If he is a dog bred at the school, he spends the first eight to twelve weeks of his life passing tests to determine whether he is a good prospect. If he passes all the tests, he goes to a foster home for the next twelve months. When he is returned to the school, he is assigned to an instructor who trains him with a string of other dogs. Work begins close to the kennel and gradually moves to the residential and business section of the town, where the dog learns how to deal with traffic, crowds and noise. Ultimately, the dog must learn to be effective when his trainer wears a blindfold.

The Foster Owner

He or she must be between nine and nineteen years old. The puppy will have been immunized against the big three when it arrives, but will need a rabies shot when it is four to six months old. The guide-dog school will pay for immunizations; some schools also pay for other veterinary expenses. The child's family is expected to pay for food and sometimes other expenses, which may average out to $10 to $15 a month. All such expenses are tax deductible.

The child gets the puppy used to people, animals, traffic, strange environments, situations and noises. Basic obedience training is encouraged and sometimes required. Although the child receives no money for caring for the puppy, the emotional satisfaction is enormous, and, surprisingly most children do not regret the fact

Robert Wichman, director of the Seeing Eye's scientific breeding station, checks up on some German Shepherd puppies.

A graduate of the Seeing Eye with her two children and her guide dog. (*Photo by Micky Fox; courtesy of the Seeing Eye, Inc.*)

that they must return the dog to the school after a year. Many children even take home another puppy and start all over again.

The Master

The guide dog is a working dog, and children are considered too immature to accept the responsibility of owning one. For this reason, the applicant must be at least sixteen years old, although there is no upper age limit. Each blind applicant is carefully considered before he is accepted into a guide-dog school. He must provide both a medical report stating that he is legally blind, and character witnesses; be interviewed by a staff member, who determines whether the applicant is temperamentally suited to life with a guide dog; and be able to show that he wants the dog for reasons of mobility and independence. He must *never* use the dog for begging, and he must be willing to take the dog for regular medical checkups.

While he is in training, the blind person establishes a regular routine with his dog. He learns when to feed, water and walk the dog and how to keep him under control at all times. He is encouraged to give his dog regular exercise, but off-leash runs "in the wild" are not necessary. These dogs are quite happy living in small city apartments—even though in many cases they have been raised in the country and had an opportunity to run free. The period of adjustment between dog and master may take as long as six months.

Most problems occur because of other people living in the same house with the blind person. The blind owner must take complete charge of the dog and provide all his food, exercise and love, in order to keep him a one-man dog. If other family members take over these duties or offer the dog too much affection, they interfere with the dog/master relationship. An occasional pat on the head is not out of line, but the blind owner should be allowed to grant and refuse permission for any such attention. If the owner dies, unless the dog is old enough to retire, he returns to the guide-dog school and is assigned another master.

Some blind people claim to have trained their own guide dogs, but this is a bad idea for several reasons. For example, the dog is trained to go around or stop in front of obstacles, and the blind person, who is unable to anticipate these obstacles himself, would be unable to train the dog to avoid them.

Throughout the United States the guide dog is allowed to go almost everywhere with his master, as long as he is properly harnessed. Airlines make special exceptions for guide dogs to travel in harness in the cabin with blind persons. Travel to the countries that enforce strict quarantines is, however, more difficult, for the guide dog is not always exempt. Before planning a trip to one of these countries, the owner should check with the nearest consulate. (See Chapter 13 for further details.) Hawaii, the one state in the United States that enforces a strict quarantine, provides special cottages at rather modest cost where the blind person may wait out the 120-day period along with his dog.

The Hearing-Ear Dog

The hearing-ear dog is a variation of the guide dog used by a person with impaired hearing. The hearing program began in Minnesota, where a deaf woman trained her dog to become an indispensable companion. When her dog died, she turned to the local SPCA for help, and it initiated the hearing-ear dog program, which received so much publicity that it soon became too much for the local organization to handle. Subsequently, the governor of Minnesota turned the program over to the American Humane Association, which still runs it.

Because mixed breeds and mutts are considered acceptable, all hearing-ear dogs come from local humane shelters. Thus a large number of dogs that would otherwise be legally destroyed are saved and trained for a worthy purpose. The program provides well-trained, cost-free dogs to any person with impaired hearing eighteen years of age or older who wants one. The dog is both obedience-trained and trained to alert his owner to certain sounds—for example, alarm clocks, smoke alarms, doorbells and knocks, telephones, intruders and burglars.

Dogs are selected by a trainer/veterinarian team. Important factors are temperament, health, intelligence and age—the dog should be between six and eighteen months old for training. Sex is not a deciding factor; both males and females are used, but both must be neutered. Once the dog is trained, which takes from three to four months, he is assigned a master and taken to his home by a trainer, who spends three to five days instructing the two. At the end of three months, the trainer returns to check the dog's progress, and if it is satisfactory, the dog becomes a certified hearing dog.

The hearing-dog program is still in the rudimentary stages, with one training center in Denver where improved training techniques and methods are being developed. The intention is that eventually training centers will be located throughout the country. The availability of dogs, however, is not limited to the population of Denver.

For more information write or call:
Administrator, Hearing-Dog Program
The American Humane Association
5351 S. Roslyn Street
Englewood, Colorado 80110
303-779-1400

INDEX

abandoned dogs, 4
abortion, 258, 261
acanthosis nigricans, 39
abscess, 106
adopting dogs from
  shelters, 43–4, 66
adrenal malfunction, 142
Affenpinscher, 31
Afghan Hound, 22, 24,
  303; training, 181, 185,
  189
aggressiveness, 47–56,
  147, 332
aging dogs, 290–3
Airedale Terrier, 29, 31
air travel, 268–75; cages,
  269–70; insurance, 274;
  rules, 268–9, 275, 349
Akita, 25
Alaskan Husky, 307
Alaskan Malamute, 25,
  185, 307, 346
allergies, 105
American Humane
  Association, 350
American Kennel Club
  (AKC), 16–18, 41, 98,
  299, 300, 302, 303, 312;
  field trials, 317, 319
  321; registration, 14,
  56, 297; types of shows,
  299
American Sighthound
  Field Association, 303,
  307

American Working
  Terrier Association, 311
anal glands, 107–8
anestrus, 238
Animalport, 272
Animal Welfare Act, 42n.,
  268
antihistamines, dosage,
  103
arthritis, 81, 96, 121,
  126–7, 291–2; see also
  hip dysplasia
artificial insemination,
  243
artificial respiration, 218,
  224
Australian Shepherd, 338,
  339, 342
Australian Terrier, 29
automatic sit, 183, 185,
  186, 188
automobiles, see cars

barking, 6, 7, 19, 22, 29,
  32, 190–1
Basenji, 22, 24, 185, 237,
  331
Basset Hound, 22, 24, 98,
  106, 181; as hunting
  dog, 317, 319, 321, 323
bathing, 6, 7, 28, 203–5;
  alcohol, 204; dry, 204
beach, dogs at, 221–3
Beagle, 22, 24, 85, 191;
  as hunting dog, 317,

319, 321, 323; training,
  181, 185
Bedlington Terrier, 29,
  31, 181
beds, 60–1
begging, 31, 32, 67–8,
  188–9
Belgian Sheepdog, 25,
  331
Bernese Mountain Dog,
  25, 181, 346
Bichon Frise, 34, 36, 181
bicycles, dogs injured by,
  220
Bide-a-Wee shelter, 44
bird dogs, 319, 321
birth control, 260–3
birth of puppies, 245–51,
  253
bitch: characteristics, 16–
  17; disease after
  delivery, 253–4; with
  newborn puppies, 251–
  2; rejection of puppies,
  254–5; reproductive
  system disorders, 258–
  60; see also birth of
  puppies; heat; pregnant
  bitch
bitch's milk, simulated,
  246, 255
Black and Tan
  Coonhound, 22, 24,
  181, 182
bladder stones, 141

blind, guides for, see
  guide dogs
blindness, 46, 290–1
bloat (gastric dilation-
  torsion complex), 80,
  233
Bloodhound, 22, 24, 36,
  181, 324
boarding dogs, 277–9
bomb detection, 325
bones, 67, 74; stuck in
  mouth, 102
Border Collie, see Collie
Border Terrier, 29, 31
Borzoi, 22, 24, 36, 182,
  270, 303
Boston Terrier, 34, 36,
  105, 221
Bouvier des Flandres, 25,
  181, 331, 346
bowls for food and water,
  57
Boxer, 25, 28, 181, 182,
  259, 326, 331, 346
breeders, 40–3
breeding, 235–6; see also
  mating
breeds, choice of, 17–39
breed sheet, 37–9
Briard, 25, 181, 331
Brittany Spaniel, 19
bronchitis, 128
brucellosis, 240, 258
Brumby, Leonard, Sr., 302
brushes, 58
brushing, 200, 201
Brussels Griffon, 31
Bulldog, 34, 36, 96, 101,
  106, 201, 221, 253;
  French, 34; training,
  180, 186
Bullmastiff, 25, 181
Bull Terrier, 29, 31;
  Staffordshire, 29, 31
bully, dog as, 192–3
burns, 224–5
buying dogs, 10–11, 13–
  17; from breeders, 40–
  2; from pet shops, 42–3

Cairn Terrier, 29
calcium, 75, 80;
  deficiency, 82, 83, 102
Canadian National
  Railroad, 267
cancer, 145; see also
  tumors
cars: chasing, 195; dogs

in, 62–4, 214–15, 265,
  266; dogs killed or
  injured by, 214–15,
  218; "down/stay in the
  car," 175; heat
  prostration of dogs in,
  221
castration, 81, 106, 263
cataracts, 99, 100, 290
central nervous system
  disorders, 142
Cheque, 262–3
Chesapeake Bay Retriever,
  18, 21
chewing, 67, 189
Chihuahua, 31, 32, 34,
  125, 190, 193
children: breeds suitable
  for, 22, 24, 28, 30, 34,
  36, 338; junior dog
  shows, 302–3; training
  guide dogs, 344, 347–8
Chow Chow, 34, 36, 102,
  181, 186
city dogs, 5–6; danger
  from windows and
  terraces, 223–4;
  exercise, 208; heat
  prostration, 221
cleft palate, 235
clipping, 205
Clumber Spaniel, 19
coccidia, 135
Cocker Spaniel, 19, 101,
  125; English, 19; as
  hunting dog, 319
colitis, 139–40
collapsing trachea, 128–9
collar, 59; corrective
  (choke), 48, 62, 148,
  150; nylon slip, 48,
  150; testing with, 53–4
Collie, 25, 28, 197;
  Bearded, 333, 336, 338–
  9, 342; Border, 326,
  333, 338–9, 342, 346;
  Scottish, 337, 342;
  training, 181, 185, 189
"come," 177, 179–80,
  183–5, 187, 188
conjunctivitis, 45, 100
Coonhound, 321; Black
  and Tan, 22, 24, 181,
  182; Walker, 307
coprophagy, 95, 191–2
Corgi, 181, 336, 338–9,
  342; Cardigan, 25, 336;
  Pembroke, 25, 336

correction, 68–9; in
  housebreaking, 92–3; in
  training, 152, 155–6
country dogs, 8–10
coursing dogs, 303–7
cruciate ligament rupture,
  126
cryptorchidism, 235, 258–
  9, 302
curbing, 4, 87
Curly-Coated Retriever,
  18
cystitis, 140, 141

Dachshund, 22, 24, 105,
  125, 311, 331; as
  hunting dog, 317, 321;
  training, 180, 181
Dalmatian, 34, 36, 181,
  307, 346
Dandie Dinmont Terrier,
  29, 181
deafness, 46, 98, 291
death, 293–4
dental care, see teeth
dermatitis, 83
detector dogs (D-dogs),
  325–6, 328
dewclaws, 39
diabetes, 82, 133
diarrhea: profuse, 233;
  simple, 134
digging, 8, 19, 22, 29,
  190
disc disease, 39, 125–6
disc fenestration, 126
diseases, see illnesses
distemper, 45–6, 82, 128,
  143
distemper, hepatitis, and
  leptospirosis (DHL)
  immunization, 3, 43,
  87, 295
distemper, hepatitis,
  leptospirosis, and
  para-influenza (DHLP)
  immunization, 278
distemper shots, 43
distemper teeth, 102
Doberman Pinscher, 25,
  28, 99, 181, 182, 326,
  331, 346
dog shows, see show dogs
"down," 166–7, 169–71,
  173–4, 183, 185–8
"down/stay," 174–5, 183,
  185, 187, 188
drover, 336

drug detection, 325–6, 328
drugs as poisons, 227–8

ear mites, 97
ears: cropping, 98–9; examination, 97–8
ear troubles, 39, 46; hematoma, 98; otitis, 97; in training, 180–1; vestibular problems, 98; wounds, 98
earth trials, 311
eclampsia, 253–4
eczema, 104
elbow dysplasia, 124
electric shock, 224
elongated soft palate, 129
emergencies, 213–33; automobile accidents, 214–15, 218; bicycle accidents, 220; burns, 224–5; electric shock, 224; fights, 220; first aid, 215–18, 222; gastrointestinal, 233; heat prostration, 221–2; muscle and bone injuries, 232–3; poisons and antidotes, 226–31; safety precautions, 213–14; shock, 215, 218; swallowed objects, 225–6; wounds, 232
English Pointer, 319
English Setter, 18, 185, 319, 346
English Toy Spaniel, 31, 181
equipment, 43, 57–61
esophageal achalasia, 140
estrus, 238; see also heat
exercise, 205–6, 208, 211–12; aging dogs, 293; pregnant bitch, 212; puppies, 206, 208
eyelids: cuts, 100; ectropian and entropian, 39
eyes: of aging dogs, 290–1; cataracts, 99, 100, 290; cherry eye, 100; conjunctivitis, 45, 100; examination, 99–100; haw, 99, 100; injury, 100

fading puppy syndrome, 254

false pregnancy, 244
fat dogs, see obesity
fear-wetting, 192
feet: examination, 106–7; of racing dogs, 307; of sled dogs, 310
female dog, see bitch
Field Spaniel, 19
field trials, 317, 319
fighting, 22, 29, 31, 193, 220
first aid, 215–18; artificial respiration, 218; burns, 225; heat prostration, 222; poisons, 227–31
Flat-Coated Retriever, 18
flea-and-tick shampoo, 204
flea collars, 104
flea powder, 104
fleas, 6, 7, 104, 105
food, 59, 71–85; for aging dogs, 78, 293; all-meat diet, 83–4; biscuits as treats, 74; canned, 71–2; carbohydrates, 75; cholesterol, 71; for city dogs, 6; dry, 72; eggs, 83, 84; fats, 71, 73, 75; fish, 82, 83; frozen, 73; for giant dogs, 28, 79–80; for herd dogs, 342; homemade, 72–3; and housebreaking, 72, 77, 90–1; for hunting dogs, 322; in illness, 82; liver, 83, 84; manufacturers' advice on, 6–7n.; nutritional requirements, 75–6; oils, 73, 84; for pregnant and lactating bitches, 80; protein, 71, 73, 75, 80; for puppies, 77–8, 251–2, 255–7; semi-moist, 72; for show dogs, 300; for sled dogs, 310; supplements, 73–4, 77, 79–81, 83, 84; table scraps, 73–4; testing with, 54–5; for toy dogs, 32, 78–9
Foxhound: American, 22, 24, 181, 307; English, 22, 24
Fox Terrier, 29, 182, 189, 190; Smooth, 31; Wire-haired, 31

fractures, 232–3
French Bulldog, 34

Gaines Research Center, 255
garbage, eating, 68, 133, 191
gastric dilation-torsion complex (bloat), 80, 233
gastrointestinal diseases, 133–40; see also worms
gastrointestinal emergencies, 233
German Shepherd Dog, 16, 25, 28, 29, 46, 48, 134, 260, 331, 337, 342; as guide dog, 345–6; as police and war dog, 326; training, 181, 182
German Shorthaired Pointer, 18, 19, 21, 317; training, 182, 185, 189
German Wirehaired Pointer, 18
giant dogs: breeding, 240; food, 28, 79–80; grooming, 28
Golden Retriever, 18, 21, 181, 189, 326; as guide dog, 319, 346
Gordon Setter, 18, 22, 185, 189
"go to your place," 175–7, 183, 188
Great Dane, 25, 99, 181, 331
Great Pyrenees, 25, 28, 181, 331, 337–9, 343
Greyhound, 22, 24, 26, 182, 270, 303, 307; Italian, 31, 270
Griffon: Brussels, 31; Wirehaired Pointing, 19
grooming, 5–6, 24, 31, 39, 197–205; herd dogs, 342; longhaired dogs, 28, 201, 203–5; puppies, 198–200; show dogs, 297–300; toy dogs, 34
guard dogs, 329–32
guide dogs, 4, 343–9; air travel, 275, 349
gun-shy dogs, 322

hair: and diet, 84; hormonal loss, 105–6; of indoor and outdoor

dogs, 205; long, in
training, 181; loss of,
103; mats, 98, 103, 107,
201
handlers, 295–6
Harrier, 22, 181
health certificate, 265–6,
276, 279–89
health examination, daily,
96–109
health insurance, 118,
120
hearing-ear dogs, 349–50
heart disease: of aging
dogs, 292; congenital,
129–30; valvular, 130
heartworm, 7, 130–2;
check, 295
heat, bitch in, 7, 8, 237–
40, 305n., 311; air
travel, 269; herd dogs,
343; hunting dogs, 323;
older dogs, 239–40;
racing dogs, 308; in
shows, 303; silent heat,
238–9; young dogs, 240
heat prostration, 221–2
"heel," 161–6, 184, 186,
188
hematoma, aural, 98
hemorrhagic gastroenter-
itis, 138–9, 143, 254
hepatitis, 143; immuniza-
tion, 3, 43, 87, 278, 295
herd dogs, 277, 332–43
heroin detection, 325–6
hip dysplasia, 22n., 28–
9, 56, 121–4, 126, 206,
235, 342
home protection, 331
hookworm, 135, 138
hot spots, 223
hounds, 22–4
housebreaking, 10, 15, 24,
29, 32, 86–94; and
feeding, 72, 77, 90–1;
and water, 74, 77
howling, 21, 25, 32, 310
hunting dogs, 315–23,
331; accidents, 323;
breeds, 319, 321; field
trials, 317, 319, 323;
training, 322
Husky: Alaskan, 307;
Siberian, 25, 28, 185,
189, 204, 304, 346
hypervitaminosis, 83
hypoglycemia, 77

Ibizan, 303
Iditarod race, 308
illnesses, 121–45; after
birth of puppies, 253–
4; on breed sheet, 39;
checklists of symptoms,
45–6, 116–17; of
reproductive system,
258–60
immunization: distemper,
43; distemper, hepatitis,
and leptospirosis
(DHL), 3, 43, 87, 295;
distemper, hepatitis,
leptospirosis, and para-
influenza (DHLP), 278;
kennel cough, 127–8,
278; rabies, 3, 144, 278
insecticides: for parasite
control, dangers of,
104; as poisons, 226,
227, 228
insurance: air travel, 274;
mortality, 265
International Air Trans-
port Association, 269–
70
International Sled Dog
Racing Association,
308, 311
introducing dog to new
home, 64–6
Irish Setter, 18, 21, 22;
training, 182, 185, 189
Irish Terrier, 29
Irish Wolfhound, 22, 24,
303
Italian Greyhound, 31,
270

Japanese Spaniel, 31
jogging, 208, 212
jumping up, 67, 193–4

Karabash, 337
Keeshond, 34, 36, 181,
186
kennel cough, 127–8, 278
kennels: for air travel,
269–70; boarding, 277–
9; colony, 44
Kerry Blue Terrier, 29
kidney diseases, 140–1,
292
kidney stones, 141
Komodor, 25, 181, 337–9,
342, 343
Kuvasz, 25, 181, 337

Labrador Retriever, 18;
85, 181, 189; as guide
dog, 319, 346; as hunt-
ing dog, 319; as police
and war dog, 319, 324,
326
Lakeland Terrier, 29
laws on dogs, 4–5, 8
leash, 4, 6, 48, 59–60,
148; breaking dog to,
156–7; testing with,
53–4; in training, 150–
2
leptospirosis, 144; im-
munization, 3, 43, 87,
278
leukemia, 145
Lhasa Apso, 34, 36, 99,
181, 221
licenses, 4, 66
liver diseases, 132
livestock: dogs interfering
with, 8; herd dogs, 277,
322–43

malabsorption syndrome,
136–8
Malamute, Alaskan, 25,
185, 307, 346
male dogs: characteristics,
16–17; mating, 241–3;
reproductive system
disorders, 258–9; re-
sponse to bitch in heat,
237, 240
malignant melanoma, 39
Malinois, Belgian, 25
Maltese, 31, 32, 34, 99,
191
Manchester Terrier, 29,
31; Toy, 31
mange: demodectic, 105;
sarcoptic, 105
March Shipping Pas-
senger Services, 268
Maremma, 337
Mastiff, 25, 36, 181, 326
mastitis, 250–1, 253
mating, 240–3
Maynard, Bud, 346
McLellan, Susan, 96, 223,
235n., 262, 263
Mech, David, 242
medical supplies, list, 60
medical guarantee, 40, 43,
46
medical problems, see
illnesses

medicine, giving to dog, 118
metritis, 254
minerals, supplementary, 59, 75–6, 78, 79, 81
mixed breeds, 13–14
Moore-McCormack, Lines, 267
mosquito as carrier of heartworm, 7, 131, 132
mounting (embracing legs), 195–6
mouth: examination, 101–2; foreign objects stuck in, 102
muscle injuries, 232

nails, clipping, 203
National Greyhound Association, 303
National Petcare, Inc., 118
nervous dogs, 47–55; training, 182–4, 190
neutered dogs, 212
Newfoundland, 25, 28, 181; water-rescue dogs, 312–15
Newfoundland Club of America (NCA), 312
non-sporting dogs, 34–6
Norwegian Elkhound, 22, 24, 346; training, 182, 185, 189
Norwich Terrier, 29
nose, examination, 100–1
nosebleed, 101
nose drops, 101

obedience training, 146–96, 315; for bad habits, 188–96; classes, 44, 146; commands, 149, 157–80, 182–8; corrective jerk, 152, 155–6; by experts, 146–7; hands used in, 148–9; personality types of dogs, 181–8; physical limitations of dogs, 180–1; repetition, 156; terriers, 29–30; toy dogs, 32, 181; voice used in, 149
obedience trials, 300, 302
obesity, 6, 77, 81, 129, 212

Old English Sheepdog, 25, 181, 185
Orthopedic Foundation for Animals (OFA), 56, 122
osteochondritis dissecans, 124
otitis, 97
Otter Hound, 22, 181
Owner Handler Association (OHA), 296

pancreas diseases, 132–3
paper training, 86–8, 94–5
Papillon, 31
para-influenza (kennel cough), 127–8, 278
patellar luxation, 34, 125, 126, 291
Pekingese, 31, 34, 101, 221; training, 180, 181
personality: tests, 48–55; types, 46–56
pet shops, 40, 42–3
Pharaoh Hound, 303
phosphorus, 75, 80, 83, 102
pica, 82
pills, giving to dog, 118
Pinscher, Miniature, 31
plants, poisonous, 8, 190, 226, 227, 231
Pocklington, Harold, 346
Pointer 18, 21, 22; English, 319; as hunting dog, 317, 319; see also German Short-haired Pointer
poisons and antidotes, 226–31; antifreeze, 7, 226, 230; battery acid, 230; cleaning agents, 229–30; detergents, 226, 230; drugs, 227–8; fertilizers, 226, 227, 231; fuel oil, 226, 227, 230; insecticides, 226, 227, 228; matches, 230; paint, 226, 227, 229; plants, 8, 190, 226, 227, 231; plaster, 229; rodenticides, 226, 227, 228; salt (from streets), 226, 227, 230; snail bait, 226, 227, 228; turpentine, 226, 229;

weedkillers, 226, 227, 231
police dogs, 324–9
Pomeranian, 31
Poodle, 34, 36, 99, 181, 201; Toy (Miniature) 31, 85, 125, 128, 190
pregnant bitch, 81, 134, 243–4; exercise, 212; false pregnancy, 244; food, 80; insecticides used, 104
proestrus, 238
Professional Handlers Association, 295
prostatic disease, 141–2
Public Health Service, 277
Pug, 31, 34, 106, 180, 181, 221
Puli, 25, 181, 182
puppies: behavior problems, 66–8; birth of, 245–51, 253; buying, 10–11, 13–16, 40–3; in cars, 62–3; equipment for, 57–61; exercise, 206, 208; fading puppy syndrome, 254; feeding, 77–8, 251–2, 255–7; first seven weeks, 251–2, 255–8; grooming, 198–200; house-breaking, 88, 90, 91; inoculations, early, 258; introducing to new home, 64–5; keeping warm, 257–8; newborn, 251; older dogs compared with, 14–16; orphaned or rejected, 254–5; paper training, 87, 94; personality, 46–8; shipping, 42n., 268; teething, 67, 102; weaning, 251–2, 255
puppy gate, 43, 61
puppy mills, 42
purebred dogs, 13–14, 40–1, 56
pyoderma, 39, 101, 106
pyometra, 259–60

quarantine for traveling dogs, 267, 276–7

rabbit dogs, 321
rabies, 144–5; immuniza-

tion, 3, 144, 278; quarantine in foreign countries, 276–7
rabies vaccination certificate, 276, 279–89
racing, 303, 307, 308; sled dogs, 307–10
reproductive cycle, 237–8
reproductive system disorders, 258–60
respiratory illnesses, 45, 101, 127–9
responsive personality, 47, 49–54, 156, 181–2
reverse sneeze, 127
Rhodesian Ridgeback, 22, 181, 185, 193, 346
Rocky Mountain spotted fever, 103
Rottweiler, 25, 185
roundworm, 134–6
runaway dog, 195

St. Bernard, 25, 28, 79, 99, 101, 181, 331
salivary gland, ruptured, 102
salt water, effects of, 221–3
Saluki, 22, 24, 181, 303
Samoyed, 25, 181, 185, 189, 307
Schipperke, 34
Schnauzer, 28, 99, 138, 185; Giant, 25, 331; Miniature, 29; Standard, 25, 331, 346
Scottish Deerhound, 22, 24, 303
Scottish Deerhound, 29, 190
Sealyham Terrier, 29
seborrhea, chronic, 39, 104–5
sedate personality, 47–54, 156, 170, 187–8
Senior, Dr. David, 237–40, 262
shake-can, 48, 52, 67, 68, 92, 148; in training, 151, 189–91, 194, 195
shampoo, 58, 104; flea-and-tick, 204; see also bathing
Shar Planinetz, 337
sheepdog trials, 332
shelters: clinics, 111; dogs adopted from, 43–4, 66

shepherd dogs, 333, 336, 338
Shetland Sheepdog (Sheltie), 25, 28, 181, 338, 342
Shih Tzu, 31, 99, 181
shock: electric, 224; first aid for, 215, 218
short-nosed dogs: air travel, 269; eye injury, 100; heat prostration, 221; respiratory problems, 101, 129; training, 180
show dogs, 17, 295–303; buying, 16; diet, 300; grooming, 299–300; handlers, 295–6; obedience trials, 300, 302; training, 300; types of shows, 297
shyness, 47–55, 306, 332; and training, 155–6, 184–5
Siberian Husky, see Husky
sighthounds (coursing dogs), 303–7
Silky Terrier, 31
"sit," 157, 182, 184, 186, 187; automatic, 183, 185, 186, 188
"sit/stay," 157–61, 182, 184, 186, 187
skin: of aging dogs, 291; diseases, 45, 83, 104–6; examination, 103–6; lesions, 106
Skye Terrier, 29, 181
sled dogs, 307–10
sleeping quarters, 61–2, 65–6
small-animal nursers, 256
smell, sense of, 291, 324
sneaky dog, 194
Soft-Coated Wheaten Terrier, 29, 181
spaniels, 18–19, 185, 326; as hunting dogs, 317, 319, 321
spaying, 261–2; and weight, 81, 262
splay feet, 82, 83
spoiling a dog, 68
sporting dogs, 18–22
Springer Spaniel, 22, 319; English, 19; Welsh, 19
Staffordshire Bull Terrier, 29, 31

Staffordshire Terrier, American, 29, 31
state regulations on dog travel, 279–89
Steingard, Dr. Jerry, 309
stomach tube for feeding, 257
stubbornness, 47–8, 50–1, 54–5, 156, 185–7
suburbs, dogs in, 6–8
sunburn, 222–3
Sussex Spaniel, 19
swallowed objects, 225–6

tail: docking, 39; examination, 107
tapeworm, 8, 104, 134–6, 139, 343
tear stains, 201
teeth, 101–2; brushing, 200; decalcification, 102; distemper teeth, 102
teething, 67, 102
temperament, see personality
temperature, 114; taking, 114–15, 117
terriers, 29–31; earth trials, 311; training, 29–30
Tervuren, Belgian, 25, 346
testicular tumor, 106
thiamine deficiency, 83
thieving, 189
throw-chain, 148, 151
Tibetan Terrier, 34, 181
tick collars, 104
tick paralysis, 103
ticks, 6, 7, 103–4; shampoo, 204
toxoplasmosis, 83–4
toy dogs, 31–4; diseases, 125, 128, 134; fighting, 193; food, 78–9; training, 32, 181
toys, 58–9
tracking dogs, 324
training: guard dogs, 329–30; guide dogs, 344–8; herd dogs, 339–40; hunting dogs, 322; police and war dogs, 327–8; show dogs, 300; sled dogs, 309; water-rescue dogs, 312, 314–15; working dogs, 25;

see also obedience
 training
traveling, 31, 34, 265–77;
 by air, 42n., 268–75,
 349; in cars, *see* cars;
 documents needed,
 265–9, 276–7, 279–89;
 equipment for, 266; in
 foreign countries, 276–
 7, 349; by railroad, 267;
 by ship, 267–8; state
 regulations on, 279–89
tumors, 145; in kidney
 and bladder, 141; mam-
 mary, 260; ovarian,
 260; testicular, 106
tying up dogs, 62

United Kennel Club, 321
urinary system diseases,
 140–2

vaccination, *see* immunization
vaginitis, 259
veterinarian, 110–17;
 medical records, 46;

symptoms requiring
 visit to, 116–17
vitamins: deficiency, 82,
 83; geriatric, 291;
 hypervitaminosis, 83;
 supplementary, 59, 75–
 6, 78, 79, 81, 84
Vizsla, 17, 19, 182, 189,
 346
vocal cords, removing,
 310
vomiting, control of, 233

Walker Coonhound, 307
war dogs, 324–6, 328
warts, 102
water, 74, 78, 80, 293;
 and housebreaking, 90–
 1, 93
water pistol, 67, 68, 148,
 151, 189, 190
water-rescue dogs, 312–
 15
Water Spaniel: American,
 18; Irish, 19
Weimaraner, 16, 19, 21,
 22, 46; as hunting dog,

317, 346; training, 182,
 185, 189, 190, 193
Welsh Corgi, *see* Corgi
Welsh Terrier, 29
West Highland White
 Terrier, 29
Westminster Show, 17,
 198
whelping, 245–51, 253
whelping box, 245
Whippet, 22, 24, 270, 303,
 306
whipworm, 135, 137
Whitney, Dr. Leon, 237
Wirehaired Pointing
 Griffon, 19
working dogs, 25–9
World Wide Pet
 Transport, 270, 272
worms, 42, 82, 102, 134–
 9; deworming, 135;
 symptoms, 45, 134–9
wounds, flesh, 232

Yorkshire Terrier, 31, 32,
 34, 77, 99, 125, 128,
 311

MATTHEW MARGOLIS is co-director, with Ira Meisler, of the National Institute of Dog Training in Los Angeles. They train dogs in the owners' homes and also operate Dog Rancho, a kennel in Monterey Park. Margolis appears regularly on *A.M. Los Angeles* as a dog-training consultant and on the *Carole Hemingway Show* (KABC Radio) every five weeks. He lives in Los Angeles with his wife and son.

CATHERINE SWAN is a Reed College graduate who received a master's degree in English from Syracuse University, where she was a Woodrow Wilson Fellow. A freelance writer who has written many articles, she is an animal lover who has always had a desire to work with dogs. This book gave her her first opportunity. She lives in New Jersey, is married and the mother of a daughter.

Veterinary consultant SUSAN MCLELLAN graduated in 1969 from the University of Illinois Veterinary School, did her internship at the University of Pennsylvania and her surgery residency at the Henry Bergh Memorial Animal Hospital of the ASPCA in New York City. She started a private practice in New York City in 1973, and in 1979 opened a second outpatient clinic. In 1978 she was elected the first woman president of the Veterinary Medical Association of New York City.